The Welshpool
and
Llanfair

by

Ralph J. Cartwright

Rail Romances

Specialist Publishers

P.O. Box 85, Chester. CH4 9ZH
United Kingdom

Ex-Antiqua locomotive No. 12 **Joan** *starts the climb of Golfa bank in 1987 with a freight train for the benefit of enthusiasts, including those travelling on Chester's No. 1 vintage bus.*

Phil Waterfield

The Welshpool
and
Llanfair . . . .

by Ralph J. Cartwright

**The Story of the Welshpool & Llanfair
Light Railway and its preservation.**

Celebrating 100 Years

1903   2003

© Ralph I. Cartwright and RailRomances 2002

ISBN 1-900622-06-8 (Hardback)

British Library Cataloguing in Publication Data
Cartwright, Ralph I.
The Welshpool and Llanfair : The story of the Welshpool &
Llanfair Light Railway - 1903-2003
1. Welshpool & Llanfair Light Railway - History
2. Welshpool & Llanfair Light Railway Preservation Company - History - 20th century.
3. Narrow Gauge Railroads - Wales - History
I. Title
385.5'3'0942951

Publishing, Typesetting and Design by:
RailRomances, PO Box 85,
Chester. CH4 9ZH
United Kingdom

Jacket Design, Special Graphics and Drawings by :
John Milner,
RailRomances, PO Box 85,
Chester. CH4 9ZH
United Kingdom

Image Setting by:
Lazertype, Laurel Bank,
Gresford, Wrexham LL12 8NT
United Kingdom

Printed by:
The Amadeus Press Ltd.,
Ezra House, West 26 Business Park,
Cleckheaton BD19 4TQ
United Kingdom

Acknowledgements

A comprehensive history of the railway by the author jointly with R.T.Russell was first compiled in 1972 (*The Welshpool & Llanfair Light Railway* published by David & Charles). Based on original research, it made use of facilities provided by the former British Transport Historical Records, Paddington, the Public Record Offices and the National Library of Wales, Aberystwyth. Especially we must acknowledge the debt we owe to Ralph Russell (sadly deceased) for the research he did into the history of locomotives and rolling stock prior to 1972. R.G. Bird kindly made available surveys of the line by his students.

Much of the earlier account has been incorporated in this book though new details have emerged. I am grateful to Martin Smith whose searches in the Public Record Office alerted me to new clues regarding the rebuilding of the original locomotives and for information subsequently uncovered by David Hyde in Swindon Works records.

For the earlier work and again more recently, reference has been made to the archives of the Welshpool & Llanfair Light Railway Preservation Co. Ltd. Much material in this book has been researched over many years and published in the *Llanfair Railway Journal.* In this connection, help was unstintingly provided in specialist areas by R. D. Darvill, R. H. Gurney, G. Horsman (Hunslet Holdings Ltd.), M. W. Knight, Peter Mircev, D. H. Taylor and C. J. Walker. I was also able to draw on information which appeared in various issues of the *Industrial Railway Record*. In gathering information initially destined for publication in the *Llanfair Railway Journal* and in addition, latterly, for this account, I have enjoyed the co-operation of Andy Carey, Keith Bide, Alan Doig, Glyn and Gareth Evans, Nick Griffiths, David Moseley, J. Pascoe Rowe and Terry Turner and many other officers and members of the Preservation Company. For this, from all of these over many years, I am very grateful. Specifically with regard to this book, I am indebted to Andy Carey, Alan Doig, Mike Lister and Colin Tickle for kindly reading sections of the text and suggesting amendments though any errors remain my responsibility.

A number of drawings by Michael Christensen have been utilised here and I acknowledge his kind permission to do so and also permission to reproduce their drawings by P. R. Booth, M. Lister and I. MacBriar. David Berry kindly allowed access to detailed drawings of the Pickering coaches which he had painstakingly produced. Thanks are due to John Clarke, Assistant Curator, National Railway Museum, for his help in obtaining images of early tickets.

To all those who readily gave permission for their photographs to be included, I offer my thanks: credits identify their work. Photographs with no acknowledgement are from the author's camera or collection. I am much indebted to John Milner for his encouragement and for his urging in the search for material of high standard. Further, I must record here my appreciation of his improvements to the original drawings.

Bibliography

A comprehensive list of printed books and articles consulted when the earlier work was published can be found in that volume. Of particular importance was *The Montgomeryshire Express* (formerly *Newtown and Welshpool Express*) - various dates 1875 - 1956; *Oswestry and Border Counties Advertizer* (formerly *The Oswestry Advertizer and Montgomeryshire Mercury* and *The Oswestry Advertizer and Montgomeryshire Herald*) - various dates 1862 - 1931. Once again, I have drawn on the publications of the Welshpool & Llanfair Light Railway Preservation Co. Ltd. - *Newsletter* (1957 - 68), *The Earl* (1959 - 67), *The Llanfair Railway Journal* (1968 on).

Further information can be found in:
Story of the Cambrian, by C.P. Gasquoine (1922)
The Cambrian Railways, Volume II by Rex Christiansen & R. W. Miller (1968)
Cambrian Railways, 1859-1947 by C.C. Green (1997)
Narrow Gauge Steam - Its origins and world-wide development by P. J.G. Ransom (1996)
Welshpool & Llanfair Light Railway - a collection of pictures by Ralph I. Cartwright (1995)
The Welshpool & Llanfair Light Railway - A Past and Present Companion by Hugh Ballantyne (2001)

Foreword

Ralph Cartwright's book, *The Welshpool & Llanfair*, is a welcome contribution to our understanding of Powys' past and to the history of railways in Britain. It provides a finely detailed history of the Welshpool and Llanfair Light Railway, which is nevertheless readable - a rare combination. In the later chapters it also documents the provenance of its engines and carriages. And there is an abundance of photographs to add a visual depth to the record. It is a useful resource both for historians interested in Mid-Wales and the borders, and also for historians of railway development, particularly that of narrow-gauge companies.

I note that in the account the Earls of Powis were always keen to be seen to be helping and supporting the Light Railway project, but that, to our shame, at times they got in the way! There has always been a family connection with the Railway and I am proud to have had the chance to contribute to this book. In the story of this railway one sees how much of a struggle uphill this scheme has had to travel. The journey has been a very long one - *one hundred years* strictly speaking - but it might be claimed to have begun in 1818 when the first attempt at rail transport began in Welshpool. From that time onwards there have been enthusiasts who have sustained and attempted to sell the vision to governments against a tide of powerful voices which have said '*No*' again and again. The determination amongst the volunteers in the Company today matches that of those visionaries in the past, and this is why the Company has managed to flourish despite government economic closures of railways elsewhere and numerous other obstacles. This book is therefore, in part, a testimony to the sustained perseverance and hard work of those who believe that a light railway has a part to play in the economics of our area.

I trust that you will enjoy reading this and find it instructive.

Powis.

The Earl of Powis
President, Welshpool & Llanfair Light Railway
Preservation Co. Ltd.

Introduction

The Llanfair Railway (as local people call it) first aroused my interest when I heard that a group of ordinary people was planning to reopen a line recently closed by the mighty British Railways. Then, this was generally regarded as audacious if not preposterous. Be that as it may, I soon discovered that narrow gauge trains with chubby storybook engines were (occasionally) still weaving through the streets and backyards in the border market town of Welshpool. The next time my attention was caught was the news that the line's river bridge had collapsed and all kinds of help was needed. Responding, I found friendly faces and unflagging optimism, but a dire shortage of funds and meagre resources of any kind. Fortune smiled, however, the bridge got mended and slowly over the years the Railway grew.

Here was, for me, a rather special little Railway. This was the first narrow gauge line built under the auspices of the 1896 Light Railways Act - surely illustrating how a rural rail link could be built simply as was implicit in the Act. Once it served a community rather than a special traffic. Use of the 2ft 6ins gauge, tangling with the town and piercing the hill country with grinding curves and capricious gradients, truly tapped the Act's spirit of purpose. At the dawn of the 20th century, it provided transport for local people and freight in a thinly populated rural area.

The birth pangs of the Welshpool & Llanfair Light Railway were the result of financial stringency. In Cambrian times it struggled to keep its head above water and the GWR quickly discovered that it was more a liability than an asset. Procrastination saved the line. So it survived to play a useful role during World War II and but for this it might not have remained to be taken into state ownership.

The preservation enterprise, too, started life poor and ill-prepared as the first attempt at something akin to *'privatisation'*. But for these pioneering enthusiasts, the allure of this wayward line was irresistible with tracks embedded in grass, weaving between hillsides tilted at unlikely angles ... and two stalwart little tank engines.

After no less than forty years under the present administration, the W&L has undergone a transformation.

Only a few traces of the town section survive: the narrow passage through the back yards together with the cottages themselves has given way to a wide stretch of new road while the site of the old passenger terminus and standard gauge sidings has become a roundabout leading on to the new Welshpool bypass. The preserved line, long since truncated, retains much of the rustic simplicity it exhibited in 1903, but the wide approaches, spacious car parking areas and raised platforms at both termini underline the changed role of the Railway.

Those eras of ramshackle charm and make-do-and-mend under BR and after reopening have given way to a much more sophisticated approach. Orderly, well tended infrastructure and regular trains, smartly turned out and with an international flavour reflect the efforts of a modern generation of supporters, many affluent way beyond the norm of early well-wishers, and access to public funds such as never thought possible. Today, supporters come to enjoy a hobby: the struggle to rescue the line from oblivion is won.

Once more, the line plays a part in the economy of mid-Wales, something local people appreciate. And in a small way, it provides transport once again for local people for whom bus services between Llanfair and Welshpool are minimal. Traffic figures may be considerably higher for narrow gauge railways in more traditional holiday areas but on the Llanfair Railway the scale of operations has allowed the preservationists to succeed in working the Railway almost entirely by voluntary efforts.

The unique nature of the Railway has been recognised by the Institute of Civil Engineers, which has registered it as a Historic Engineering Work. The W&L is a rare instance (in Britain) of the 2ft 6ins gauge, chosen for its flexibility and economy with minimum sacrifice of capacity for handling substantial loads. A hundred years after the line was opened, the preservation enterprise is safeguarding all this for posterity along with fine examples of British and foreign locomotive building. May the shrill shriek of a steam locomotive whistle long echo and re-echo across the hills of Powys for lovers of little railways . . . truly a paradise here in mid-Wales.

Ralph I. Cartwright, Owl Halt, 2001

This book is dedicated to those volunteers and well-wishers who persisted, with aspiration undiminished, through the difficult years when funds were scarce and challenges unabating.

Contents

Chapter 1

Early Schemes and Rival Plans

The thirteenth century borough of Welshpool lies only three miles inside the Welsh border where English plain meets Welsh mountain. Westwards, stretches ridge after ridge of the Berwyn Mountains, rounded off rather below 2,000 feet and from here the stone-strewn Afon Banwy plunges inland towards the border. This is Powys, a constituent part of which is the old county of Montgomeryshire with its motto "*Powys, Paradwys Cymru - Paradise of Wales*".

Welshpool's chief attraction for border people for over 700 years has been its markets especially that for livestock, held regularly on Mondays, bank holidays notwithstanding. Its industries once included malting, tanning and flannel weaving while the now disused Standard Quarry and, out of town, the long-working Buttington brickworks and Briedden quarries were evidence of other industrial activity.

Llanfair Caereinion lay on the old road from Shrewsbury to Aberystwyth and grew up as a market centre for the area of central moorlands, clinging to the steep hillsides flanking the River Banwy. The little township experienced industrial prosperity for a brief span in the nineteenth century, at the same time as the inns were busy with drovers. Then, they came for Llanfair's fairs or were herding pigs or Welsh Black cattle towards the English Midlands. But even when Llanfair's trading function was increasing in importance, communications remained tedious. The river passes through and then turns sharply northwards, spurning the Severn a few miles away and goes on to dally with the Afon Vyrnwy in the picturesque Vale of Meifod. Thus to reach Welshpool, there is a climb over the watershed in the Pass of Golfa at 620ft (189m) above sea-level, between the crests of Pen-y-foel and Y Golfa. A steep descent then follows beside the stream known first as the Sylfaen Brook, then as the Nant-y-caws Brook and in Welshpool as the Lledan Brook. A less direct route between Welshpool and Llanfair uses a gap at 700ft (213m) southwards from the village of Castle Caereinion but this also involves a considerable climb.

Communications for Welshpool and its hinterland began to improve when the canal reached Montgomeryshire. The Ellesmere and Montgomeryshire Canal Acts of 1793-4 also granted powers for the building of rail feeders up to three miles in length to connect with the new waterway. Promoted by Welshpool's Earl of Powis (probably Edward, 2nd Lord Clive), the Welsh Pool Rail Road was constructed about 1818 to carry granite from the Standard Quarry. Though it only survived just over thirty years, it was remarkable in its use so early, apparently, of chaired track and significant in that it indicated a way of cleaving through the town beside the Lledan Brook.

Dreams and Realities

During the Railway Mania of the 1840s, a number of schemes were proposed to bring railways to the area. In 1845, Isambard Kingdom Brunel drew up plans for an impressive scheme to lay broad gauge metals across the Welsh massif. Fulfilment would have put Llanfair Caereinion in early possession of good communication with both London and the west coast. Once already, however, a GWR plan for crossing Wales to carry the Irish traffic to a new port at Porth Dinlleyn in Caernarvonshire (present-day Gwynedd) had been frustrated when Holyhead and the route of the Chester and Crewe Railway were favoured by the Railway Commissioners.

This new attempt, allied to the GWR Company cause, was called the Worcester and Porthdinlleyn Railway. Entering

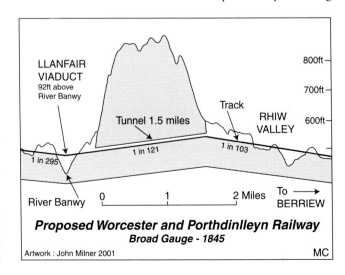

LLANFAIR VIADUCT 92ft above River Banwy

Tunnel 1.5 miles

Track

RHIW VALLEY

1 in 295

1 in 121

1 in 103

River Banwy

800ft
700ft
600ft

0   1   2 Miles   To → BERRIEW

Proposed Worcester and Porthdinlleyn Railway
Broad Gauge - 1845

Artwork : John Milner 2001   MC

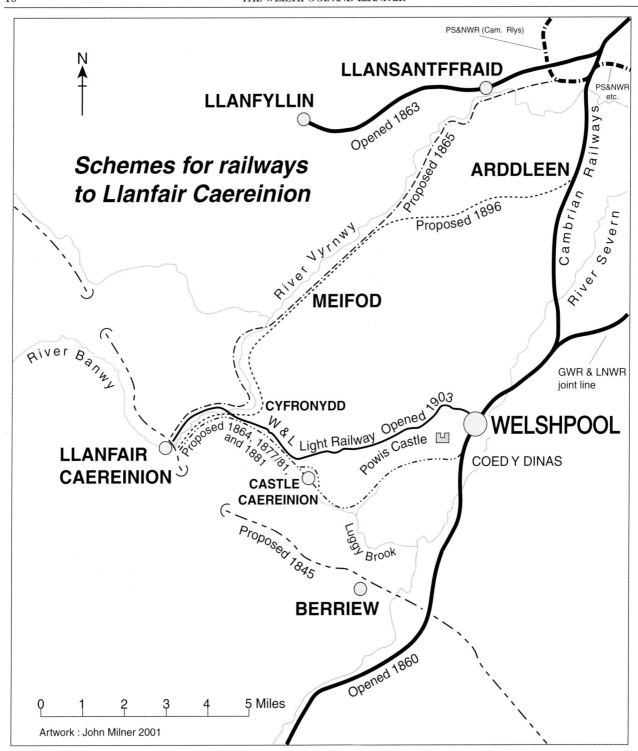

Schemes for railways to Llanfair Caereinion

Artwork : John Milner 2001

Montgomeryshire, the railway would have pierced the Aran range with tremendous feats of cutting, bridging and tunnelling. Westward from Berriew (south of Welshpool), Brunel envisaged a five mile climb steepening to 1 in 103. Deep cuttings were to lead to the summit and the entrance to the 1½ mile Llanfair tunnel. The appreciable incline into the Banwy valley in the tunnel confines would have provided fearsome conditions for crews on the open footplates of the early engines, especially those slogging eastward. A dramatic

viaduct, 92ft (28m) above the river, would have carried the line over Llanfair Caereinion. The Bill was not proceeded with, apparently because it became certain in 1846 that Parliament was to prohibit new broad gauge construction. There is little doubt that cost would anyway have been a seriously inhibiting factor.

The scheme which was eventually successful in bringing the first railway to Montgomeryshire was the Oswestry, Welchpool (*sic*) and Newtown Railway, proposed in 1854.

Tremendous ceremony marked the opening at Welshpool on 4th August 1860, although ten months passed before the line was completed right through to Newtown.

Within the next few years, a great deal of agitation arose for railway connections for many small towns and villages in the vicinity, possession of a railway being regarded by many people in the Welsh valleys as something of a panacea. The busy market centre of Llanfair Caereinion (population 2,584) was no exception. Demand for improved communications with the lowlands was fanned by the introduction of daily services to Welshpool by horse-bus or wagonette although the nine mile journey was slow and uncomfortable. The first wagonettes used offered patrons little protection from the elements. Indeed it is reputed that one poor soul froze to death en route on one occasion! The services were soon arranged to connect with the mid-morning and evening trains at Welshpool but those who were obliged to transfer from rail to road must have been acutely aware of the shortcomings of the only available means of public transport to Llanfair.

The summer months of 1862 saw a definite scheme being hatched out for a railway from Welshpool, the motivation being provided chiefly by Abraham Howell (a solicitor, and the mayor of Welshpool), Capt. Pryce (of Cyfronydd), Major Davis (of Brynglas) and Charles Humphreys (of Llanfair). The proposed route was from Welshpool station, across the canal near the Smithfield Market, by tunnel under the town and on to Llanfair via Golfa. However, the Earl of Powis objected to the route which would have interfered with a favourite road of his.

In September, however, a new route was announced, largely '*suggested by the Earl*'. This used the Dysserth Dingle and Luggy valley, starting from the Oswestry and Newtown Railway, three furlongs (600 metres) south of Welshpool, then skirting the southeastern flanks of the Powis Estate to reach Castle Caereinion (pop. 350), and continuing to Llanfair on the south bank of the River Banwy. Not only did this remove the Earl's earlier opposition but it avoided the expensive necessity of tunnelling to get past the centre of Welshpool which occupied the gap between two hills.

Further public meetings were held in 1862 and it seems that the idea was for a standard gauge branch to be made by a mainline company, at a possible cost of £50,000. The branch would have run at least to Llanfair, perhaps even to Machynlleth, with landowners as far as possible taking shares in payment for their land. Heralding a dispute which was to reach its height thirty-five years later, there was already a lack

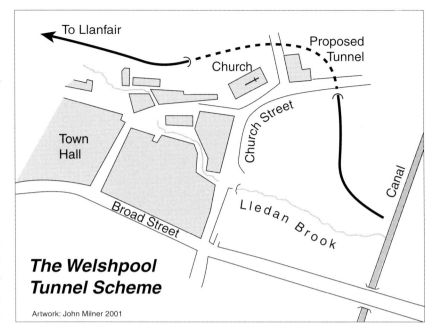

The Welshpool Tunnel Scheme

Artwork: John Milner 2001

of unanimity with regard to the route, some being in favour of a railway from Llanfair leading to Newtown via Forden and others of using the Meifod valley to reach Llansantffraid. The committee consulted David Davies (1818-90) of Llandinam, currently being acclaimed for his feats of construction on the mainline railways of Wales, but the scheme failed to get his support. Thus the matter ended, at least for the time being.

The First Narrow Gauge Scheme . . . . and Opposition

In 1864 Abraham Howell (1810-93), who had taken a prominent part in the promotion of the railways which were to become the backbone of the Cambrian, decided to persuade David Davies to re-examine the scheme he had earlier condemned. One summer's day they set out together to walk over the route past Trefnant Hall, south of Welshpool, along the Luggy Brook and over the summit. Despite the splendour of the Dysserth woods and the magnificence of the views on the descent into the Banwy valley, the expedition only served to convince Davies that he was justified in withholding support. It was a month or two later that an event took place which inspired him with a solution. Over the mountains at Portmadoc (now Porthmadog), the Festiniog Railway, of only 1ft 11$\frac{1}{2}$ ins gauge, was experimenting with steam locomotives after nearly thirty years of slate carrying by gravity and horse. About this time, it was inspected by Capt. Tyler for the Board of Trade. Not only did he pronounce it fit to carry passengers - the first line of less than standard gauge to be so favoured - but he also commended the narrow gauge locomotives as an economic proposition and an example to cheap lines in undeveloped areas. Here, then, was a solution to help the people of Llanfair Caereinion.

The influential gentlemen who had so far been frustrated in their efforts now saw their chance to promote a railway which would be a viable proposition. By 30th November 1864, they had deposited the plans, hoping soon to gain Parliamentary sanction and to be able to raise sufficient money to construct the railway to a narrow gauge. The ten miles of the 'Llanfair Railway', as they called it, were to start on the south bank of the River Banwy close to Llanfair bridge. Eastwards, the line would be close to the river as far as Cyfronydd, rising then for over a mile at 1 in 45 to go under the road at Dolarddyn before cutting round to the north of Castle Caereinion village. It would then descend with long stretches of steep gradients as severe as 1 in 40 via the Luggy valley to the Oswestry and Newtown Railway about a mile south of Welshpool. It was proposed to lay a third rail along the main line and have running powers over mixed gauge track into Welshpool station.

Having now prepared for parliamentary action, it was vital to ensure that financial support would be forthcoming. At a meeting at Llanfair's Goat Inn soon afterwards, it was explained that the scheme, including rolling stock, could be carried through for £33,000. Optimistic though the promoters were, their hopes were once more dashed, for by the spring of 1865 it became apparent that support would be insufficient. Some scorned anything less than 4ft 8½ins, while the newly formed Cambrian Railways Company was quick to disown any affiliation. So lapsed a scheme for what might have been only the second passenger carrying narrow gauge line in the country.

Failure at this stage was also partly due to an alternative scheme which was being mooted, not for the first time nor by any means the last. The inhabitants of Meifod, five miles to the north east of Llanfair, were also anxious to have the benefits of rail communication. They felt that it was physically easier to construct a line of railway along their wide, flat valley floor and through the Banwy gap to Llanfair, while it would provide a more direct route to the limestone quarries, the North Wales coal mines and the livestock markets at Oswestry and beyond. The Meifodians approached Mr. Richard Samuel France, the owner of limestone quarries at Llanymynech, who was interested in railway construction, particularly where it gave him better distribution for his products. He was promoting the Shrewsbury and North Wales Railway, soon to become the Potteries, Shrewsbury and North Wales and later the Shropshire and Montgomeryshire Light Railway.

During 1865, he was asked to add to his plans a lengthy, standard gauge branch from Carreghofa near Llanymynech to Llanfair Caereinion. It was to pass along the Vale of Meifod and up the side of the River Banwy, to reach a station close to the vicarage in Llanfair town. The ruling gradient would have been 1 in 100. By the time his Bill was being considered by a Parliamentary Committee in May 1866, Mr. France was having to explain that the part relating to the Meifod extension was to be deleted due to the lack of funds to carry out its construction.

A Light Railway… and more Narrow Gauge Schemes

A number of years now elapsed before the next move. Towards the end of 1874, at a public meeting the people of Caereinion debated various proposals and plumped for a scheme taking the same direction as the 1864 route - east to

An early twentieth century view of Llanfair Caereinion. The main part of the town is behind the church. Like the Light Railway built, earlier proposals for railways from Welshpool aimed to use the valley in the middle distance to approach the bottom of the town.

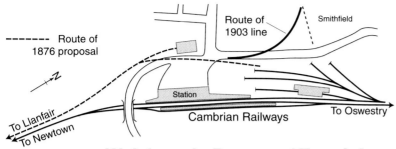

Welshpool : Proposed Termini

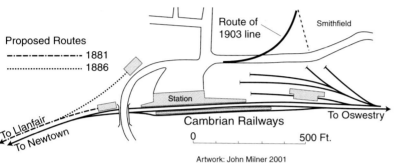

Artwork: John Milner 2001

rather halfhearted in their backing, and as time went by (five years were allowed by the Act for construction) it seemed that the powers at last granted would lapse. It would anyway have been a difficult and expensive line to work with gradients as steep as 1 in 44 and 1 in 51 approaching Castle Caereinion from the Welshpool side and two and half miles of 1 in 64 to reach the village from the west.

But now events took place which were almost a repetition of those of 1864. In 1881, with time running out, the promoters saw an example on the west coast of what they must do. Four years previously the North Wales Narrow Gauge Railway, the Welsh Highland of later years, had opened a line of similar length. The figures available for their train mileage and working expenses convinced the Montgomeryshire promoters that they would be able to pay a $4^1/_2$ per cent dividend on capital of £34,000 which was the estimated cost, including rolling stock, of a narrow gauge line to Llanfair. They argued that a narrow gauge line could be built more cheaply with easier gradients and they hoped receipts would approach the £3,676 of the Llanfyllin branch in 1880 (a depression year) against working expenses in line with the £2,131 of the North Wales Narrow Gauge Railway for that year. They were now able to gain the support of most landowners and promises to take up shares were invited on the understanding that the scheme would be abandoned if less than £22,500 was secured. The Earl of Powis lent his support by taking up £4,000 in shares. Preparations were made to get authority for the change of gauge, to extend the time allowed under the Act for construction and to run the narrow gauge metals into Welshpool to a terminus just south of the main line station. But subscriptions still flagged and in the 1882 parliamentary session, authority was granted for total abandonment of the 1877 scheme.

Some of the leading figures in the struggle for a railway into Caereinion lost heart, including the now ageing Capt. R. D. Pryce of Cyfronydd. But moves now started outside the area, ostensibly to help the people of this part of Mid-Wales to secure what they needed but could not themselves afford. A firm of civil engineers, Simpson, Davies and Hurst of London, was behind this proposition, the last named appearing at a public meeting in the Cross Foxes Hotel at Llanfair Caereinion on 8th October 1886. He promised to raise the balance of the cost if local support could be obtained to the tune of £15,000. Evidence was again provided of the viability of narrow gauge construction. The whole scheme was to cost £40,000 with a 3ft gauge line just over 10 miles in length, again with its own

Welshpool. In the following spring, under the Chairmanship of Capt. R. D. Pryce (then deputy chairman of the Cambrian Railways), a Board was set up consisting of twenty-five landowners. As the summer passed, over £17,000 was promised including a substantial amount from the Earl of Powis who was willing to allow the proposed line to cross his estate, and by the autumn the route was surveyed. Detailed plans were drawn up, this time for a standard gauge line to Welshpool, and further meetings were held at Llanfair to enlist support.

The new plan proposed the western terminus roughly where the present-day station is, shortly crossing the river on a 90ft (27.4m) three-span bridge. After leaving the Banwy valley, it was to climb into Castle Caereinion village, before descending to the Luggy Brook to join the Cambrian's Oswestry and Newtown railway at Coed-y-dinas, a mile south of Welshpool. For £40,000, it was planned to build a light railway for working at a maximum speed of 20mph - a prophetic touch in view of the Light Railway Order quarter of a century later. LNWR and Cambrian Railways' trains were envisaged running over it. There was to be a spur at Welshpool to a separate station.

On 10th August 1877, an Act authorised the construction of a railway from near Welshpool to Llanfair. The line was to be a little over $9^1/_2$ miles long, with an interchange siding for the use of the Dysserth Estate and could be worked by the Cambrian Railways Company. A clause had been inserted authorising the construction of a new carriage road from Pont Sychcoed (Cyfronydd Bridge) to Mathrafal Castle on the Meifod road to give convenient access from the vale to the north. Yet even with such a sop to the Meifodians, insufficient financial support was forthcoming. Some of the residents of Llanfair had been

station in Welshpool just across the road on the west of the Cambrian's. Leaving the side of the main line at Coed-y-dinas, it was to strike out for the Luggy Brook and pass south of Castle Caereinion, crossing the Dolarddyn road on a 25ft (7.6m) span bridge before following the line of the later Light Railway construction. Gradients were to be as steep as ever, including a mile at 1 in 40.

The narrow gauge was becoming more acceptable and, in an editorial column, the *Oswestry Advertizer and Border Counties Herald* enthusiastically advocated support for the latest Llanfair Railway scheme. On 23rd August 1887, Parliament sanctioned the construction. Clauses protected the Earl of Powis's private drive en route and the nearby Dysserth Estate's valuable timber. Although five years were again allowed for completion of the line, contributions once more faltered and the promoters lost interest in favour of potentially more profitable schemes which they departed to survey.

The Light Railways Act

On the horizon, however, there was now appearing the means to provide that necessary extra source of finance. In the nineties, a new Railway Act was anticipated in the valleys of eastern Wales, as in other places, with hopes of rail communications for all and sundry. In November 1895, a meeting in Llanfair Caereinion framed a resolution for their Member of Parliament (A. C. Humphreys-Owen) to take to London. They asked for action by the Government, and shortly afterwards they arranged for a similar demand to be sent to HM Treasury and various Members of Parliament. They wanted public funds, both central and local, to be directed towards railway construction - particularly, of course, for a line to Llanfair. Private enterprise had failed to provide improved communications for these farming communities with slender financial resources.

The agitation was to bear fruit. On 14th August 1896, the Light Railways Act became law. It was an early attempt to develop hitherto economically backward areas by publicly subsidising communications. Finance could be provided, within prescribed limits, from Treasury funds (up to half the total cost) and by local authority subscriptions. Expenses were cut by abolishing the need to obtain authorisation by Act of Parliament, a Parliamentary Order confirmed by the Board of Trade now being sufficient. Furthermore, railways so authorised were to be exempt from the provisions of various Railway Acts in the interests of economy. In view of such relaxation a relatively low overall speed limit was to be imposed, and junctions had to avoid interference with the rails of existing lines as far as possible. The financial assistance was conditional upon an existing railway company constructing and operating the Light Railway, while land for the lines had to be given free

as far as possible and '*all reasonable assistance*' by landowners was expected by the Act. Even before it reached the statute book, Powysians were optimistically calculating the benefits the Light Railways Act would bestow. Quick off the mark, meetings at Llanfair under the auspices of the Parish Council had appointed a committee which was planning a Light Railway before the end of 1895.

The committee's attention was initially drawn to a number of routes - to Welshpool station either by Golfa and through the town centre, or via Dysserth Dingle and the Luggy valley, or via Berriew; to Pool Quay via Golfa and Guilsfield; and via Meifod to Four Crosses or Llanymynech. They visualised standard gauge trains working up the Banwy valley and their findings influenced the 300 parishioners who attended a meeting in May 1896 into deciding - still ahead of the passing of the new Act - upon the Meifod route. That the initiative should come from the people of Llanfair, and that they should apparently be in favour of a line to the north, irked townspeople in Welshpool. Welshpool Town Council now realised that they, too, must act and appointed a committee to investigate and make recommendations.

The Rival Plans

Plans for the Llanfair and Meifod Light Railway were meanwhile taking shape. For an estimated £41,000 it was hoped to build a line, 13½ miles in length, from a station in the vicarage field at Llanfair Caereinion, along the south bank of the River Banwy, past Pont-sychcoed (near Cyfronydd), through Meifod and up a mile-long stretch of 1 in 70 through Sarney to join the Oswestry and Welshpool main line at Arddleen. The chief personality behind the scheme was Dr. C. E. Humphreys of Llanfair, who canvassed the surrounding area for support. In December 1896 the *Border Counties Advertizer* reported the lodging of the application for a Light Railway Order, claiming '*it was the first application from any part of Britain*'.

In Welshpool, while news from their committee was awaited with impatience, various suggestions were voiced. Some were prompted by memories of earlier schemes such as that for a new road to approach Cyfronydd station from the north (to placate Meifodians) and that for a tunnel under part of Welshpool. By October the investigation committee was ready to report to the Town Council which was quick to put the matter to approving townspeople at a public meeting. With thoughts of the light railway system in Belgium in mind, a route was recommended by the roadside (except for the Smithfield Market - Church Street portion in Welshpool and the ascent of Golfa bank). Already, a gauge of 2ft 6ins was mooted. It was commended for its economy, for its facility for sharp curves, for its suitability for extension westwards into the hills and for its capacity for comparatively powerful locomotives with

Welshpool station, opened in 1860, to serve the Cambrian Railways and the L&NWR. Seen over a hundred years later, this was the terminus which the schemes of 1862 and 1864 would have used. The Light Railway that was built eventually connected with sidings at the far end, on the left.

Copyright: R.K.Blencowe collection

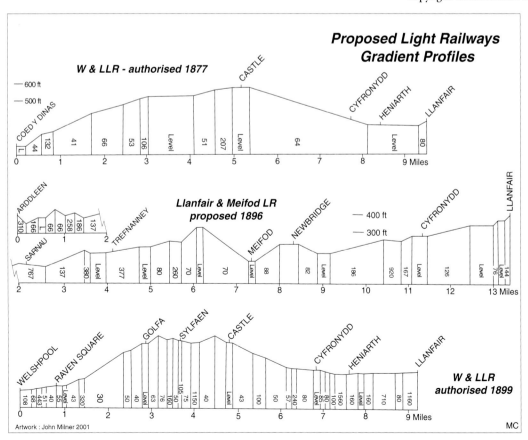

Proposed Light Railways Gradient Profiles

Artwork : John Milner 2001

suitable rail. First estimates of the cost of the scheme including rolling stock put it at £25,000. Messrs. Moorsam and Ward, a Welshpool firm of engineers, prepared a survey of the route, now including a slight diversion across the fields to pass near the small farming community of Castle Caereinion.

On 28th January 1897 a meeting held in Welshpool Town Hall elected a promotion committee, consisting of no less than ninety local worthies including the whole of Welshpool Corporation and Castle Caereinion Parish Council. The chairman was William Forrester-Addie (1851-1921) who, for the second year running, was mayor of the town. The committee soon decided to adopt the projected 2ft 6ins gauge and further resolved that the line should go through the Pass of Golfa, although it was not satisfied with the idea of following the turnpike road as opposition was anticipated from the county council. It was agreed to divert the railway off the roadside all the way west of Raven Square - and also out of Brook Street in Welshpool, cutting through the nearby fields instead. It was now to cross the River Banwy, not at Cyfronydd, but as it neared Llanfair. A projected new street in Welshpool to provide a route for the line between Church Street and Brook Street would have involved the demolition of a dozen shops and houses. It was eventually scaled down to a narrow alley of which the longitudinal bridge over the Lledan Brook was a continuation, the alley requiring the destruction of only three houses. To minimise delays to through rail traffic at Welshpool, the committee envisaged using transporter wagons. Light railway specialist E. R. Calthrop was quoted as saying that transhipment by this means would only take three minutes.

The scheme was explained at Llanfair when a deputation led by Forrester-Addie met the Llanfair Parish Council in April, 1897. The division of support between rival schemes was obviously undesirable, but the parish councillors remained intransigent, the village doctor being particularly critical of the Welshpool scheme. Rebuffed, the delegation returned to Welshpool. At 10.30 on the morning of 7th May 1897, they deposited their £50 with the Clerk to Montgomeryshire County Council together with their plans and application for an Order for a Light Railway of '9 *miles 1 furlong and 1*$^1/_2$ *chains*' (14.71kms) in length.

The Inquiry

The morning of Tuesday 3rd August was fine and warm as a Great Western express with a through coach to Aberystwyth pulled out of Paddington station. Aboard were three men on whose report depended the future of new railways in the Border country - the Earl of Jersey, Colonel Boughey RE and Mr. G. A. R. Fitzgerald, all Light Railway Commissioners. Leaving the train at Welshpool, they reached Llanfair Caereinion to start at 3.30 pm, the official inquiry required by Section VII of the 1896 Light Railways Act. This was only the second inquiry held concerning a narrow gauge line. In the Board School, a large crowd from the surrounding area had gathered to hear the arguments to be put forward for and against the two rival schemes.

Having made their application first, the promoters of the proposed Llanfair and Meifod Light Railway appeared first. Backed by the Mayor of Oswestry and the Cambrian Railways, they detailed the support they had from the parish and district councils along the route. But cross-examination exposed weaknesses in the proposal and local landowners also objected.

It was afternoon on the second day that evidence began relating to the narrow gauge project. W. Forrester-Addie described the merits of the route to Welshpool and the advantages of the proposed gauge, mentioning the possibility of a later extension to Llanerfyl or beyond. Persuasive evidence followed from E. R. Calthrop, formerly engineer to the Barsi Light Railway in India. He neutralised objections to unmanned

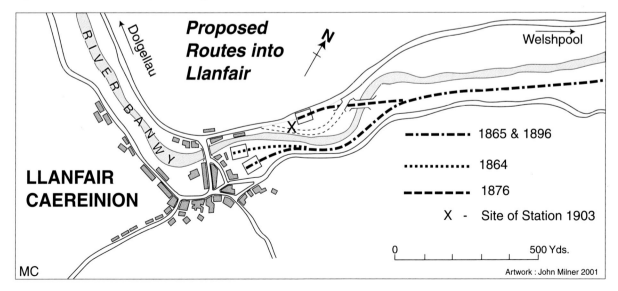

public level crossings and met worries about the need to transfer goods at Welshpool with proposals for transporter wagons. This new and swift method of transhipment was in use in India but, apart from successful tests by Liverpool Corporation, had not yet been adopted in Britain.

His transporter wagon for British railways, apparently, had a narrow body with a platform along each side beside the wheels. This was grooved to take the wheels of standard gauge wagons which were moved on from a ramp-cum-stop block. Hinged flap plates between the side-platforms of each narrow gauge car were designed to allow a whole train of main line wagons to be run on or off at once.

More evidence, equally telling, was provided by Mr. J. R. Dix, manager of the 2ft 3ins gauge Corris Railway, who considered that a narrow gauge line would be able to cope adequately with the traffic. Messages of support were heard from Welshpool merchants and others. Evidence given in favour of the Welshpool scheme had been well marshalled (at no little expense) and scarcely any logical objections were raised.

With admirable speed, the commissioners reviewed the evidence presented at Llanfair Caereinion. On 4th September 1897, letters to the parties concerned informed them that:

'with reference to the application made by Messrs William Addie, John Morris and others to the Light Railway Commissioners for an Order to authorise the proposed Welshpool and Llanfair Light Railway, I am directed to inform you, that after consideration, they have decided to submit in due course to the Board of Trade an Order authorising the line proposed.'

Rejoicing at the news in Welshpool was accompanied by disappointment in Llanfair where, however, they were consoled by the knowledge that a railway to the town was at last decided on, even if their own scheme had failed.

The Light Railway Order

Mr. Forrester-Addie's committee members met once more on 10th March 1898, expressing their thanks for the energetic way he had steered the undertaking since its inception. They nominated the Company's first directors: this Board consisted of the Earl of Powis, Capt. A. R. Pryce, R. C. Anwyl, J. C. Hilton and representing Welshpool Corporation - W. F. Addie, David Jones and W. A. Rogers. Frustratingly, two years were to drag by before the Light Railway Order became applicable. There were several reasons for this delay. The implications of the new Act of 1896 were still being unravelled, the draft Order

submitted needed considerable amendment and negotiations were protracted regarding the company to work the line.

News came in January 1899 that HM Treasury had agreed to a free grant of £7,000 subject to certain conditions, including all the land needed being acquired for £3,000. At the same time the Light Railway Order had been issued by the Commissioners, but during the ensuing months there were still modifications to be made to it by the Board of Trade.

When the Order was finally confirmed on 8th September 1899, it had 95 sections and two schedules and was the 56th to be confirmed. The powers of deviation were limited. In Welshpool, the canal was to be crossed on a bridge that was '*good and substantial*' and clear of the water level by at least 7ft 6ins (2.28m), while power was specifically denied for use of the Order for the compulsory purchase of land belonging to the Shropshire Union Canal Company. A maximum speed limit of 20mph was now specified, further reduced on steep gradients, sharp curves, unfenced sections and road crossings. A maximum axle load of 8 tons was laid down. No less than sixteen clauses were devoted to provisions made for the use of electric power. The possibilities of electrification were currently being advocated - 30 miles northward, the 3ft 6ins gauge Wrexham and Rhos electric tramway was opened early in 1903. Its opening ceremony was to coincide with that of the W&L. Beyond Welshpool, the Order required the provision of at least four fixed stations or stopping places with convenient approaches at which traffic of all kinds would be forwarded and received. These were near Castle Caereinion, Cyfronydd, Heniarth Gate and Llanfair Caereinion. All carriages had to have a '*proper and convenient means of access*' if the company was to avoid the obligation to provide raised platforms. The maximum fare for all third class passengers was to be 1d per mile and no power was granted to carry mails as previously proposed.

Early requirements included signals where trains might cross (although no distant signal was necessary where the home was visible for a quarter of a mile), rail of at least 41½lb per yard, checkrails and metal ties on curves of *under* three chains (198ft/60.5m) radius and specifications for the securing of flat-bottom rail to the sleepers at joints. A turntable was not required, although the stipulation was added that engines running tender first were limited to 15 mph. None of the powers conferred by the Order came into force until the sum of £1,000 had been deposited with the Paymaster General. The compulsory purchase powers were valid for two years, while three years were allowed for completion of the construction of the Railway. But many months would elapse before work could start.

The first motor 'bus' between Welshpool and Llanfair was operated by Tom Norton as the railway was being planned. This was one of his vehicles.

Courtesy : The Automobile Palace Ltd

Welshpool's ornate main line station building which was to be the interchange for the W&LLR's passengers. Freight yards (and the W&LLR terminus) were to the left of the picture.

Chapter 2

Building the Line

Almost from the time the Light Railway Commissioners' decision was announced, the W&L had been negotiating with the Cambrian Railways Company. It also made contact with the LNW and GW joint organisation responsible for the Welshpool - Shrewsbury railway and with the Shropshire Union Railways and Canal Company. The matters involved were the site of the actual terminus in Welshpool and facilities for interchange traffic, as well as the construction and working of the Light Railway. However, only the Cambrian was really interested in the new line. Though the agreement was bandied about for almost twelve months, the W&L had to accede to the Cambrian's insistence that the plans for a swing bridge over the Shropshire Union canal and for a siding to the canal should be scrapped, the clauses in the Light Railway Order amended and the line carried over the waterway at a higher level. Agreement was further delayed while the W&L secured an understanding that the Cambrian and not the Light Railway would accept liability for renewal of the rolling stock.

On 6th March 1900 both parties were able to put their signatures to the agreement. Under the 99 year undertaking, the W&L would provide all necessary rolling stock as approved by the Cambrian while the main line company undertook to construct the line within two years of the land being made available, and to maintain it. It was also to work the line at its own expense, and provide a *'reasonable and sufficient passenger and goods train service.'* Of the gross receipts, the W&L was to get 40 per cent.

During the negotiations, arrangements had also been made for Alfred J. Collin (Cambrian Railways' Chief Engineer, 1898 -1904) to take charge of the engineering work at a fee equivalent to $5^1/_2$ per cent of the cost of the work. In other ways, things seemed to move slowly through the year 1900 as money was raised and as land was acquired, but not without difficulty. When the Cambrian made a detailed estimate of the cost of the project, it totalled £43,204. The figure included £2,950 for the purchase of the land and buildings, £29,530 for the construction and materials and £8,100 for rolling stock. This was considerably more than had first been thought and the W&L immediately took steps to raise additional capital.

The Treasury agreed to increase the free grant from £7,000 to £14,500. Local authorities were asked to increase their contributions and application was successfully made for an amending Order.

Still costs rose and the flow of vital funds flagged. During the summer of 1902, a further approach was made to the Treasury and the free grant was increased to £17,500. But even with this increase in the grant, the Company's financial powers were to prove inadequate.

When tenders were invited, the firm of Guest, Keen and Co. of South Wales successfully quoted £5-1s-0d (£5.05) per ton for 800 tons of Bessemer steel rails, and the six tenders submitted for the civil engineering works ranged from £21,365 to £33,232. Additionally some permanent way materials and various buildings and other items were to be provided by local contractors. Investigations into the standing of a Manchester firm, which submitted the lowest tender for the civil engineering works, proved it to be unsatisfactory. Of the others, the lowest was £24,290 tendered by John Strachan of Cardiff. It was this Welsh firm to which the contract for the civil engineering works was offered in April 1901.

Construction Starts

John Strachan not only accepted but also, to the delight of the W&L Board, agreed to take part payment in shares. A contemporary issue of *Building News* recorded that this was the first contract to be let for a railway authorised by the Light Railways Act of 1896. Swifter progress at last became apparent. On Thursday, 30th May 1901, the first sod was cut in Welshpool with tremendous ceremony. The gaily decorated streets were lined with crowds as the official procession, headed by the band of the Montgomeryshire Imperial Yeomanry, set off from the Town Hall at 12.30 pm. Not only railway officials and councillors were present, but Members of Parliament, the principal landowners, past mayors, magistrates, the police and the fire brigade! Soon after assembling in Colonel Hutchins' field, a burst of cheering from the crowd heralded the approach of a carriage drawn by a pair of superb bay horses and

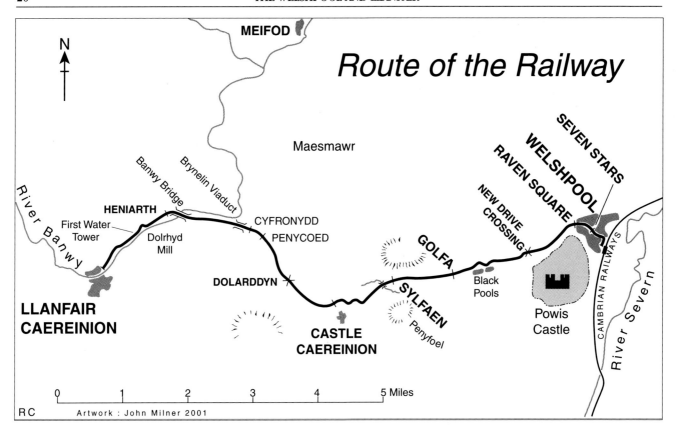

accompanied by outriders. From this alighted Viscount Clive together with his parents, the Earl and the Countess of Powis. W&L director, Mr. J. C. Hilton, then presented the Countess with an oak wheelbarrow adorned with silver mountings. To the young Lord Clive, Mr. Hilton presented an ornate spade (which still exists in the Powysland Museum, Welshpool).

Lord Clive dug the spade into the ground, cutting the letters WLLR and removing the turf in the ceremonial wheelbarrow. In a short speech which followed, the Earl claimed his son had played a part '*in connection with the first light railway which had been undertaken under the Light Railway Act.*' Then the band led the procession back to the Town Hall for luncheon and more speech making. A. C. Humphreys-Owen, MP and Chairman of the Cambrian Railways, compared the earlier failure of private enterprise to build a railway to Llanfair with the result of the united efforts of public bodies, ratepayers' representatives and private persons. A. J. Collin, the engineer, spoke of how they expected to complete the Railway within a few months - in fact it was to take little short of two years. Lord Powis, applauding the generous terms the Cambrian Company had agreed to for running the line, predicted (more truly than he knew) that it would take more than that Company's 60 per cent share of the receipts to work the line.

This grand occasion was quickly followed by commencement of the construction work. Strachan's men began on Monday 2nd June 1901, the third day after the sod-cutting, and a hundred men were soon engaged on the project.

Resident Engineer, A. J. Collin, set up office at the Standard Quarry. During the first few months, work included the arching of the Lledan Brook in Welshpool and preparatory work for all the bridges and cattle creeps, the foundations being ready for all these by the end of July. Early the following year, when Welshpool Council complained about the risk of flooding arising from the way the Brook was being arched over in the town, the bridges in the Brook Street area had to be rebuilt. Nevertheless, the town section including the canal bridge was completed during the spring of that year, apart from the buildings. By now, half the formation of the whole line and the fencing had been done. For about a mile and a half out of Welshpool, the rails were in position and spiked down, though not yet ballasted, and a temporary line continued to Golfa to carry the contractor's materials forward. Beyond this point, earthworks were progressing at various points almost as far west as Cyfronydd and other work was going on still further up the valley.

A start had been made on building the two main viaducts - the Brynelin Viaduct over a ravine near Cyfronydd and the girder bridge to carry the line over the River Banwy on the approach to Heniarth station. Both gave trouble to the engineer. In August 1901, members of the Board of the W&L had toured the works in progress and after visiting the Banwy Bridge works they had complained to the Cambrian Railways Company about the '*perishable nature*' of the stone with which it was being built. As a result, A. J. Collin, the engineer,

On 30th May 1901, as the band played, the young Viscount Clive cut the first sod at Welshpool watched by crowds in the beflagged grandstand erected by John Strachan.

Courtesy : Peter Coward

The silver spade used at the sod cutting ceremony and the oak wheelbarrow, with silver mountings. The spade is inscribed :

Presented to the
Right Honourable The Viscount Clive
by the Directors & Shareholders of the
W&LLR COMPANY
on the occasion of this
Cutting the first sod
of that
Railway at Welshpool
May 30th 1901

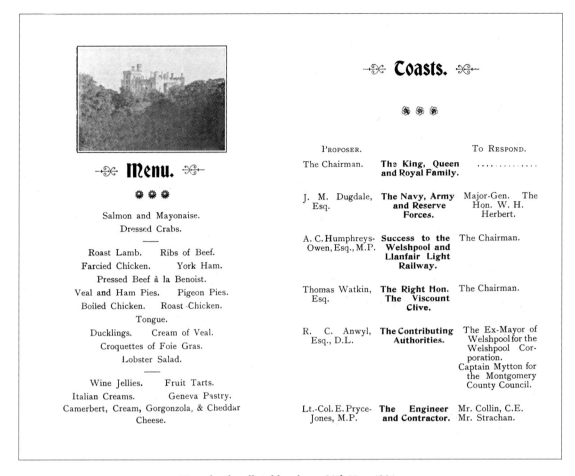

⇜⇝ Menu. ⇜⇝

❀ ❀ ❀

Salmon and Mayonaise.
Dressed Crabs.
———
Roast Lamb.   Ribs of Beef.
Farcied Chicken.   York Ham.
Pressed Beef à la Benoist.
Veal and Ham Pies.   Pigeon Pies.
Boiled Chicken.   Roast -Chicken.
Tongue.
Ducklings.   Cream of Veal.
Croquettes of Foie Gras.
Lobster Salad.
———
Wine Jellies.   Fruit Tarts.
Italian Creams.   Geneva Pastry.
Camerbert, Cream, Gorgonzola, & Cheddar
Cheese.

⇜⇝ Toasts. ⇜⇝

❀ ❀ ❀

PROPOSER.		TO RESPOND.
The Chairman.	**The King, Queen and Royal Family.**	············
J. M. Dugdale, Esq.	**The Navy, Army and Reserve Forces.**	Major-Gen. The Hon. W. H. Herbert.
A. C. Humphreys-Owen, Esq., M.P.	**Success to the Welshpool and Llanfair Light Railway.**	The Chairman.
Thomas Watkin, Esq.	**The Right Hon. The Viscount Clive.**	The Chairman.
R. C. Anwyl, Esq., D.L.	**The Contributing Authorities.**	The Ex-Mayor of Welshpool for the Welshpool Corporation. Captain Mytton for the Montgomery County Council.
Lt.-Col. E. Pryce-Jones, M.P.	**The Engineer and Contractor.**	Mr. Collin, C.E. Mr. Strachan.

Menu for the official luncheon, 30th May, 1901

agreed that it should be rebuilt with better material. That there was an error in siting one of the piers was not to be discovered until many years later.

Near Cyfronydd, the Cwmbaw stream occupied a deep, wooded defile just before it emerged to join the Banwy. Over this defile, the 32ft (9.75m) high Brynelin Viaduct was being constructed of local stone. It was to have six 25ft (7.62m) arches. Difficulties were encountered in the making of the foundations and by the time they had been laid for six of the seven piers, a spell of cold weather (in February 1902) delayed the laying of masonry and concrete even further. The time had come for an inspection of the works in progress by Major Druitt from the Board of Trade's Railway Department. Forrester-Addie and Collin were in attendance. As a result, the Treasury released £7,250, half of the grant then promised.

Strachan's Men and Equipment

Construction gangs generally worked ten hours a day and 'excavators' on the contract were paid 8d (3½p) an hour, although less was paid for boys and a penny or two more for craftsmen such as stonemasons. Strachan's blacksmiths were paid 1s 6d (7½p) an hour. While working on the line near Castle Caereinion in 1902, a number of them caused the village constable acute embarrassment by not only getting drunk but becoming aggressive and insulting and harassing the inhabitants of the small hill-top village. Unfortunately, there was no cell in the village where they could be locked up. How they were eventually restrained is not recorded but soon afterwards they had to appear before the local magistrates and were duly fined. On an earlier occasion, in November 1901, their abundant energy and high spirits had been tapped to form a joint Welshpool and Llanfair and Tanat Valley Light Railway contractor's team for a rugby match against the Oswestry town team.

During the building of the Railway, the contractor provided the men with his own primitive rolling stock, typical of that commonly employed for such projects. At least three small 2ft 6ins gauge locomotives were used. Until the permanent water tank at the Llanfair end was completed, a temporary tank was erected on the Banwy bridge, lifting its water from the river to service these diminutive locomotives.

The best documented is *Strachan No. 9*, an 0-4-0 saddle tank, makers' No. 1655. It left W. G. Bagnall's Castle Engine

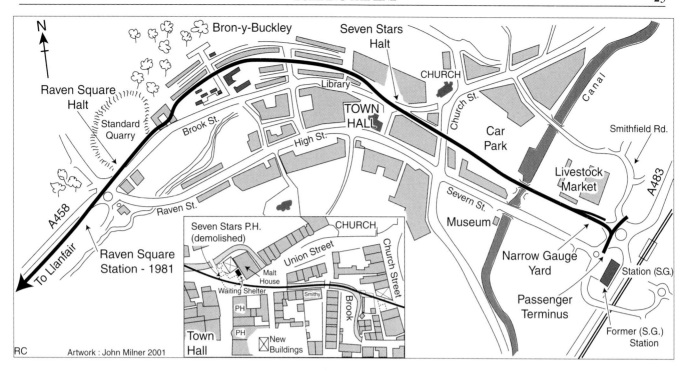

The town section superimposed on a map of Welshpool today. Inset: The town centre in 1903.

To get through the town, a longitudinal bridge was built over the Lledan Brook and the line poked its way through a tangle of backyards. The scene in 1965 was little changed from the day it was built.

Works, Stafford, on 17th September 1901 for delivery new to the W&L contract. Another locomotive on this contract was built by the Hunslet Engine Company, Leeds, in 1883, makers' No. 307. This was a standard type 0-4-0 saddle tank with 7ins by 10ins cylinders and 1ft 8ins wheels. It was employed in Northamptonshire until about 1900 and by autumn 1902, it was at Welshpool.

The third narrow gauge engine known to have been on the contract was *Strachan No. 8*. A photograph of the Banwy Bridge, reputedly taken in 1902, shows a tiny cabless 0-4-0 side or pannier tank with outside frames and cylinders standing on the centre. The tanks extend to the front of the smokebox. Details suggest the maker was the Falcon Engine Works, Loughborough, in the late 1880s, or just possibly Black, Hawthorn and Company Limited of Gateshead.

Of the contractor's rolling stock there is little record. Bagnall supplied new steel 'V' type tipping wagons in 1902 and old prints show wooden bodied tippers. There was an auction of Strachan's equipment at Standard Quarry, Welshpool, on 15th May 1903 but little is known of the fate of much of the stock. Of the locomotives, Bagnall No. 1655 was definitely not sold. The makers supplied spares for it in June 1903, suggesting that some contractors' work was still proceeding, indeed the Bagnall tipping wagons were still in use in August 1903. By September 1903, however, *Strachan No. 9* had been transferred to Strachan's contract for the construction of Welham marshalling yard, L&NWR, near Market Harborough, eventually passing to Jees Hartshill Granite and

The Banwy Bridge was completed in 1902 at a cost of £998. Until the permanent water tank near Dolrhyd Mill was completed, the temporary tank on the left raised water from the river for Strachan's locomotives. Strachan No 8 stands near the middle.

Brick Company Limited for their 2ft 6ins gauge system at Hartshill, near Nuneaton, Warwickshire. It survived there, named *Butcher,* until scrapped in 1945. It seems certain that the W&L had no interest in the contractors' stock at the sale in 1903 and one can only assume that the other two narrow gauge locomotives (*Strachan No. 8* and Hunslet 307) left for pastures new.

At Welshpool there was for a time a temporary standard gauge track. It ran through the site of the narrow gauge goods yard and here John Strachan had a standard gauge 0-4-0 saddle tank engine named *Strachan No. 3.* This 4ft 8½ins gauge locomotive was built by Hunslet, makers' No. 365, in 1885, for the contractors Holme and King at Brentwood, Essex. Then called *Phyllis,* it had 10ins by 15ins cylinders and 2ft 9ins wheels. Strachan was using this engine at a contract at Stafford in 1897 and besides his Welshpool contract, he used it on his Tanat Valley contract 1899–1904. During the final stages of construction, the contractor hired *The Earl* (for £50) to haul trains conveying his men to work, its tractive effort being appreciated on the considerable gradients along the line.

Delays

Although at one time it was thought that the Railway might be ready by August 1902, there was more trouble ahead and meanwhile costs were rising. Excavations were encountering rock unexpectedly and doubt about the accuracy of the surveyor's levels necessitated changes in the planned gradients. The engineer and contractor were having to execute considerable extra work at Heniarth to transform the narrow, twisting, steeply graded track from the main road into a satisfactory approach to the station. The necessity for widening, lowering and metalling this lane was to be contested later when the company and the contractor became involved in a lawsuit, but timber hauliers using the approach in later years were no doubt grateful for the improvements.

During the summer of 1902, it was necessary to apply to the Board of Trade for an extension of the time granted by the Light Railway Order for construction. It was agreed to extend the expiry of this period from September 1902 to 7th March 1903. This seemed more than adequate for, in the early autumn of 1902, the engineer considered that work was nearing completion and there was discussion of a formal opening date towards the end of November. But this was reckoning without the wiles of the local climate. To the consternation of the construction gangs, the end of 1902 brought almost continuous heavy rain, something for which this upland area tends to be notorious. This hampered work considerably and the *Border Counties Advertizer* reported that the opening would be delayed until the middle of December, although even this proved to be over-optimistic.

The wet weather caused slips in some of the cuttings, and these had to be cleared out, the slopes made flatter and extra drains inserted. Near Dolrhyd Mill, between Heniarth and Llanfair, the river rose in angry and menacing torrents and finally flowed over on to the line, washing away the new ballast and spoiling much of the work which had been done. Eventually, as the water receded, the river walls were built up an extra twelve inches (300mm) to help prevent a recurrence of the disaster. In all, the inhospitable Welsh weather cost the

Company many weeks delay and an extra £760 for the measures made necessary. Happily, the construction was eventually finished with a complete '*immunity from accidents*' to the men, as the contractor afterwards claimed.

While construction workers were striving to complete the task in the face of these set-backs, another struggle was becoming serious. This was in the boardroom; how best could the now inadequate finances be eked out? In July 1902 the Board of Trade had announced the increase in the free grant (to £17,500), but even with this it was clear that the Company would be short of the total capital required. Various attempts to raise more were made throughout the summer, including canvassing the residents of Welshpool.

One way of reducing capital costs was to eliminate the cost of signalling apparatus. It was at this time that the Cambrian Railways Company was persuaded to agree to work the line on a '*one engine in steam*' basis. The Cambrian also agreed that plans for a locomotive shed at Llanfair could be dropped but not those for a carriage shed at Welshpool, though this was to be shortened to accommodate only two coaches. A suggestion to shorten the transhipment shed at Welshpool was rejected by the Cambrian's General Manager C.S. Denniss as it had to hold two mainline wagons at once. The W&L Board was right to cut back in the circumstances. A hint of future

Strachan No 9 was renamed Butcher *after leaving the W&L project. It was one of Bagnall's standard Margaret class locomotives with 7ins by 12ins cylinders, a 3ft 6ins wheelbase and the maker's characteristic circular firebox.*

Collection: Frank Jones

The Welshpool shunter. Strachan No 3 stands in what was to be the narrow gauge goods yard on a temporary standard gauge siding in front of the cattle pens. This standard gauge Hunslet 0-4-0 saddle tank built in 1885 presumably handled the delivery of construction materials arriving via the main line.

CAMBRIAN RAILWAYS COMPANY.

TENDER FOR

The Construction of

THE

WELSHPOOL & LLANFAIR

LIGHT RAILWAY.

To the Directors of the Cambrian Railways Company.

GENTLEMEN,

    I hereby propose to execute and complete to the entire satisfaction of the Company's Engineer, the whole of the works required in the construction of the Welshpool and Llanfair Light Railway, in strict accordance with the Plans and Specifications, and the terms and conditions mentioned therein, and exhibited to *me* , and will provide all labour, materials, and everything requisite to complete the same, for the sum of

✗ £ *26,290.0.0* less 2½ per cent. discount.

£24282... *See correction in Summary*

    The whole to be completed within **Fifteen Months** *after receiving the order to proceed, under a penalty of £50 per week for each and every week, should the works be incomplete after that date.*

    And *I* further agree to uphold and maintain in perfect repair, and at *my* expense, the whole of the works for **Twelve Months** *after receiving the final Certificate of Completion, and undertake to enter into a Contract and to provide a satisfactory Bond for the due performance of this Contract if required.*

As witness *my* hand 18 this *12th* day of *Mar* 1901.

John Strachan's navvies pause during the building of a cattle creep on Golfa bank. The besuited gentleman on the right may be inspecting progress.

Near the summit between Golfa and Sylfaen, navvies work on the shallow cutting using only picks, shovels, wheelbarrows and a horse.

In the summer of 1902, the western-most (left-hand) arch of Brynelin Viaduct awaited its keystone. Meanwhile, the centring has been removed from arches just completed. Temporary track has been laid across the work in progress.

developments might well have been seen, if it could have been appreciated, when the first public motor service between Llanfair and Welshpool had started on 3rd December 1900. Augmenting the existing horse-drawn omnibus, Tom Norton's covered wagonette ran twice daily in a journey time of 50 minutes - quicker than the new train service when that started.

Choosing the Rolling Stock

The W&L minutes of 19th December 1900 record agreement with the Cambrian Railways, as future operators, for the following stock to be available for the opening of the W&L at a total estimated cost of £6,350:

2 locomotives	£3,200
2 coaches	£900
1 extra coach	£200
40 wagons	£1,000
4 covered wagons	£240
2 cattle wagons	£170
1 travelling crane	£150
10 timber trucks	£250
2 break vans (*sic*)	£240

Mr. H. E. Jones, the Cambrian Railways locomotive superintendent (1899-1918), was given responsibility for preparation of designs for the stock. These were submitted in January 1901 with a recommendation that the crane be excluded if the W&L Board had to make further economies. The Cambrian Railways made strenuous efforts to persuade

the W&L Board to include a third locomotive in the estimates (together with a small shed at Llanfair to house it), but lack of capital precluded this.

The first vehicles ordered for the line were the two tank engines. In March 1902, their construction at Beyer Peacock's Gorton Works near Manchester had been delayed and the Cambrian was explaining that this was because they had had to be specially designed. In view of this, the W&L was considering hiring a locomotive from W. G. Bagnall and Co. of Stafford for the opening, but during August the first of their own was completed. It arrived at the Cambrian Railways station in Welshpool in September 1902, on what a contemporary newspaper called a '*special trolley*'. *The Earl*, as it was destined to be, was temporarily stowed under a tarpaulin and three weeks later the sister engine arrived.

Well before the end of 1902, the initial goods and passenger vehicles had arrived from the Lanarkshire firm of R. Y. Pickering and Co. Generally, the goods vehicles were scaled down versions of main line stock; however, H.E. Jones' expertise with regard to the designs was disputed by E. R. Calthrop, the specialist on light railways who had spoken at the Inquiry in 1897. He was currently engineer to the Leek & Manifold Light Railway, also under construction. Calthrop believed that long steel-framed 8-wheel freight vehicles with a low axle load and with his patent centre buffer coupling would have been better for this gauge. He criticised cheap, heavy, wooden framed wagons like those at Welshpool and he was scornful of the choice of Norwegian hook couplings. He referred to the excessive slack between the buffer heads and to jamming which would occur when short and long vehicles, coupled together,

To minimise costs, cuttings like this were made only when unavoidable. Temporary track was worked by horses until the formation was sufficiently advanced for Strachan's little locomotives.

The Shropshire Union canal was crossed by this steel plate girder bridge which is still in situ. It has a single span of 33ft 4ins (10.6m). A siding to the canal eventually agreed in July 1902 was never constructed. In the foreground, the Lledan Brook passed under the canal.

Below : *Looking west over the canal bridge. The approach was on a 1 in 33 incline.*

W&LLR Pres. Co.

were hauled round curves.

Even though the work on the line was incomplete, no time was lost in making use of the new stock as soon as the permanent way reached Llanfair. On 30th September 1902, Strachan conveyed the first wagon of coal behind one of his little four-coupled locomotives and on 3rd October, the directors of the W&L set out behind *The Earl*. Their accommodation consisted of seats in one of the open wagons. After some distance, *The Earl* was replaced by one of the contractor's much smaller machines, probably to facilitate progress over incompletely ballasted track. When the party eventually reached Llanfair, the event was celebrated with champagne before the somewhat precarious return journey began.

Perhaps they had been lucky: difficulties were experienced with the new freight stock soon afterwards. In November 1902, some of the wagons loaded with stone broke away on Golfa incline and careered down the bank before crashing into the Standard Quarry. Jones went out on to the nearly finished line to conduct tests and his report confirmed that some wagons were coming loose. He alleged that that they were not being properly coupled together but concluded that the '*excessive gradients and curves*' as he put it, called for extra precautions. He therefore advocated side chains with which all the stock had to be fitted by the time the line opened.

The Line Described

In January 1903, A. J. Collin, the chief engineer, decided that the line was sufficiently complete for approval by the Board of Trade. This followed prodding by the W&L directors who had reminded Collin of the approach of the time limit

set for construction.

There now existed a 2ft 6ins gauge railway starting from a point in Welshpool's Smithfield Road and close to the Cambrian Railways' goods and passenger station (240ft/73m above sea level). Its length was 9.06 miles (14.48 km), station to station; later spurs at Welshpool added another 154 yds (141 metres) of track. At this terminus, there was a gravel 'platform' and a waiting room with a booking office complete with awning. A short siding swung away into the Cambrian Railways' yard to the transhipment shed, while the main line of the new narrow gauge construction curved off from Smithfield Road. Entering enclosed property, it passed the run round loop on the left and the three sidings on the right which formed single roads

View of Golfa bank, newly built, looking east. Note the coarse ballast and the steep drop to the Black Pools.

into the goods shed, the engine shed and the longer carriage shed adjoining. A steep climb took the Railway over the Shropshire Union canal before crossing the main road (Church Street) on the level.

Then the track dived through the newly opened gap between the buildings to reach the Lledan Brook. Above the watercourse, the rails were borne on longitudinal bearers supported by steel cross girders to enable the railway to reach and cross Union Street, where the Seven Stars public house and adjoining Malthouse had had to be demolished and where trains would make a stop for passengers. Disappearing behind the cottages with two more stretches of viaduct, the route lay behind the Armoury to pass by the Standard granite quarry, where a siding was soon to be connected, and so to Raven Square. On the town side of the intersection, a line-side gravelled area marked the third station.

Gaining its own reservation again beyond the road crossing, and protected here as in most places westwards by a cattle guard, the line at first paralleled the main Dolgellau road. Later it swung away a little, to ease the gradient. Even so, it climbed at a nominal gradient of 1 in 30 for about a mile up the later renowned Golfa bank, with the track winding through some of the deepest cuttings on the line, being up to 15ft (4.5m) deep. The ascent eased approaching a crossing over a minor

road (Cwm Lane), and here Golfa station consisted of an 80ft (24.4m) platform and a 120ft (36.6m) loop. Over the first summit, 603ft (184m) above sea level and coming alongside the Dolgellau road again, a siding had been constructed for Sylfaen Farm with standing room for four trucks. It was not envisaged as a regular passenger station at this stage.

Veering across the fields again, the second summit at 578ft (176m) was attained at the junction with another minor road (Coppice Lane) before passing beneath a wooden accommodation bridge, the only overbridge on the line. The descent was made through a cutting into Castle Caereinion station, distinguished by a 120ft (36.6m) gravel platform with a waiting shed and a somewhat longer loop than at Golfa. The loop was worked from ground frames, there being no signal box at this time.

A lengthy descent, at first at 1 in 33, then at 1 in 51, led to Dolarddyn road crossing. Eventually the line passed through Cyfronydd station, which boasted a loop and another 80ft (24.4m) gravel platform replete with waiting shed. A little further on, the Cwmbaw stream was crossed by the 50yd (45.9m) long six arch Brynelin Viaduct, and a short descent at 1 in 25 brought the line close to the River Banwy. At about 7½ miles from Welshpool, a girder bridge supported by two stone piers crossed the river on the skew in two spans of 32ft

Near Castle Caereinion, the line's only overbridge served farmers whose landholdings had been divided. It imposed a maximum loading height of 12ft. It lasted until 1932.

9ins (9.98m) and one of 34ft (10.3m). Beyond this, Heniarth Gate station was built, having a shelter for passengers together with the usual 80ft (24.4m) gravelled alighting area and a 120ft (36.6m) loop siding.

Little over half a mile west of the station was situated Dolrhyd Corn Mill. The original plans were for the Railway to pass along the slope between the Mill and the main road, but a last minute change of plan (which involved deviating beyond the limits authorised) saw the contractor squeeze the formation between the Mill and the river. This saved the cost of buying property and land but necessitated the remarkably sharp curves which are still a feature of this part of the line. On the west of

the Mill, a water tower was constructed. It was fed by a ram, a device using the pressure of inflowing river water to lift water, at a rate of three gallons a minute, to the tank.

Following closely alongside the river, the Railway ran past the timber yard of E. Jones and Sons (Tanllan corner) and then into Llanfair Caereinion station. The terminal was laid out with a 120ft (36.6m) gravel platform a few inches high, a loop and two sidings. On the platform stood the combined booking office and waiting room, wrought in corrugated iron with an awning projecting helpfully, while further along stood a urinal. The original goods shed was 30ft by 12ft (9.1m x 3.6m).

Land for the line had been obtained from numerous owners, mostly in small parcels except for the three miles between the Armoury in Welshpool and a point near Sylfaen, all of which the Earl of Powis had owned. He had donated this land to the Company, this and other gifts of land making up about half the total length and being valued at £2,400. The remainder of the land and buildings eventually cost £6,753, somewhat more than had been anticipated. Probably one of the most expensive single transactions had been the purchase for £1,175 of the Seven Stars public house in Welshpool. A troublesome acquisition was that of land below Golfa Hall, which belonged to the Rev. G. R. Pugh, and the Order specifically protected the reverend gentleman from compulsory purchase. When agreement with

The route past Dolrhyd Mill

LLANFAIR ←   PUBLIC ROAD   → WELSHPOOL

WT   Mill Race

MELIN DOLRHYD

RIVER   WEIR   BANWY

Boat House

0   200 Ft.

- - - Limits of Deviation authorised in 1897.
X   Probable site of request Halt.
WT   Site of early Water Tower.

Artwork : John Milner 2001   MC

him seemed unattainable, Collin drew up plans to re-route the line. Clauses relating to this were drafted for inclusion in the Amendment Order 1901, but were repealed when agreement was at last reached later that year.

The two major bridging works have already been mentioned. The line had also been carried over thirteen smaller underbridges, mainly over watercourses, and formed by timber baulks bearing each rail and mostly under 10ft 6ins (3.2m) in span. In two locations, however, masonry was used to build arches to provide cattle creeps beneath the line.

Board of Trade Inspections

This was the new line of Light Railway which the Railway Department of the Board of Trade sent Major E. Druitt RE to inspect on Tuesday 3rd February 1903. His examination was no less thorough than usual and included a careful survey of the ground frame equipment and rolling stock as well as the trackwork. He was dissatisfied with a number of matters, although they were points which could readily be put right. Before the line could be opened, the inspector required check rails on all sharp curves on high banks and across the main bridges and steel ties on the sharp curves. He thought that in view of the 10ft (3m) fixed wheelbase of the locomotives, the gauge should be eased on the sharper curves by up to half an inch (13mm). Along the line, he recommended the fixing of mile and quarter mile posts, these increasing the construction costs by £36.

The ballast needed attention in places and the sidings at Sylfaen, Heniarth and Llanfair required slewing away from the main line to give more clearance opposite the trap points. He also considered that the centre buffer couplings on the rolling stock should have more lateral movement, otherwise they

---

CAMBRIAN RAILWAYS.

PUBLIC NOTICE.

THE LINE BETWEEN WELSHPOOL AND LLANFAIR
IS NOW OPEN
FOR
GOODS, MINERAL AND LIVE STOCK TRAFFIC.

RATES and other information may be obtained from the Company's Agents at Welshpool and Llanfair, or from Mr. W. H. GOUGH, Traffic Superintendent, Oswestry.

C. S. DENNISS,
Secretary and General Manager.
Oswestry, March, 1903.

Llanfair station soon after completion. The siding is filled with private owner wagons carrying coal. Beyond, is the goods shed (in its original shorter form) while in the distance is a simple ramp for loading cattle which was later replaced by a larger stone-faced dock. For passengers, only a low level platform is provided. Inset : *Announcement in the* Oswestry and Border Counties Advertizer, *11th March 1903. It was repeated in several subsequent issues.*

would be dangerous on the numerous curves. Below Golfa, the sharp reverse curves would have to be subject to a 5mph limit.

About two weeks later, on 20th February, Major Druitt paid a return visit. Many of the modifications he had asked for had been completed including the alterations to the couplings. Accompanied by the chief and resident engineers, W. F. Addie and H. E. Jones together with C. P. Winnall (the W&L solicitor), he traversed the whole line in a train which was considered to be typical of the likely formation of an ordinary mixed train. It consisted of a passenger coach, two covered vans, three open wagons and a brake van. It emerged that John Strachan's men had still more work to do. One of the results of the inspector's imposition of a 5mph speed limit on the Golfa bank curves was that alterations to the super-elevation of the track were required. Check rails at potential danger spots positioned 3ins (77mm) from the running rails, as he had suggested, now proved to be half an inch (13mm) too far out as the wheels of the rolling stock were narrower than those of the engines and could possibly drop between the parallel rails on each side. Making out his second report, Major Druitt was cautious about certifying the line as safe and gave only a conditional recommendation that the line could open for passenger traffic.

This meant that the Board of Trade had still to await the engineer's report that measures imposed with regard to the sharp curves were completed. The ground frames also had to be properly connected up and working was to be subject to an overall speed limit of 15mph (until the formation had consolidated). In addition, the Cambrian Railways Company had to formally apply for permission to run mixed trains.

Opening Approved

Anticipating that these details would swiftly be attended to, the W&L Board now made preparations for the long looked for opening. Provisionally, it was to be on Tuesday 31st March. As the Earl was away in India, a telegram was dispatched to Bombay informing him of the imminence of the opening of the Railway he had done so much to help, and asking him to return to preside at the ceremony. With little delay, the Board of Trade was able formally to agree that the line had been brought up to a satisfactory standard. On 4th March 1903, they wrote to Harrison and Winnall, the Company's solicitors, at Welshpool sanctioning the opening of the Railway for passenger traffic.

Arrangements were quickly made to start running freight services. With the Chairman, the Earl, still on his way back from India, the ceremony marking the opening of passenger services was not expected before the last day of that month. On the Monday after the communication from the Board of Trade, 9th March 1903, Mr. Price, the Welshpool stationmaster,

supervised the making up of the first official freight train consisting of fifty tons of grain and coal. Some unscheduled dispatch of freight to various points along the line had apparently already occurred, but nevertheless a small crowd, including Welshpool's town clerk, gathered in the yard to cheer away the train on this occasion. Starting away at 11.30am, it was *The Countess*, which, with warning whistles, gamely hauled the load up the gradient through Welshpool's houses, fighting stretches of slippery rail as she continued.

Knots of spectators awaited the passing of the train at various points and the first stop, apart from road crossings, was made at Heniarth to detach a wagon of coal for someone in that neighbourhood. The train reached Llanfair station in just under an hour, to be heartily welcomed by a large crowd. Starting at 1.45pm, the return journey took a little longer despite stopping at intermediate stations to pick up empties. A second trip was worked the same day and two more the next day, even before a proper advertisement had appeared in the local press.

Arrangements had to be finalised to start passenger services, and application was made to the Treasury for payment of the balance of the free grant. Bureaucracy now took a hand. Under an agreement made in 1901 with the Cambrian Railways and the W&L, the Treasury had undertaken to pay the second instalment of the free grant if the line should '*open within the time limited by the Order . . . . for public traffic*'. Correspondence passed to and fro between HM Treasury and the Board of Trade while the meaning of '*public traffic*' in the agreement was disputed. As long as the Board of Trade could only certify that the Railway had opened for goods traffic, the Treasury was reluctant to part with the funds. It was decided to ask the W&L to render a statutory declaration from the working company that the line had actually been opened. With this, the Board of Trade's Railway Department felt able to issue certificate No. R.3680 which, at last, the Treasury accepted as evidence that it could forward the £10,250 needed by the W&L. Signed by Sir Herbert Jekyll, assistant secretary to the Board of Trade, on 3rd April 1903, the last paragraph read:

And whereas on the 4th day of March 1903, the Board of Trade, having considered the terms of the said report (viz. Major Druitt's) and being satisfied that the said Light Railway had been properly completed, sanctioned the use of the line for the public conveyance of passengers. Now therefore the Board of Trade do hereby certify that the Welshpool and Llanfair Light Railway has been completed to their satisfaction and is fit for public traffic.

*Signed by Order of the Board of Trade,
this 3rd day of April 1903.*

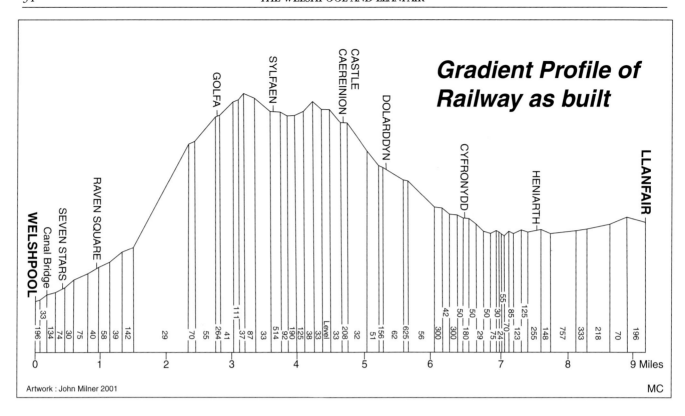

Gradient Profile of Railway as built

WELSHPOOL

Canal Bridge

SEVEN STARS

RAVEN SQUARE

GOLFA

SYLFAEN

CASTLE
CAEREINION

DOLARDDYN

CYFRONYDD

HENIARTH

LLANFAIR

Level

0   1   2   3   4   5   6   7   8   9 Miles

Artwork : John Milner 2001

MC

At Llanfair station, soon after the railway opened, staff (and some elegantly attired ladies) pose in front of the corrugated iron booking office-cum-waiting room. The train seems ready to depart with the composite coach and a couple of wagons.

W&LLR Pres Co.

Chapter 3

The Cambrian Era

Saturday 4th April 1903 was finally chosen as the day for the inauguration of passenger services. At Welshpool, the day brought with it cold and rainy conditions although these were ameliorated by the gay appearance of the town which was decorated with flags and coloured bunting. The Earl of Powis, Chairman of the Company, directors W. Forrester-Addie and C. Shuker, together with Mr. John Evans, the W&L secretary, met briefly to fix the Company's common seal to an Agreement with the Cambrian that the line would be worked in accordance with Board of Trade requirements.

In Smithfield Road, the special train was drawn up with *The Countess* simmering at the head of the three bronze-green and white coaches. The engine, smartly painted in black and lined in orange yellow, was embellished with green and red art muslin, red rosettes sporting yellow centres and the traditional daffodils. Displayed on the smokebox door and on the rear bunker panel were the Prince of Wales feathers surrounded by leeks, while white letters on a red background on the boiler side proclaimed '*Success to the W&LLR*'. By eleven o'clock, several hundred people had gathered in the nearby road. A warm welcome was accorded the Earl of Powis when he drove up in his dogcart to be joined by his co-directors. In turn they welcomed the officials of the Cambrian Railways Company who alighted at the main line station from a special train from Oswestry.

Shortly after 11.15 am, the signal was given for the train to start, with Herbert Jones, the Cambrian's locomotive superintendent, on the footplate. Amid the cheering of the crowds along the route, the ringing of bells and a fusillade of detonators, the *special* steamed forward through Welshpool town. At every vantage point the inhabitants gathered to give the '*little train*' a hearty cheer and at the Standard Quarry, rocks were blasted as it approached. Some guests arriving late from Shrewsbury made use of the bus from the Royal Oak Hotel to enable them to dash to Llanerchydol Gates (Raven Square) where the train made a brief stop to pick them up before setting out on the rural journey. At various points along the line, small groups of country folk had gathered and gave the *special* a vociferous welcome. A stop was made at

Cyfronydd, to entrain Captain Pryce, the Company's deputy chairman who chose to start his ceremonial ride from the neighbourhood of his home.

At Llanfair terminus, the train passed under a huge arch of greenery and entered the crowded station to the accompaniment of fog signals and sustained loud cheering. More evergreen arches had been erected near the entrance and the little station was decorated overall with flags and banners. It is recorded that even one of the Llanfair busmen, who expected to be superseded, paraded alongside in the road with his horse and vehicle decked out in ribbons and bright colours. The day was taken as a holiday in Llanfair; the church bells had been ringing all morning and the waiting villagers had been entertained by the Llanfair band. The passengers

---

WELSHPOOL AND LLANFAIR LIGHT RAILWAY.

OPENING CEREMONY.

SATURDAY, APRIL 4th 1903.

OFFICIAL PROGRAMME.

11-15 a.m. — Special Train will leave Welshpool Station for Llanfair.
(Free Railway Passes—not transferable— will be sent on application to all Share-holders of £15 and upwards).

12-15 p.m. — Reception at Llanfair Station.

1-0 p.m. — Special Train leaves Llanfair.

1.45 p.m. — Special Train arrives at Welshpool.

2.0 p.m. — Public Luncheon at the Royal Oak Hotel, Welshpool. Chairman : The Earl of Powis. Tickets, 3/6 each.

The Directors much regret that the small space at their disposal obliges them to limit the issue of Free Railway Passes.

To ensure seats being reserved at the Luncheon Table, Tickets should be taken at the Royal Oak Hotel, Welshpool, not later than Tuesday, March 31st.

JOHN EVANS.
24, Broad street, Secretary.
Welshpool, 23rd March, 1903   12

Advertisement for opening ceremony in the Border Counties Advertizer, 1st April 1903

Tremendous celebrations marked the opening on 4th April 1903. The Earl of Powis, W&LLR directors and representatives of the Cambrian Railways Co. (to the right) were present, contrasting with more lowly townspeople. The train stands in Smithfield Road - the W&LLR was too poor to provide a proper station though, for ten years, there was a waiting room-cum-booking office.

Courtesy: Powysland Museum

now alighted from the inaugural train and, from the waiting room, biscuits and jugs of champagne were dispensed, supplied by the proprietor of Llanfair's Wynnstay Arms Hotel. These were the days when champagne cost 6s (30p) per bottle. Mr. W. A. Jehu (whose land had been used for that end of the line) found a vantage point on a large boulder, and on behalf of the inhabitants of the district welcomed the new railway. The Earl replied, mentioning the near £50,000 spent and their inability to find funds to equip the line to run more than one engine in steam.

When it was time for the train to return, many of the folk from Llanfair saw the opportunity for a free ride to Welshpool. The station-master, Mr. Barrow-Griffiths, and his helpers had great difficulty in closing the gates of the new coaches. Thus it was a little past the scheduled departure time of 1.00pm when *The Countess* was able to pull out, reaching Seven Stars in Welshpool less than three quarters of an hour later. A large party alighted and repaired to the Royal Oak Hotel for luncheon

with more speechmaking. In final commemoration of the occasion, a medal was struck bearing the arms of the borough.

The opening of the line, sought after for so many years, had been celebrated in fine style, yet this did not stifle criticism from some quarters. Keen to derive maximum benefit from the new railway, which many of them had wanted to come from Arddleen and Llanymynech, the inhabitants of Llanfair held public meetings during the first month of operation to convince the Cambrian that its freight rates were too high and its passenger timetable inconvenient and slow. In response, the working company quickly made some reduction in its rates, although not enough to satisfy all its critics. Two years later it was able to lop a quarter of an hour off the journey time, reducing it to 55 minutes each way. Some of the people of Caereinion were disappointed that there were only three trains each day at first and that none arrived at Llanfair later than 6.05 pm, but soon a later working was introduced.

After the opening of the W&L in 1903, passenger services

Medal struck to mark the opening of the railway

seem to have been almost unexpectedly well patronised, though as things settled down, mid-week services attracted a lighter pattern of traffic. The first Monday market trains were heavily laden with passengers packed '*like sardines in a tin*' according to a contemporary report. On at least one occasion, the services of the Welshpool Constabulary were required to keep order among the crowds wishing to return to Llanfair in the evening. The visit to Welshpool market had formerly been something of a special occasion, but now for many inhabitants of Llanfair Caereinion and its hinterland it became a regular habit. The Up morning trains were packed, their passengers clutching baskets of cheese, butter, eggs and other produce. Frightened chickens and ducks stared down from the hampers in bewilderment as the carriages jolted and lurched. Stops at intermediate stations often occasioned a mad scramble to squeeze on to the already overcrowded coaches. Fortunately, for travellers, trains on most other days offered a rather pleasanter, less cramped journey.

Business in Welshpool improved, but somewhat paradoxically so did trade in Llanfair. The boom there was the result of the incursion into the little town of many farmers from the upper parts of the Banwy basin and from over the hill to the south, the folk of Cefn Coch and Adfa forsaking the trek down the Bechan valley. From Llanfair station was collected coal and lime which had previously been carted from Llanfyllin and Newtown. Llanfair Caereinion also hoped that its tourist trade would develop; it advocated its sulphur springs to health seekers and advertised the splendid scenery which now could be so easily reached. The Wynnstay Arms pronounced itself a '*First Class Hotel for Families, Tourists & Commercial Gentlemen*', arranged for a conveyance to meet all trains and supplied its clientele with its noted homebrewed beer. Excursion facilities to Llanfair were offered from Cambrian Railways' stations and, in 1903, there were reports of a considerable influx of visitors on Saturdays. This perhaps accounted for numbers of would-be passengers being left behind in Welshpool by morning trains crammed to capacity.

Financial Difficulties

In the years ahead, shortage of capital was to prove restrictive and irksome. Even at the inaugural ceremony on 4th April 1903, the optimism customary in the speechmaking on such occasions had been tempered with mention of financial stringency. The cost of the ceremony itself had eventually to be paid out of the pockets of the directors of the W&L at £38-19s-9d (£38.99) per head. Not that these gentlemen did not make some efforts to raise more capital. Only three days after the official opening, a canvass was being planned to sell more shares. This brought some success and some outstanding creditors who were now charging interest on their accounts, such as Beyer Peacock & Co. Ltd and R. Y. Pickering & Co., were paid off.

But within a year, and with the contractor's bill not yet completely settled, application was necessary for an extra Treasury grant. It was explained to the Board of Trade, where the application was received, that £47,364 had already been expended but the total cost of the Railway and its equipment had reached £56,945 (equivalent to £3½ million today). Much of the balance was still owing. The Earl and Forrester-Addie pressed the Board's Grants Committee and explained the need for £3,600 additional to the deficit. This was for signalling equipment, a passing place to allow the second engine to operate, the purchase of an additional locomotive, carriage and timber wagons and more sidings at Llanfair. In August 1904, the Treasury made its offer - a loan of £5,700 at 3¼ per cent to cover the deficiency. The Company was no nearer to getting a third engine or implementing thoughts of trains crossing at Castle Caereinion.

In 1905, an Order was obtained which increased the borrowing powers. The capital finally authorised and the amount actually raised is tabulated:

	Authorised	Raised
Ordinary Share Capital	£12,000	£ 11,065
Loans or Shares:		
Local Authorities	£19,350	£19,350
Free Grant	£17,500	£17,500
Treasury Loan	£5,700	£5,700
Mortgage (debentures)	£7,000	£3,000
Total	£61,550	£56,615

Despite H. P. Jones' one-time satisfaction with the rolling stock, the effect of financial constraint on what was ordered soon became apparent. Even before the line opened, concern had been growing locally as to the ability of the railway to cope with the expected traffic. It was strongly rumoured that timber longer than 30ft (9.1m) would not be carried. Indeed, at that stage, a local timber merchant had been advised by

The Earl *is ready to depart from Llanfair station with a typical train of two coaches and at least one wagon.*

Real Photographs/Ian Allan

The Countess *with the third class coach and one of the composites at the first water tower close to Dolrhyd Mill.*

W&LLR Pres. Co.

An early view at Llanfair station. The Earl *has arrived with the usual mixed train.*

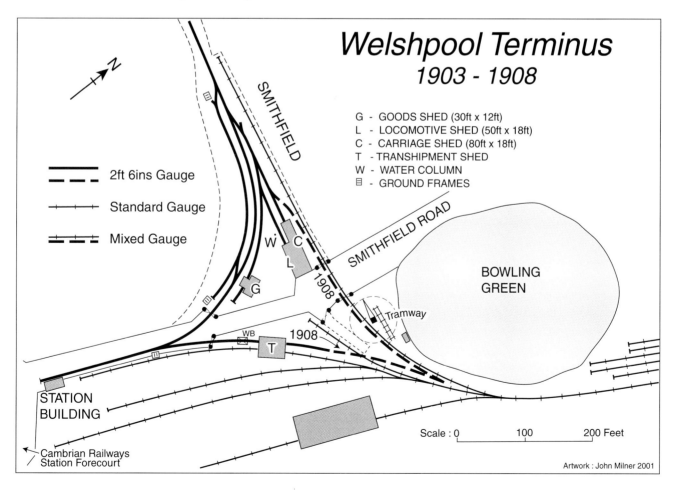

Welshpool Terminus
1903 - 1908

SMITHFIELD

N

G - GOODS SHED (30ft x 12ft)
L - LOCOMOTIVE SHED (50ft x 18ft)
C - CARRIAGE SHED (80ft x 18ft)
T - TRANSHIPMENT SHED
W - WATER COLUMN
▤ - GROUND FRAMES

2ft 6ins Gauge

Standard Gauge

Mixed Gauge

W   C

L

G

1908

SMITHFIELD ROAD

BOWLING
GREEN

Tramway

WB

T   1908

STATION
BUILDING

Cambrian Railways
Station Forecourt

Scale : 0   100   200 Feet

Artwork : John Milner 2001

In Welshpool yard circa 1904, a timber train awaits shunting to the stacking grounds across Smithfield Road. Round timber was carried in special trains with long lengths supported on two separated trucks connected by a drag chain with match trucks where necessary. Here, a pole seems to have been used between the bolsters on the right. Both brake vans have been used.

Collection: R.W. Miller

Mr. Denniss that no provision was being made at either terminal for loading and unloading such traffic. However, a couple of months after the opening ceremony it was agreed that suitable rolling stock for carrying long timber ought after all to be purchased. The order, for ten trucks, was finally placed at the end of that year. The W&L was dissuaded from ordering timber stock which was unsprung and poorly equipped but cheap. Savings of nearly £20 on each £44 truck could have been made in this way, but as a solution to its financial problems the W&L accepted an offer of a form of hire-purchase spread over a five year period. Some trial vehicles were to be dispatched in advance and during 1904 six of these arrived. Two years went by, the remaining timber bolsters were not delivered, finances did not improve and the remainder of the order was cancelled.

There were other monetary problems in 1904. Strachan, the contractor, was demanding settlement of his outstanding account. There was some dispute over his bill for extra work carried out during the construction, including that caused by flooding and the alterations required by Major Druitt.

Eventually, the dispute went to arbitration and Strachan was awarded £2,565 with costs. On top of all this, the W&L had £300 to find for the solicitors representing them at the hearing. In July 1906, the Company paid off £1,200 of the award, '*and thereby prevented the issue of a writ*' as the minutes recorded. But capital was still so desperately short that the Cambrian had to advance the balance.

Traffic

Overall, traffic never exceeded expectations. Freight rates remained higher than the rates for conveyance by road, and the old donkey carts continued running for some time in competition. At the end of the first year, the W&L as owning company took £661 (less tax) from the gross receipts. This was swallowed up mainly by interest charges, and there was nothing left with which to pay dividends. As the years came and went, the Company was in fact, never able to pay a dividend. At the end of 1903, after paying working expenses, the Cambrian Railways Company was faced with a loss on the line, although in ensuing years profits gradually improved. Results for most years up to 1922 came near to the estimate of annual traffic made before the line opened by C. S. Denniss, the Cambrian's general manager.

Raven Square halt was in Brook Street near the Standard Quarry. This 1920s view shows Countess *unusually working bunker first towards Llanfair.*

Traffic Receipts

	Estimated	Actual receipts for	
		1905	1911
Passengers	£1,250	£1,365	£1,226
Coal & Minerals	£ 500	£ 631	£ 520
Other Goods	£1,500	£ 735	£1,016
Parcels	£ 150	£ 177	£ 182
Livestock	—	£ 10	£ 94
Total	£3,405	£2,918	£3,046*
Working Expenses	£2,043	£1,859	£1,835
Net Revenue	£1,362	£1,062	£1,211

*includes some miscellaneous receipts

This was not as satisfactory a picture as it looked, for the W&L had to be paid its 40 per cent share of the gross takings and at times its share exceeded the net revenue (i.e. receipts less working expenses). In those early years the acclaimed generosity of the Cambrian in the working agreement became apparent, as the cost of working the line came to more than its share of the takings.

In 1906, a typical pre-war year, evidence indicates that about 50,000 passengers were carried, accounting, with parcels traffic, for about half of the total receipts. Freight would have included about 3,500 tons of general merchandise and some 4,000 tons of mineral traffic (mainly coal), though the latter traffic made it a poor third in importance. Livestock accounted for only 1½ per cent of total receipts. Much of the livestock continued to move by road despite the opening of the Railway, perhaps understandable as there were just two cattle vans. In February 1911, to provide facilities for the carriage of more sheep, the Cambrian was asked to convert four of the goods wagons into livestock vehicles.

Before World War I the cost of running the line gradually decreased, despite substantial engineering costs. In 1909, for example, these totalled £521 as against £375 for coal (for 26,079 train miles) and £797 in respect of wages for traffic and locomotive staff. At Welshpool, two transhipping goods porters were employed for the narrow gauge traffic. More men were required at Llanfair Caereinion where the staff included a stationmaster in the early years, as well as the booking porters and several goods porters. Other stations were unstaffed. Before World War I, the porters and porter - guards received 18s (90p) per week or 10s (50p) if they were juniors. Wages escalated during the war and after, the same porters' weekly wages reaching £3-7s-0d (£3.35) in 1921 before wage rates declined somewhat during the depression years.

Alterations at the Termini

Financial constraints, and the resulting inadequacy of the yard accommodation at Llanfair Caereinion station, were referred to by the Cambrian's general manager on opening day. The following month, the works committee of the W&L considered suggestions from Mr. Denniss sparked off by difficulties in dealing with the coal traffic. The committee consulted A. J. Collin who estimated that it would be possible for £200 to fill in the low-lying part of the yard from the coal siding to the fence and lay in extra lengths of siding. Although it was agreed to ask the Cambrian to carry out the scheme, eight months later the expansion of facilities at Llanfair yard was still under discussion. Plans had been drawn up for the construction of an access road on the river side of the yard as well as for lengthening the siding to which it would lead. But the scheme was deferred due to difficulties with regard to paying out John Strachan, the contractor.

A few weeks later, in April 1904, the construction of some additional facilities at Llanfair was agreed. These were to cope with timber traffic (the new bolsters had just arrived) and further plans had been produced for a relatively cheap scheme, not actually in the yard at the terminus but quarter of a mile to the east beside E.0. Jones' sawmill at Tanllan corner. By cutting away the bank on the curve, 90yds (82.5m) of siding were laid in, albeit inclined at the somewhat steep gradient of 1 in 70. These works were completed by the Cambrian Railways Company for £130. The W&L agreed it would contribute £60 when it was 'in a position to do so', and Jones & Son agreed to put up the remainder in return for a rebate of 3d per ton on their traffic. They had just purchased a large quantity of good timber which they were anxious to move.

The timber traffic included the handling of considerable lengths, loads up to 72ft (23m) long being carried. Timber trains were subject to an overall speed limit of 10mph. One contract secured in 1907 was for the conveyance of 50,000cu ft (1,400 cub metres) belonging to a Mr. Barker of Shrewsbury. In connection with such traffic, the working company put in a cross-over from the W&L carriage shed road in Welshpool to the middle of the standard gauge Smithfield siding alongside. A third rail to give a mixed gauge section of track then led across the Smithfield Road to a stacking ground on the other side. The exact date of completion of this is not known, although an agreement had been approved in December 1908 between the W&L, Welshpool Corporation and the Cambrian Railways for the use of the siding, presumably for this traffic.

Completion of this work must have inspired the idea of a reversing triangle. A peculiar system of moveable rails was installed in the Cambrian Railways' yard to link the Smithfield siding with the narrow gauge transhipment siding when

In Welshpool's Church Street a house (on the left side) was demolished to provide a route for the new railway. Ahead of this passenger train in the 1920s is the narrow passage over the bridge along the Lledan Brook.

Collection: R.W. Miller

Emerging from 'The Narrows' where the line was built over the Lledan Brook, this train, early in the Cambrian era, is crossing Union Street to reach the first halt.

No trains today! Seven Stars Halt, the 'town station', took its name from the public house demolished to make way for the railway. Floods, possibly in 1919, have covered the track. Behind the enamel 'Bovril' advertisement, is part of a shelter of some sort.

required. Carriages (and very occasionally locomotives) were turned on this formation to even the wear on wheel flanges.

Signals at Castle Caereinion

Along the line, a number of alterations were carried out in connection with the handling of timber traffic. The most important of these was at Castle Caereinion. In the spring of 1907, the Cambrian once again raised the idea of crossing trains here, using the second engine to head the separate trips necessary to work down the timber traffic. The W&L agreed to be responsible for the £190 bill and the operating company put in hand the work necessary to gain Board of Trade sanction for use of the loop to cross trains. Home and distant signals were installed and the opportunity was taken to construct a siding, presumably where wagons consigned to local people could stand without blocking the running lines.

Lt-Col. E. Druitt, who had been promoted in 1904, came to inspect the installation for the Board of Trade. His report appears below:

15th June 1907
The Assistant Secretary,
Railway Dept.
Board of Trade,

Sir,

I have the honour to report for the information of the Board of Trade that in compliance with the instructions contained in your Minute of the 7th June. I have inspected the new works at Castle Caereinion on the Welshpool and Llanfair Light Railway worked by the Cambrian Railways.

At this place a passing place has been laid down in the single line between Welshpool and Llanfair. A small signal box has been built containing 9 working levers and 1 spare lever. The interlocking and signalling arrangements are satisfactory.

This railway is a light one of 2ft 6in gauge and has hitherto been worked by one engine in steam but will be worked shortly on the Train staff and ticket system combined with the absolute block telegraph system. It is proposed to transmit the block signals by means of telephones at the three stations instead of by the usual block instruments.

I see no objection to this proposal but the Company should send a copy of the Regulations proposed to be used and also a fresh undertaking as to the mode of working signed by both owning and working Companies.

Subject to the above and to the new points and signals being correctly connected up, I can recommend the Board of Trade to sanction the use of the new works in question.

I have, etc,
(Sd) E.Druit
Lt Col RE

Details of the new mode of working duly submitted to the Board of Trade indicated that the passing place was only to be used for short periods and normally the points would be disconnected from the signal box and the outside lever frame would be used. This somewhat whimsical arrangement may be presumed to have preserved the original Tyers two-lever ground frames. The new regulations took effect from 23rd September 1907, defining the two staff sections and stipulating that passing was permitted at Castle Caereinion only.

During November of that year, the new signal box was opened to allow a ballast train to work on the line simultaneously with the regular train. The box was closed again within five weeks and the months passed without the crossing place being used, as the W&L recorded in its minutes. Over two years after construction, the Cambrian agreed to reduce the interest rate on the W&L's debt for the new layout until such time as it should be brought into use.

Three years after Lt-Col. Druitt's visit to Castle Caereinion, the Cambrian cut the number of trains and the hours worked by the men as it was now contended that the services were under-used. Even so, a day's working still required two shifts of men to work the trains, as the Cambrian's secretary noted critically. A third train crew to man the second engine in steam seems by that time to have been unlikely on financial grounds although, after the rifle range opened on Gwncefn, near Castle Caereinion village, extra trains needing the crossing facilities might have been expected. But even for the opening ceremony of the range in April 1910, the inauguration party used the 11.45am service train. So the new signal box was left locked, opened normally only by the guards who always carried a key so that they were able to operate the Phonophone instrument. Lt-Col. Druitt had recommended the continuing use of the telephone but by the early 1930s, the box is believed to have fallen into disuse.

In 1909, alterations were made at Heniarth so that Mr. Barker could transfer his timber loading operations from Tanllan corner siding, Llanfair. A sleeper crossing was built to give easier access to the loop which was lengthened two years later. At this time, a crane was located at Heniarth. Later, in 1913, a crane was erected for Mr. Barker's use at Cyfronydd station and quantities of timber from the Maesmawr Estate to the north were loaded here. The W&L had to widen the gates to the station yard.

At the same time, traffic from the Standard Quarry in Welshpool was such as to warrant the Cambrian Railways Company planning '*a new loading and unloading place for stone*', as a contemporary newspaper report put it. This was not altogether a new idea as Denniss had proposed in 1905 that a narrow gauge siding and transhipment apparatus should be built adjacent to the Smithfield metals. The scheme under consideration just before World War I involved the extension through the Cambrian Railways' yard in Welshpool and alongside the standard gauge main line to new transship sidings, with shoots from the narrow gauge to the standard gauge.

More plans for a similar extension were prepared in 1920, this time for unloading round timber for a local timber merchant who had established a yard beside the main line during the war. The plans are believed to have been backed by the Ministry of Transport. The W&L felt unable to provide the £140 asked of it for the construction, nor a further larger sum which might have been needed for additional wagons for the traffic. The scheme was left to the GWR to implement a few years later, adding about another 88 yards (81 metres) to the narrow gauge system. Swindon Works built suitable timber bolsters. The extension seems to have been dismantled just before World War II.

In 1914, with war in the offing, there was enough traffic to require the expansion of storage facilities at Llanfair Caereinion station. Still poverty stricken, the W&L acceded to the Cambrian's demands but declared that payment would have to be by instalments; £50 down and £10 per annum for 10 years! By December 1915, the alterations had been carried out. Moving the western-most loop points towards the booking office had made it possible to lengthen the warehouse by 10ft (3m). Siding accommodation beyond the loop was increased. It was hoped that this would make the handling of goods more convenient for customers and would encourage more traffic. Other measures, which had been taken in an effort to expand business, included suggesting to the Cambrian's traffic manager in February 1911 that he arrange the carriage of mails with the Postmaster General. It had been envisaged when the draft Light Railway Order was put together, but it was omitted from the Order which was authorised. The 1911 attempt was equally abortive.

Passenger Facilities

Two years before this, an additional halt had been agreed to at Dolrhyd Mill. Here Mr. R. C. Anwyl, a director, wished to have a platform made and a hut erected at his own expense. First mooted in 1902, a 'flag' station at this place was being used by Mr. Anwyl's tenants, most of whom lived across the River Banwy. Parcels and papers were left here by the trains from Welshpool. A weir across the river maintained sufficient depth of water for a punt to be able to cross, the occupants hauling the craft across by means of a

wire stretched from bank to bank. In December 1912, however, there was a calamity. Involved were a chauffeur and a serving maid who were intending to catch the train due out of Llanfair at 2.15 pm. The surging, brown torrent, swollen by recent heavy rain and snow, seized the punt and hurled it over the weir, drowning the unfortunate couple.

At Dolarddyn level crossing, half a mile west of Castle Caereinion station, another stopping place had been advertised in the timetable since July 1904. (The Dolrhyd Mill halt was never shown.) Trains were scheduled to halt at Dolarddyn on Mondays only, though parties could make use of it on other days, everyone being charged to or from Cyfronydd and being issued with tickets accordingly.

Many travellers to or from Welshpool used the halt at Seven Stars in Brook Street. Surprisingly, no shelter there is recorded until the line had been working for nearly ten years. Then it cost the W&L £24-17s-0d (£24.85). And it was even later, in 1915, that any shelter was provided for passengers using Sylfaen halt, a bleak spot in winter. It had been decided late in 1904 to erect a waiting hut here, but the critical financial position at the time caused the erection to be deferred, although criticism continued in ensuing years from people who objected to waiting in the wet. At that time, there was not even a signboard here.

29

Welshpool & Llanfair Light Railway (Narrow Gauge.)

Miles from Welshpool		DOWN.		1 Goods A	3 Goods 1st & 3rd Mons. in month.	5 ¶ Mixed	7 Mixed Mons. except.	9 Mixed Mons. only.	11 Mixed	13 Mixed
M.	C.			a. m.	a.m.	a.m.	a.m.	p.m.	p.m.	p.m.
		Welshp'l Station dep	..	5 10	6 0	8 10	11 45	12 45	3 55	7 5
	35	Welshp'l Sev' St's ,,	..	..	...	*	*	*	*	*
1	0	Raven Square .. ,,	..	..	...	*	*	*	*	*
1	66	Golfa .. ,,	..	..	...	*	*	*	*	*
3	59	Sylfaen Halt .. ,,	..	.	...	*	*	*	*	*
4	65	Castle Caereinion ,,	..	..	...	8 30	12 5	1 5	4 15	7 25
6	57	Cyfronydd .. ,,	..	..	...	*	*	*	*	*
7	54	Heniarth.. .. ,.	..	..	...	*	*	*	*	*
9	4	Llanfair .. .. ar	..	6 15	7 10	9 5	12 40	1 40	4 50	7 55

Miles from Llanfair.		UP.		2 Mixed A	4 Mixed 1st & 3-d Mons. in month.	6 Mixed	8 Mixed	10 Mixed	12 Goods. Thurs. & Sats. excepted.	14 Mixed Thurs. & Sats. & Llanfair Fair Days.
M.	C.			a.m.	a.m.	a.m.	p.m.	p.m.	p.m.	p.m.
		Llanfair .. ..dep	..	6 30	7 30	9 40	2 15	5 30	8 10	8 0
1	10	Heniarth .. ,,	..	*	*	*	*	*	..	*
2	27	Cyfronydd .. ,,	..	*	*	*	*	*	..	*
4	20	Castle Caereinion ,,	..	6 50	7 50	10 0	2 35	5 50	..	8 25
5	26	Sylfaen Halt .. ,,	..	*	*	*	*	*	..	*
6	19	Golfa .. ,,	..	*	*	*	*	*	..	*
8	5	Raven Square .. ,.	..	*	*	*	*	*	..	*
8	50	Welshp'l Sev' St's ,,	..	*	*	*	*	*	...	*
9	4	Welshpool Station arr	..	7 20	8 20	10 30	3 5	6 20	9 25	8 55

* Trains **must stop** at all stations to pick up or set down passengers.
¶ On Llanfair Fair days No. 5 will run 20 minutes earlier, and on First and Third Mondays in each month 25 minutes later.
A—Runs on Fourth Monday in November, February, and May only.
On Mondays all Up and Down trains will stop at the Crossing at Dolarddyn to pick up or set down passengers to or from Welshpool. Passengers must take Cyfronydd tickets. Trains will also stop at Dolarddyn on other days for picnic parties. S.88701.

Extract from Cambrian Railways Service Timetable, 1915

The former waiting shelter at Seven Stars which was duly converted for other use after the end of passenger services.

With passenger traffic (at least) well up to expectations, there were accommodation difficulties. Even passengers travelling first class were grumbling about overcrowding at this time. In 1913, the Cambrian therefore urged the W&L to provide a fourth coach, but in view of the lack of resources, the request was refused. Nor would the W&L pay for improved lighting in the coaches which the Cambrian was asking for. As gas lighting was now standard in their main line stock, it seems that the Cambrian felt that the oil lamps provided in the W&L coaches were obsolete.

Most services were operated by mixed trains, and it is said that the goods brake van coped with some of the overflow of passengers. The basic pattern of services up to the end of 1908 included four mixed trains each way on weekdays. No services ever ran on Sundays. On Mondays, Tuesdays and Wednesdays, an additional train, goods only, left Welshpool just after 5am, working back about 6.30am with a passenger coach attached. The first passengers could be conveyed out of Welshpool about 8.00am; the exact time varied slightly from year to year. The last train left Welshpool just after 7.00 pm and the latest returning from Llanfair departed at 8.00 pm (passenger only). No additional workings for freight were actually timetabled although some probably ran, notably those conveying timber.

During and after 1909, cuts were made affecting the first and last trains from Llanfair. Before the end of World War I, the evening passenger trains were discontinued completely, although in 1920 they were restored on certain days. But on Mondays, Thursdays and Fridays, people for Llanfair had to leave Welshpool no later than 3.50pm.

There were thoughts of connections westwards early in 1919 when the County Council consulted Welshpool Town Council about suggestions for improving transport facilities in Montgomeryshire. The Town Council offered to support any scheme for the continuation of the Light Railway towards Llanerfyl and Garthbeibo. It also suggested a Light Railway, or alternatively a '*motor transport system*', to open up the New Mills and Tregynon area, south of Llanfair Caereinion.

Welshpool Town Council had been involved with the W&L more closely, a little earlier, in 1913. After some investigation it was decided to support the Cambrian Railways' Bill which would allow the line of the Light Railway to be reconstructed near the passenger station in Welshpool. The Bill also ratified the construction of the third rail of the mixed gauge laid along the corporation's Smithfield siding from the connection with the narrow gauge yard eastwards. The Bill became law on 4th July 1913, giving the W&L running powers over the Smithfield siding backdated to 4th April 1913. For this, the Cambrian had to pay the corporation a small annual rent. Work commenced on 27th October 1913 and during the following week, passengers boarded and alighted by the locomotive shed. Staff were instructed to work freight to and from the transhipment shed by means of the Smithfield siding and the temporary connection in the main line goods yard.

Welshpool Council welcomed the reconstruction of the passenger spur as it swung the railway inside the Cambrian's yard, removing the station from the roadway. It had been agitating for this for at least seven years. Trains at the terminus were now fenced off from the road and road traffic was unencumbered, except when arriving and departing trains crossed the road. A red lamp at the crossing was required to be lit during the hours that street lamps were on. A moveable stopblock was operated by a key to allow trains from the narrow gauge yard to move on to the road crossing.

In the summer of the next year, the Railway experienced a period of mechanical crisis. On the first Friday in May, which was Llanfair Fair Day, the train came to a halt with a jerk on

Brynelin viaduct. When the crew climbed down and peered beneath *The Earl*, they discovered to their dismay that an axle had snapped. There was nothing for the passengers to do but to complete their journeys on foot, and meanwhile No. 1 struggled into the loop siding at Cyfronydd. Services later resumed hauled by *The Countess*. It was only three weeks later that No. 2 was also in trouble. *The Countess* had hauled the early morning goods to Llanfair and was shunting the yard there when it became obvious that something was wrong. Examination showed that *The Countess* too, had broken an axle. Services had to be suspended, a breakdown gang was sent for and, while arrangements were made to convey passengers the length of the line by road vehicles, No. 2 limped back to Welshpool. The problem was now acute as both locomotives were unfit for service. Not to be beaten, the Cambrian's fitters removed a set of serviceable wheels from *The Earl* and feverish activity saw them fitted to *The Countess* in time for her to resume work the next day.

A close-down, even for a short period, was to be avoided at this time as the Railway was beginning to look more profitable. For the last two years, receipts had been greater than in any previous year while working expenses were about the lowest ever. Nevertheless, shortage of capital remained an embarrassment and even the regular income paid to the W&L automatically each year from revenue was barely adequate even to cover the interest on loans, let alone repay the principal or

build up any reserves. In 1914, local authorities which had made loans agreed to wait yet another seven years for repayment. Perhaps they had little choice.

Preparations for Absorption

During the post-World War I period, the Company had joined the Association of Smaller Railway Companies, the better to seek compensation for revenue which it was considered had been lost while subject to government control during and after the war. Claims became eligible under the Railways Act of 1921 and the W&L's case was based on losses from the arrest of traffic growth in progress in 1913 and income lost by the diversion of traffic from rail to road.

In July 1922, the W&L was awarded £2,667, being slightly more than anticipated and a useful contribution to the normally empty coffers. But at this time the directors were preoccupied with bigger things. For some months, negotiations had been going on with regard to the impending absorption of the W&L by the GWR under the Grouping of Railways Act of August 1921. The Cambrian had been absorbed already in March 1922. The Earl of Powis and Major D. Davies MP represented the Company in its attempt to arrange for the best possible financial terms. In June 1922, the Great Western offered £19,345, admitting that this was less than the full nominal amount of stock and loans. However, the W&L was

The transhipment shed at Welshpool was reached by shunting across Smithfield Road and for some years was part of the triangle which could be temporarily completed using a moveable section of rail behind the shed.

not willing to accept this and four months later managed to wring better terms from Paddington.

The W&L got £23,236 in cash, including revenue and government compensation due to it up to the end of the year. The GWR agreed to take over rent charges and, in effect absolve the W&L from its remaining capital debt to the erstwhile Cambrian which amounted to £2,387. Negotiations now started with debenture holders, local authorities and HM Treasury with regard to the repayment of what was due to them. Eventually it was agreed that the money would be allocated to the major lenders, as follows:

Debenture Holders - 90% of holding
HM Treasury (£5,700 loan) - 81%
Local Authorities (£14,625 in loans) - 80%.

Allowing a small sum for winding up expenses, this left ordinary shareholders with 4s-11d (24½p) per pound share. The last entry in the minute book of the W&LLR Company is dated 14th December 1922; from 1st January 1923, the company ceased to exist. After 23 years of nominally independent existence, the W&L, like its foster-parent the Cambrian a few months earlier, was swallowed up by what became an even greater Great Western. In financial terms, the flirtation with what was really a communal railway project had been a dear one for the locality: individually and communally they had lost about £14,000 of what they had put in (to say nothing of dividends forgone). It had also cost the exchequer £18,500.

Freight traffic westbound included much in the way of agricultural supplies. In the transhipment shed at Welshpool, a load of basic slag for Llanfair is transferred the hard way.

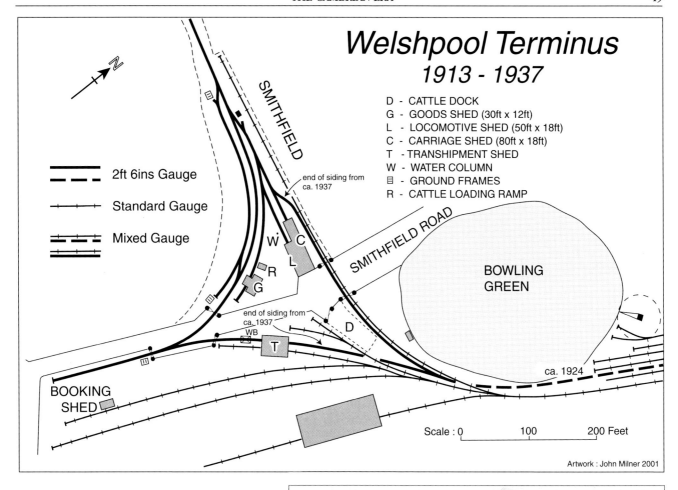

Welshpool Terminus
1913 - 1937

D - CATTLE DOCK
G - GOODS SHED (30ft x 12ft)
L - LOCOMOTIVE SHED (50ft x 18ft)
C - CARRIAGE SHED (80ft x 18ft)
T - TRANSHIPMENT SHED
W - WATER COLUMN
⊞ - GROUND FRAMES
R - CATTLE LOADING RAMP

2ft 6ins Gauge

Standard Gauge

Mixed Gauge

SMITHFIELD

end of siding from ca. 1937

SMITHFIELD ROAD

BOWLING GREEN

W C
R L
G

end of siding from ca. 1937

WB

D

T

ca. 1924

BOOKING SHED

Scale : 0   100   200 Feet

Artwork : John Milner 2001

The narrow gauge yard at Welshpool boasted this corrugated iron warehouse. Access for road vehicles was on the other side and reached from Smithfield Road. Part of the ramp for livestock can be seen on the left of the shed. The cattle vans are those provided by the GWR.

PEK Morgan/G&D NG

At Welshpool, the mixed gauge Smithfield siding crossed the road making the north side of 'the triangle'. The cattle transfer dock was on the left.

GWR No. 823 Countess *(name now abbreviated) heads the waiting train, ca.1925. The Welshpool terminus was now in the standard gauge yard with Smithfield Road behind.*

Real Photos/Ian Allan

GWR No. 822 The Earl *(rebuilt) passes through the narrow gauge goods yard, ca. 1930. Standard gauge cattle wagons stand on the mixed gauge Smithfield siding behind. Note the flat wagons converted from opens.*

Chapter 4

New Owners

When the GWR took over the W&L, there was a basic service of three mixed trains each way daily, and a fourth three times weekly. Extra workings were introduced on special days for agricultural shows, fetes and so on. The Powys Provincial Eisteddfod at Llanfair on 16th June 1927 called for a service of seven trains in each direction, for example, and the last one returned to Welshpool half an hour after midnight. Sometimes the last trip out of Welshpool was worked by road motor bus. Typical examples of this practice were the late night connections put on from Welshpool to Llanfair for passengers returning from the circuses at Newtown on 5th and 12th March 1927.

In 1930, the cutting back of rail services began with the cessation of the thrice weekly working. For five years GWR petrol buses had been connecting Welshpool with Llanfair. Before the chocolate and cream painted buses were introduced on the Llanfair run, the GWR was already complaining of road competition in the area. The Company realised that if it did not have its own motor service on the road to Llanfair, someone else would. Its road service started on 27th July 1925 and ran three times daily. It turned off the main road near Castle Caereinion and made for Llanfair over the hill road, one service continuing to Dinas Mawddwy. Two GWR buses also started to run from Oswestry to Llanfair.

Perhaps the somewhat primitive single-decker vehicles proved unsuitable for the stiff ascents and dangerous descents between Castle Caereinion and Llanfair, for within five months they were following the main road, parallel to the Railway all the way. It began to look more like sabotage of the Company's own rail facilities, even though the bus services from Welshpool to Llanfair were soon reduced to two on most days. Four years later, however, the Railway was closed to passenger traffic and six road services were necessary, more on Mondays and Saturdays. The journey time was 37 minutes. The Great Western Railway was no longer running the buses by then, the services having been taken over by the Western Transport Company, soon to be merged with Crosville Motors whose buses continued to serve the area for more than sixty years.

Freight Traffic

In the twenties, traffic was, if anything, slightly greater than in the pre-World War I period. Passenger receipts were very similar and there was rather less coal carried but milk, timber and livestock had expanded. In 1925, a typical year, figures for freight carried were:

Coal and Minerals	5,639	tons
Goods	2,579	tons
Milk	1,368	cans
Livestock	344	trucks

East-bound freight included timber from Pen-y-coed (between Cyfronydd and Dolarddyn) for Messrs Boys and Boden's sawmills in Welshpool, and sheep and lambs to places such as Oswestry and Manchester. There were sheep trucks holding 25 and 32 beasts. A variety of materials was imported into the Banwy valley and, of course, the GWR quoted through rates inclusive of transhipping at Welshpool from standard to narrow gauge. Much grain and oilcake was carried from Chester and Ellesmere Port, iron and steel from Newport in South Wales and roadstone from the Standard Quarry. A great deal of basic slag came up the line from various places such as Aberdovey, Middlesbrough, Scunthorpe, Minera (North Wales) and Staffordshire. It was unloaded at all stations from Golfa onwards. Before the Railway was built, farmers had required lime for their soils but basic slag had come to be preferred.

Wagons were apparently left in the loops for the customers to unload. It is said that when wagons of coal arrived at Castle Caereinion, delivery was announced to the probably distant owners by a recognised system of whistles sounded by the engine. When eventually emptied, the wagon was sometimes used, undoubtedly unofficially, as a means of transport to Llanfair. Castle Caereinion station is situated some 200ft above the river, alongside which the line runs to its western terminus and the descent commences with a 1 in 32 gradient. Reputedly, a *'good'* wagon could be set rolling across the level crossing (locked pointwork notwithstanding!) and then, with all aboard, would coast down Dolarddyn bank, pass Cyfronydd and even Heniarth before stopping. Negotiating the road crossings must have been a hazardous business, nor were these the only danger spots. Regular train crews were used to this irregular practice and when they came up from Welshpool with the first train of the day and found the wagon gone from the loop siding, they knew to keep a sharp lookout for it on the line ahead. There was no telling where it would have come to rest!

On average, three loaded trucks or vans would be brought up the line by each train; two-thirds of those wagons hauled eastwards would be empty. Freight traffic brought in over £3,000 in 1925 and passenger fares added a further £1,200. 1924 had been very similar. But this was insufficient. It fell short of the cost of maintenance, renewal and working expenses by some £2,000. Wages were rising. Drivers at this time got about £4-10s-0d (£4.50) per week and working hours were being reduced, making more men necessary. The engines were uneconomical, partly because of the steep grades they had to tackle; coal consumption averaged about 7cwts (350kgs) for the return journey. Staff were being employed to work lighter loads than on an easier line, so that the cost of train running alone was more than twice as much per mile than the average for the whole system of the GWR.

The End for Passenger Services

Realising that some of its new acquisitions were turning out to be expensive liabilities, it was inevitable that Paddington headquarters should instigate an inquiry into the future of them. This it did as early as 1926 and the working of the W&L

was closely scrutinised. The terms of reference were not simply whether to keep it open or close it but whether more economical working was possible. The feasibility of replacing steam with a rail motor and trailer or even of removing the rails and converting it into a motor road was to be borne in mind!

The distance of the stations from the villages they served, though certainly not as great as some on other lines, was considered a handicap in the matter of attracting passengers. Furthermore, passengers on mixed trains were being delayed while freight stock was shunted. It was suggested that small goods which had to be transhipped could just as easily be transferred to a railway lorry and could be delivered direct. Though GWR lorries had not started running in this area in 1926, they were introduced within three years. It was not considered possible to reduce the running costs by replacing *The Earl* and *The Countess* as rail motors were unsuitable for the difficult inclines on the branch. In view of these findings and the deficit the line was sustaining, the report recommended closure. It was observed that under contemporary conditions, the W&L would never have been built. Had the recommendation been implemented, the Railway would have been doomed after only 23 years' existence.

As Board of Trade permission would probably be a prerequisite of closure, an alternative was mooted. This was to restrict all activities to an eight hour span daily, using road motors for those passengers who must be conveyed outside these times. It was anticipated that this would avoid the employment of a second shift of men on the Railway.

Fortunately, however, Paddington dallied. Meanwhile,

A GWR coal train negotiates 'The Narrows'. The track over the Lledan Brook squeezed behind the cottages between Church Street and Union Street. When trains ran, washing was in danger of being smothered in smuts.

In Llanfair yard c.1930, wagons appear to have been shunted on to the coal road for unloading. Note the 2 ton hand crane.

Collection: R.W. Miller

economic pressure was mounting and traffic on the line was diminishing. Though about eighty passengers used the train on market days, many other days saw trains running without any. Cheap returns (at the single fare), introduced to increase traffic, failed to do so and reduced passenger receipts by more than a third. Then, in January 1931, an announcement was made. Not closure as recommended, but the withdrawal of passenger facilities. A notice appeared in the local press, applicable also to the standard gauge Kerry branch, and mentioning the Western Transport Company's *compensatory* road passenger services to Llanfair.

It immediately caused an outcry. Welshpool Municipal Association quickly raised a petition; at Llanfair Caereinion, a special Parish Council meeting was hurriedly called and it drafted a protest letter to send to the railway company. They asked for an inquiry to be held at which they could state their views about the closure of passenger services and at which the Company would have to prove the line's failure. It was stated that bus facilities were quite inadequate to deal with market traffic and bus fares were excessive. They made out a case of hardship that would be caused to farmers and smallholders in the Llanfair valley and suggested that there would be sufficient traffic on Mondays, Saturdays and special fair days to justify retention of passenger services on these days. Angrily they demanded to

GREAT WESTERN RAILWAY.

Welshpool & Llanfair Branch.
Abermule & Kerry Branch.

THE GREAT WESTERN RAILWAY COMPANY give NOTICE that owing to the losses which are being incurred on the Welshpool and Llanfair and the Abermule and Kerry Branches, the Passenger Train facilities now afforded by the Company will be WITHDRAWN on and from FEBRUARY 9th, 1931.

The WESTERN TRANSPORT COMPANY will arrange compensatory ROAD PASSENGER SERVICES on the WELSHPOOL AND LLANFAIR BRANCH.

The Great Western Company will continue to afford facilities for the CONVEYANCE OF PARCELS, MERCHANDISE & MINERALS over the two Branches.

Particulars of the arrangements may be obtained from the Company's local representative.

JAMES MILNE,
General Manager.

Paddington Station,
London. W.2.,
January, 1931.

Notice of closure in the Montgomeryshire Express,
3rd February 1931

know why passengers could not still be carried on the goods workings which were to continue.

Soon afterwards, the Mayor of Welshpool met Mr. H. Warwick, the GWR District Superintendent. Officials of the Municipal Association were also present. Mr. Warwick laid some of the blame for the line's losses on the eight hour working day which necessitated the employment of two shifts of men. Considerable savings were expected if they reduced maintenance to the standards of a mineral line. The deputation criticised the Company's recent fare-cutting and a timetable was suggested for market days which the superintendent agreed could be worked by only one shift of men. He was persuaded to consult headquarters at Paddington.

Alas, the GWR rejected the deputation's suggestions remaining adamant about its decision. Still dissatisfied, the Municipal Association afterwards claimed that there was no provision in the Light Railways Act for closure, sought legal advice and, in the meantime, protested to the Ministry of Agriculture. Sadly, it was to no avail.

At 4.00pm on Saturday, 7th February 1931, the last passenger train drew out of Welshpool station. It faltered up the incline to the town, then, with premonitory shrieks from the engine, wound its way through the alleyways pausing at Seven Stars halt for passengers to step up from the road. Some commiserated about the savings they had put into the Railway years before and lost. They didn't mind too much but they did not expect the line to close to the travelling public. So the train puffed manfully uphill with the solitary guard waving frantically in response to onlookers' sad stares of farewell. Even the GWR seemed reluctant to write 'finis' to the passenger services, for the coaches, removed to Swindon Works, languished there for five years.

During the next 25 years, the Branch Lines Investigation Committee was to reconsider the fate of the W&L several times. Each time it was assumed that fencing and some maintenance costs would still be incurred if the line were closed. Meanwhile the line was worked on most days by one trip each way leaving Welshpool at 11.00am and returning about 2.00pm. Trains, each with a brake van, were made up in accordance with the following limitations:

Coal and Minerals	Maximum 7 wagons
General Merchandise	Maximum 11 wagons or vans
Empties	Maximum 14 wagons and vans

Some of the staff were transferred in 1931 to duties on other parts of the former Cambrian system. There was no need for two shifts of crew-men any more; in previous years work had even started as early as 4.00am to prepare for the 8.00am departure from Welshpool. Steam raising was a long process, sometimes drawn out for as much as eight hours if the engine had been spare for some time, but it was much improved after the GWR fitted new boilers. In 1929 and 1930, men from the former Cambrian Works at Oswestry arrived to load the locomotives, in turn, on to flat wagons. On their return from Oswestry, 'westernised', they were more popular with the crews.

Cyfronydd station was provided with a waiting shelter and, in 1937, with a simple ramp for loading livestock.

W&LLR Pres. Co.

GWR buses providing an alternative service from Welshpool ran into the centre of Llanfair Caereinion. In July 1928, this Thornycroft A1 seating about 19 passengers, waits outside the Lion Hotel (nowadays the Red Lion). It displays a Dinas Mawddwy destination board.

Collection: Richard Hayden

Maintenance of the Line

Maintenance gangs were also reduced after the end of passenger traffic. Whereas two gangs of four men had been responsible for each of the two sections, split at Castle Caereinion, one gang was given charge of the whole line. For the first time, they were given their own transport. A velocipede (a one-man rail cycle) and a pump trolley were converted to 2ft 6ins gauge. But it was soon reported that they were of little use in view of the severe gradients. In 1940, a motor trolley arrived, a four seater with the engine under the seat, and the other contraptions languished in Welshpool yard.

The gang started work at 7.00am and finished at 5.00pm and normally had possession of the line until 10.30am each day. Maintenance included patching the permanent way, two or three sleepers at a time, repairing the wire fencing (especially in spring with the birth of the ubiquitous lambs) and mowing the line-side grass by scythe each summer. The hay eventually went to feed railway horses. Major resleepering and ballasting operations were restricted to Sundays and ash used for cheapness. Another economy introduced by the GWR

was the practice of cutting main-line sleepers in half for use on the line.

A recurrent headache during the summer months was the creeping and bending of the track, and in an attempt to forestall this, a great deal of time was spent oiling the fish-plates and also taking up the expansion gaps to pull the rails uphill. Even so, instances still occurred where it was necessary to remove or shorten rails and the gangs always had to be prepared to restore the lengths when the colder weather returned. One of the most troublesome stretches was the long straight east of Sylfaen. On occasions, the trolley was called out with crowbars to slew back the track snaking from ditch to ditch while the train from Llanfair waited until it was safe enough to pass. Several lengths at this point were eventually relaid with heavier rail.

The GWR Divisional Engineer examined the bridges on the line periodically through the thirties. During this period no repairs were ever required on the stone Brynelin viaduct (except painting the handrails), though on the 114ft (34.7m) long viaduct over the shifting River Banwy decaying transverse timbers had had to be renewed in 1929. It was estimated that

Sheep and cattle for Welshpool. During 1947, No. 822 The Earl *was photographed climbing Sylfaen bank with a livestock train. It includes vehicles converted from open wagons, two of which have been strengthened for cattle.*

S.P. Higgins Collection/National Railway Museum, York

Cartons of cake and a consignment of coal are the day's traffic to Llanfair. This train is loading at the old passenger terminus in Welshpool in the 1950s. The connection across Smithfield Road into the standard gauge yard was used for the transfer of parcels into the brakevan and gave access to the transhipment siding.

Hugh Ballantyne

The Earl *and* Countess *(foremost) pose outside the loco shed at Welshpool in 1949. Note the water crane beside The Earl. The carriage shed is to the left.*

Copyright: E.T. Gill/R.K. Blencowe collection

Beyond the crossing at Seven Stars in 1951, No. 822 begins the climb towards the housing estate.

F.W. Shuttleworth

Rail to road. At Llanfair in October 1951, agricultural supplies are collected by a local merchant. The canopy on the old booking office has been removed to give access along the former platform.

F.W. Shuttleworth

Another view in BR days of the (usually) daily goods for Llanfair ready to leave from the old passenger terminus at Welshpool.

Robin Butterell

the whole structure would require rebuilding in the year 2050! East of Castle Caereinion station, a wooden overbridge spanned the track where it curves through the cutting. It had been erected to placate the owner of the fields which had been severed by the building of the line. In 1932, the GWR decided to dismantle the structure and, at first, planned to replace it with a steel girder span. When the lineside landowner refused to contribute towards the cost, he was left instead with an accommodation crossing at the east end of the cutting.

Fighting for Traffic

The GWR was quite worried about the activities of local road hauliers who were emerging and extending their activities now that motor lorries were becoming more reliable. In the early thirties there were no less than nine carriers at Welshpool and one each at Llanfair Caereinion, Chirbury and the more distant Aberystwyth. The GWR classed half of these firms as *anti-railway* and noted those which received nothing by rail. When the opportunity occurred, the railway authorities opposed applications made by the road hauliers for extensions of their licences. A special watch was kept on a carrier based at Llanfair Caereinion as the firm was considered to be hauling traffic abstracted from the railway. Basic slag and manure from North Wales were being carried direct to the farmers; no more unloading at the stations and carting home as with rail-borne deliveries. Sheep were taken to Welshpool and Oswestry markets on Mondays and Wednesdays and, in season, to Birmingham.

Meanwhile, the GWR went into ways of attracting, or retaining, rail-borne traffic. From 1936, private wagon users on the standard gauge no longer had to pay for the hire of narrow gauge wagons from Welshpool to Llanfair. This did not apply to collieries. The 10d (4p) per ton charge for transhipment at Welshpool was retained, however, despite concern at its effect. To help secure a greater share of the livestock traffic, loading facilities were installed at Cyfronydd station late in 1937. Cattle loading docks were also used at Llanfair and Castle Caereinion stations, as well as in Welshpool yard. Covered storage facilities at Llanfair included the former waiting room as well as the warehouse and, in 1938, they were augmented by the building of a galvanised iron store shed. The awning of the old waiting room-cum-booking office, and two lamps, were removed to allow small lorries to traverse the one-time platform to collect sacks of meal.

Wartime Boom and the After Years

On the roads, motor lorries were making plain the little railway's disadvantages, but the course that world events now took staved off the final reckoning. The 1939-45 World War

brought a scarcity of fuel for road vehicles and exhortations to farmers to produce as much as they could to feed the nation. By 1942, two trains were running each Monday. A livestock working came down from Llanfair at 9.00am and returned with animals from Welshpool Smithfield market at 4.00pm. In September, the 'sheep season', up to five trips per day were not unknown with the wagons and vans crammed, the doors of the latter vehicles having to be left ajar to provide adequate ventilation. At Welshpool, the beasts were unloaded in the narrow gauge yard and driven across the Smithfield Road to the transhipment pens; the mixed gauge connection having been severed in the 1930s. The driving of animals along the road from the Llanfair valley to Welshpool was now much rarer than it had been before the war.

Once developed, the livestock traffic continued even after the end of the war. In one week in October 1946, for example, 530 sheep were carried from Llanfair destined for Macclesfield, New Mills and Manchester. At the beginning of December 1947, as well as 20 cattle consigned to Hanley, Staffordshire, there were 500 sheep for various Midland towns. Increasing traffic in feeding stuffs taxed storage space at Llanfair station and once again facilities had to be expanded. Condemned pre-1900 standard gauge coach bodies had been brought by road for this purpose and installed along the northern side of the station, the first arriving in February 1940 and another and a van body during the ensuing war years. As so many able-bodied men were required in the armed services, the traffic generated by the war was kept flowing with the aid of female track workers. Two women worked in the gang with two men. Equipped with the motor trolley, they maintained the full length of the Railway.

Though busier than for many years, it was not always possible to overcome the harshness of the notorious Montgomeryshire winters which had caused so much trouble during the building of the line. In severe cold spells, watering the engines could be difficult. Locomotives usually filled up at the water tower near Llanfair, apparently erected by the GWR in 1931. It replaced the original tank at Dolrhyd Mill and was gravity fed by a stream or by the use of a hand pump which lifted water from the river. But once in a while even the Banwy was known to freeze over. On these occasions, wily crews ingeniously nursed their engines until they reached a stream bridge near Sylfaen which, experience taught them, was sufficiently fast flowing to avoid freezing over. It was not the pleasantest of jobs, even for dedicated enginemen, to raise the amount of water required by the bucketful from beneath the under-bridge to the opening on the top of the tank.

Despite such resourcefulness, the weather managed to get the upper hand in the winters of 1940 and 1947 when coal lay frozen beneath a deep mantle of snow and prevented services for weeks at a time. Floods were another hazard. There were occasions when the river rose to cover the track west of Heniarth. Part of the bank was washed away following one storm just after the war. It may have been the same violent storm which seriously damaged a large culvert down Golfa bank. It had to be replaced with a 'temporary' wooden bridge which survived until the Preservation Company rebuilt the line to Welshpool.

By contrast, summertime on the line could be delightful. Crews had time to stop to collect sticks for the peas and beans on their allotments at home and, as the season advanced, their halts were prolonged to enable them to gather the hazel nuts and ripe blackberries, which hung in profusion at numerous favoured spots along the line. Small wonder that it was known among railwaymen as 'the holiday line'.

Nationalisation from 1st January 1948 seemed to have little noticeable effect on the running of the line. At the time of the changeover, British Railways proclaimed in the *Montgomeryshire Express* that they would '*do their best to preserve the fine traditions they inherit and . . . to provide a standard of service worthy of the rising national effort*'.

During the fifties, at about 11.30am on most days, a train of about six wagons left Welshpool for Llanfair, astonishing an ever-growing stream of motorists when the locomotive emerged to cross Church Street. Trains were nearly always subjected to delays on reaching Union Street, where the Seven Stars halt had once been, while attempts were made to clear parked cars from the metals. About 100 tons of freight each week were conveyed westwards, perhaps half that of the line's heyday in the Cambrian era, and while coal and coke continued to form the mainstay of the traffic, trains often included the odd wagon of basic slag, bricks or cement. Agricultural implements, meal and oats also were carried from time to time, but general merchandise was now only handled at infrequent intervals. The collection of stone from the Standard Quarry

Glimpse of Arcady. Countess *dallies at Castle Caereinion while unloading proceeds unhurriedly. The corrugated iron shelter survives long after the end of passenger services while the distant signal box is a relic of the 1907 scheme for passing trains here. Behind No. 823 is the cattle loading ramp (and the loop siding).*

Maurice Deane

A verdant scene on the descent from Cyfronydd in the 1940s. No. 822 The Earl *is hauling a coal train up to Llanfair.*

S.P. Higgins Collection/National Railway Museum, York.

Converse with the cottagers. The Earl, *with a train load of coal for Llanfair, pauses in The Narrrows, Welshpool, on 17th May 1956.*

T.B. Owen

BR days: some of the last employees are seen at Llanfair. From the left: N. Foulkes (station foreman), platelayers W. Gough and W. Allan, P. Cochrane (ganger), G.H. Jones (driver), W.N. New (fireman) and H. Williams (guard).

had long since ceased, the quarry having closed in 1939.

The trains which drew out of Llanfair yard now usually consisted of empties. Perhaps once or twice a week, there would be a wagon of wool or bundles of empty sacks. Occasionally traffic was forwarded from or received at Castle Caereinion and Heniarth, but only rarely did it make a complete wagon load.

The End is Near

Even without competition from speedier and more convenient motor transport, it seems inevitable that the Railway could not have developed as the thriving economic proposition it was once hoped it would be. The number of inhabitants in the rural districts that it served was diminishing. Since the middle of the nineteenth century, the population of Llanfair Caereinion had halved and the process accelerated notably after the early 1930s.

The future of the W&L became more and more uncertain. In 1947, with closure under consideration but still not decided on, costly locomotive repairs could no longer be postponed. Execution was stayed to get some return for this expenditure, but in the summer of 1950, British Railways, nearly three years old and becoming increasingly sensitive to the unprofitability of the W&L, was again actively considering closing it. The Divisional Superintendent Traffic Manager from Oswestry informed Welshpool Town Council that alternative road transport arrangements would be made. The reception this suggestion met with was mixed. Some members of the Council regarded the Railway as a continuing nuisance. Others,

however, secured approval of a motion asking BR to reconsider the matter. A few weeks later the District Traffic Superintendent explained the Railway Executive's case to Council delegates. After that, the Council took the view that no further action could be taken.

Meanwhile, interest amongst enthusiasts was fanned by the Birmingham Locomotive Club who found a way of persuading BR Western Region to run an innovative excursion over the line on 2nd July 1949. It must have been quite an adventure! Headed by No. 823 *Countess,* accommodation was in four open wagons in which chairs and benches had been placed for the day. In the next few years, several other railway societies managed to run similar excursions.

Early in 1951, representatives of the parish councils along the line deplored the proposed closure but showed less militancy of opposition than Welshpool Council. Surprisingly, closure did not come. There were rumours of strings pulled in high places and in 1952 a Western Region spokesman denied that any decision had been taken to close, although he admitted that it was under consideration. This statement was in response to an enquiry from Eric G. Cope, a founder secretary of the Narrow Gauge Railway Society, who was now initiating a move to take over and preserve the W&L. Having been informed that, if it did close, BR would not object to selling the line and, inspired by the efforts of the Talyllyn Railway Preservation Society at Towyn, Mr. Cope suggested either a national appeal or a private company to save the W&L. He communicated with the Welshpool Town Council seeking help. However, the council would have none of this, having now made its own plans for building a car park and for widening roads where

The GWR erected the stream-fed water tower beside the River Banwy just over half a mile east of Llanfair station. A Welshpool-bound train in the early 1950s pauses to replenish the tanks of No. 822.

John Milner

the line ran. Some support was voiced for the project if a terminal could be provided near Raven Square; shades of things to come, thirty years later!

Some consignees were complaining of delays and damage to their goods. The stationmaster at Welshpool explained to his superiors that the rolling stock was '*of poor and old quality*', while the traders agitated for delivery by lorry from Welshpool and threatened to transfer their business to road hauliers. Meanwhile, trains continued to run and their occasional clatter through the back streets of the town chattered defiance at those who wished to be rid of something which was nothing if not a local institution. But when both locomotives needed urgent repairs, no trains ran for several weeks. Lifting of some of the narrow gauge sidings at Welshpool heralded the inevitable. Early in 1956 *The Countess* was removed to Oswestry Works and closure again seemed imminent. Finally, the announcement was made by British Railways (Western Region) that '*on and from 5th November 1956, the freight train service between Welshpool and Llanfair Caereinion will be withdrawn and the line closed for all purposes*'.

Saying Goodbye

During the last month of operation, the now doomed freight trains conveyed 117 wagon-loads to Llanfair. The last goods working on 2nd November consisted of five wagons of coal, while the previous day six wagons of coal, one of sheep racks and one of general goods had been hauled up the line.

Towards the end of October, the Festiniog Railway Society organised a farewell trip on the Railway for its members and expressed an interest in acquiring some mementoes such as a few of the couplings and, possibly, even the rail when lifted. Disposal of *The Earl* was still to be settled. There were suggestions that it might be sent to the Narrow Gauge Railway Museum at Towyn, while about forty wagons and vans were to be made available to the demolition contractor. The engine made a brave show as it stormed out of the Welshpool terminus with the FRS '*last*' trip. Rumbling through the town, the customary stops were made at Church Street, Union Street and Raven Square for the fireman to dismount and signal the train across as he displayed his red flag.

Up Golfa bank, watched by the inspector accompanying the trip, 16 year old fireman Ted Williams had to work hard as the engine poked its way undaunted along the twisting, climbing line. Across the deepening valley, the tints of autumn made an impressive display among the trees on the hillside. With a stop at Castle Caereinion where a traction engine was rusting beside the line, they reached Llanfair terminus with an hour to spare before the return started. From Heniarth, the train was followed by the motor trolley conveying the gang

which had been dismantling the long disused waiting shelter there. Gaining the lower end of the line with a mile to go through the town, the Mayor of Welshpool took over the controls, guiding the '*Llanfair Jinny*', as it was affectionately known, on its sad journey to the terminus.

During the last week of scheduled operations, the small guard's van on the freight trains pulling out of Welshpool was crammed with passengers who had asked for a last ride to Llanfair. Some were local people recalling the days of the passenger services, some were staff from the main-line station and a number were enthusiasts. The privilege of performing the last rites, however, fell to the Stephenson Locomotive Society on Saturday, 3rd November 1956. The train of nine wagons and two brake vans was equipped with seats 'borrowed', once again, from the platforms of the mainline station. In the yard across the road from the terminus, some of the W&L cattle trucks were being dismantled while, significantly, a sleek maroon and cream cattle lorry stood beside them. The journey was described in the *Railway Magazine* of January 1957:

The co-operation of the Western Region of British Railways was secured for the issue of specially-printed tickets and in the recovery of one of the nameplates of The Earl *which was attached to locomotive No. 822. The Newtown Silver Band was present and played at Welshpool and Llanfair and intermediate points. There were 120 members of the Society on the train of open wagons and many more were unable to attend because accommodation was strictly limited. Considerable local interest was aroused. Some of the houses adjoining the line in Welshpool and particularly those in the new housing estate through which it runs, bore decorations which suggested a Royal visit to the narrow gauge railway.*

The train started from Welshpool at 2.30pm and the occupants of a large number of cars vied with each other for vantage points on the way to Llanfair to secure photographs. At Castle Caereinion, official photographs were taken of invited guests.

The special returned from Llanfair at 4pm to the accompaniment of cheering crowds, the music of the band, and continuous whistling of The Earl. *The latter's efforts became even more effective from Raven Square (on the outskirts of Welshpool) to the main-line station, and few residents could have failed to hear it. The climax was reached as the train approached the station where a '2200' class 0-6-0 and a 'Manor' 4-6-0 joined in with gusto on their whistles till the train drew to a halt. Then the stillness descended, and only the band playing Handel's Funeral March could be heard - a fitting ending. On any standards, no branch line could have had its last day commemorated more tangibly or with more appropriate ceremony.*

Standing room only! The farewell trip was assigned to the Stephenson Locomotive Society on 3rd November 1956. Near New Drive crossing, the nine little wagons and two brakevans filled with 120 society members make an amazing sight.

Ivo Peters

Last rites. At Castle Caereinion, the Newtown Silver Band had been playing in salute to the line's last train. On the return to Welshpool, the band finished the day with Handel's Funeral March. Never was there such a big finale for such a little railway!

Ivo Peters

Chapter 5

Rescue and Revival

When the take-over of the W&L had first been mooted, in 1952, the idea of acquiring and resuscitating a doomed railway was quite new. The only attempt then working was that of the Talyllyn Railway Preservation Society at Towyn (Tywyn) on the west coast and that venture was but two years old. The Narrow Gauge Railway Society's inquiries regarding the W&L had led to nothing, although negotiations throughout July, August and September of 1952 indicated an initial willingness on the part of the British Transport Commission to be co-operative. Representatives of the NGRS had got so far as discussing a tentative price of £6,000 for the line and £300 for the two locomotives. Details of running and maintenance expenses had been given to them too. Perhaps it was the suggestion that these expenses could reach £3,500 per year that caused the NGRS to inform British Railways that, in the event of closure, their interest would be confined to purchasing the two locomotives for preservation, preferably in Welshpool yard. Had closure come at that time it seems doubtful whether the line itself would have been saved.

With closure again proposed in 1955, Llanfair Parish Council was told by the British Transport Commission that £7,100 was needed for resleepering and other repairs to the line and £1,600 for repairs to the locomotives at a time when a year's receipts only amounted to £4,269. The farming community, its leaders meeting at Llanfair, were fearful of increased costs for haulage of basic slag and coal from Welshpool by road but Welshpool Town Council saw closure as an opportunity to acquire the trackbed for other purposes.

A letter to the *Railway World* magazine in 1955 had suggested a scheme for a non-profit-making society involving diesel passenger services to serve the town section. Although nothing came of this immediately, it showed how interest was stirring. A fine photograph appeared in the *Observer* in the spring of the next year and in July Llanfair Parish Council invited inquiries from railway enthusiasts who might be interested in taking the Railway over as a private enterprise, on the lines of the Talyllyn Railway Preservation Society. When the end finally came, the Talyllyn Railway scheme was meeting with success and the Festiniog Railway had been taken over

two years previously. Prospects at Portmadoc (Porthmadog) looked promising. Such hope and enthusiasm was infectious and encouraged new interest in saving the line at Welshpool. Throughout the summer of 1956, special excursions along the line with passengers in open wagons, fanned interest and a Welshpool and Llanfair Railway section of the Branch Line Society sprang up.

Hard on the heels of this came news of another scheme. During August 1956, William Morris, a London printer, was busy trying to initiate a society expressly for the preservation of the Railway and he began making contact with British Railways. Preceded by a letter to the *Railway Magazine* to mobilise support, William Morris organised a special trip over the line. It attracted about seventy enthusiasts who were carried in four drop-sided freight wagons after handing over the usual signed indemnities to the Welshpool station staff.

The date was 15th September 1956 and it was a significant day for the Railway. Following the exhilarating ride up the Banwy valley and back, a historic meeting was held in the narrow gauge yard at Welshpool. Addressing the gathering, William Morris outlined his ideas for saving the line. Many of those present accepted his invitation to pay a subscription and become members of a new society to achieve the objectives Morris had referred to. The Branch Line Society's W&L section also canvassed for members on this occasion without much support. Within the next few months their organisation agreed to hand over the assets of their W&L section to the new Society, dithering however for two years whilst they awaited details of the new Society's constitution. The cheque amounted to the princely sum of £22 and a few pence. Meanwhile the Society founded by Morris held its first general meeting in London on Friday, 23rd November 1956, approving a brief constitution and electing its committee including William Morris as secretary and Stanley H. Keyse as legal advisor.

They were pioneers more truly than they knew. The situation at Welshpool was not directly comparable with the two earlier preservation schemes at Tywyn and Porthmadog. It was the first attempt to rescue a railway owned by British Railways, and formidable financial and legal problems presented themselves.

After descending the notorious Golfa incline (in unfitted stock!) this LCGB special in June 1956 has just crossed Raven Square roundabout where later the line was to be cut. Travelling on the line in freight wagons would never have been allowed today!

Ivo Peters

The Society Struggles

Early discouragements included a spurious claim by British Railways that the Light Railway Order stipulated that the line must be operated by an existing company. Within a year of closure, the fledgling Society was wondering whether to wind up but decided they should threaten to take the problem to the Minister of Transport. News of the Society's professed determination to reopen the line dismayed Welshpool Town Council and in January 1958 some councillors conceded that they might have to accept a terminus near the old Seven Stars. Morris was trying to convince the council of the advantages of the Railway re-opening, painting a prospect of 50,000 passengers a year being attracted.

About this time, the possibility of leasing the line (instead of buying) was mentioned for the first time. Meanwhile, the Clerk to Llanfair Parish Council was reported to be activating local interest, but at Welshpool strong objections were being raised to the town section remaining in use, presaging a truncating of the line which was to rankle deeply. The disquieting news from Welshpool was shortly followed by an

intimation from British Railways that the transfer they were now willing to negotiate would be limited to the section west of Raven Square. Furthermore, on 7th May 1958, locomotive No. 822 *The Earl* was removed from Welshpool, albeit to better cover at Oswestry Works, while membership had only risen to 200 and hoped-for local financial help had not materialised. The outlook was disconcerting.

Other factors, too, militated against success. The Society of those early days was short of officials with maturity and expertise. But admirably, the committee's enthusiasm somehow kept things together when progress was minimal and membership numbers were growing at snail's pace. At first, only a few people came forward who were talented and experienced in the organising of such a movement as had been formed. Nor did the Society attract wealthy and generous well-wishers on the scale that some similar projects did. In the early years, these troubles also tended to dog the company which succeeded the Society.

One of the legal tangles which faced the project was that the old Light Railway Company, unlike the Talyllyn and the Festiniog Railway Companies, had ceased to exist on 31st

December 1922. If the British Transport Commission was to assign its rights and obligations with regard to the W&L, it had to be to a body approved by the Ministry of Transport. Sounding out the Ministry for its views, it appeared that it would be necessary to secure the incorporation of a limited liability company to be responsible for operating the Railway. At first, some members expected that the Society would continue with control over the Company which it was now proposed should be formed.

The spring of 1959 brought news of a provisional agreement and proposed terms which, hearteningly, seemed to be within the reach of the preservation organisation. With little hope of funds being forthcoming for the purchase of the Railway, it was very fortunate that the somewhat unusual procedure of leasing the line was offered. The proposal was for a lease on a 42 year basis and the rolling stock was to be paid for by hire purchase over a ten year period, recalling the purchase of the first timber bolsters over half a century earlier. Agreement was subject to Ministry of Transport approval of the Company carrying passengers. July 1959 saw the first working parties clearing the line, at first along the town section, and, as summer passed, on Golfa bank, where brambles were vying with rapidly sprouting saplings for possession of the track. At about this time, a selection was made of the W&L rolling stock which was to be purchased. Apart from the two locomotives, for which considerable sums had to be raised in due course, a representative range of the freight stock was chosen.

The transfer of the latter from the Welshpool terminus to Raven Square or beyond seemed desirable, but the Society had neither motive power nor legal powers to operate the Railway. In September, while the agreement of BR to the movement of the stock awaited a report that clearance of the track had been completed to their satisfaction, a working party, in somewhat cavalier fashion, went ahead. They solved the haulage problem by borrowing a pair of sturdy carthorses which were newly shod for the occasion. Quite a number of trips were required to complete the movement, the steep gradients in some parts necessitating 'banking' at the rear provided by half a dozen Society members.

The Company is Set Up

The year 1960 brought with it an important event in the saga of the railway's preservation. On 4th January occurred the incorporation of the Welshpool and Llanfair Light Railway Preservation Company Ltd, to be followed five days later by the Company's first meeting at a Paddington public house. Though well-advised, the formation of the Company had not been achieved without a certain amount of controversy, and the issue was the founder-

secretary. The Society lingered for over a year after the Company was incorporated. Finally, after a meeting in Birmingham on 11th March 1961, four and a half years after its formation, the Society was wound up and its funds transferred to the new Company which most of the members had already joined.

Before incorporation, it had to be decided what kind of company was required. A private company would not have been appropriate but there are two main kinds of public company. One, like the original company which built the line, is open to all to subscribe to up to the limit of the share capital authorised. Here, the Society would have had to acquire at least 51 per cent of the issued shares to retain control. Had such a company been set up, it would have been hoped to attract some of the much-needed capital with the offer of the remaining shares. However, the principle of equal voting powers for all prevailed over all other considerations and the company formed was of the kind 'limited by guarantee and not having a share capital'.

One vote at the Company's general meetings is gained by each person who pays the full membership subscription. This was felt to be a democratic formula appropriate to an organisation dependent upon the combined efforts of individual and manifold talents, freely donated in a crusading spirit. The inability of any individual to gain financial control of the Company under this arrangement was particularly welcomed. Special provision was made for supporters under eighteen years old to pay a reduced subscription as non-voting associates.

The legal status of the newly registered Company was a highly desirable feature in view of its engaging in trade of various kinds and the need for liability to the general public to devolve upon the Company and not upon individual members. Disappointingly, many summer months were yet to wax and wane without public train services running, resulting in the loss of much-needed revenue and testing morale. However, spirits were boosted by the operation of special trains for members. Many thrilled to the sound of the reverberating exhausts as the engines climbed Golfa bank.

Throughout 1960, attempts were being made to work out details of the lease. It was realised that, with the exclusion of the Welshpool town section from the contract, the motive power depot would have to be at Llanfair Caereinion. It seemed that plans would have to be made for a new terminus on the west of Raven Square. The unsuitability of this arrangement resulted in a board representative visiting Western Region headquarters where he was able to persuade British Railways to amend the draft lease to include the line as far east as the Standard Quarry. This would have given much better scope for providing a new station with space for congregating and the parking of cars. A term of 21 years was, unfortunately, the longest that could now be wrung out of the authorities at Paddington; neither was there included any option to renew the lease on expiry.

About this time, Welshpool Town Council secured terms for the acquisition of the town section but in a gesture of goodwill, they decided that efforts should be made to buy the site near the quarry to provide for the proposed station on the east side of Raven Square.

Another winter passed before details of the proposed lease were eventually agreed by both sides. By dint of judicious negotiations, these terms had been kept within the scope of the Preservation Company's rather precarious finances. A relatively nominal initial rent had been agreed. For the first five years, £100 was to be paid annually increasing thereafter in two stages. The summer months of 1961 were occupied with track clearing and the acquisition of the necessary rolling stock. By November, it was possible to apply to the Ministry of Transport for a Light Railway (Leasing and Transfer) Order. It was four months later, in March 1962, that the first visit took place from a Ministry official who intimated what restrictions (with regard to speed and so on) were likely to be imposed. Two months later came another visit, this time mainly to discuss the position at Raven Square. The official heard the Company's

views regarding the siting of the terminus, but gave little hope of the Ministry agreeing to the Railway being allowed to run across the road there on the level.

Some of the members were understandably becoming weary of the continual postponement of the re-opening but, at long last, on 3rd October 1962 the British Transport Commission (Welshpool and Llanfair) Light Railway (Leasing and Transfer) Order was issued. Effective from 12th October, it specified the south-west side of Raven Square as the eastern terminal. Of the loss of the crossing over Raven Square, the late Lt.-Col. Sir Thomas H. Salt Bt., chairman of the company 1960-65, wrote:

> *'...the result of the line the Minister took will be felt through the years. In every way, the Railway will be harder to make a commercial success, less pleasant from the visitor's point of view and we will have to put up with second best solutions to countless problems not only at Raven Square but all over the Railway'.*

Nevertheless, history was to show that the enforced choice of Llanfair as the base was, in the end, the most practical point from which the nascent enterprise could develop.

Trains Again

By the time the Order was eventually issued, a set of rolling stock had been acquired which was sufficient to satisfy the new management's basic requirements. Though acutely short of capital, the Company overcame the complete lack of stock with pluck and initiative. By the autumn of 1962, the line possessed the original two locomotives, *The Earl* and *The Countess*, two 4-wheel diesel locomotives, two smaller motor trolleys and five modern (if basic) bogie carriages. In addition, there was a collection of wagons and vans including stock suitable for permanent way work. Although one of the trolleys had been brought up from the old yard at Welshpool soon after working parties were allowed on the line, news of the first engine capable of hauling engineering trains was received with delight. It arrived on a Tuesday towards the end of March 1961, a modest enough diesel-powered machine. It was nonetheless welcomed and was named *Raven*, after the inn of that name at the Welshpool end of the line. Its departure from the Nettleton Top ironstone mines in Lincolnshire had unfortunately been postponed some months, partly through the delay in transit of a pair of new which were

S&T workers east of Heniarth in 1962 with humble No 3 Raven, the former ironstone mines diesel. The track has disappeared beneath the grass cover.

W&LLR Pres. Co.

In 1959, when it seemed that stock would be isolated if the authorities decided to lift the track through the town, a spirited member hired a horse and harness and pulled all the rolling stock through to Raven Square. A crowd has gathered as two of the vans emerge into Union Street. When British Railways heard about the movement, they were not very pleased but by then the deed was done.

At Raven Square in 1961, Chairman Sir Thomas Salt accompanied by Lady Salt was shown the homemade Austin trolley, based on an old hand-pump vehicle. Standing is Derek Mayman, an early benefactor and now a vice-president. Sir Thomas Salt's railway interest stemmed from family links with the North Staffordshire Railway and in particular with the 2ft 6ins gauge Leek & Manifold Light Railway.

When The Earl *returned in 1961, it was shunted on to the market siding to be unloaded by the Salop steam crane.*

W&LLR Pres. Co.

diminutive machine was to perform heroically on the line.

Before the Society was superseded by the new Company, the search had begun for suitable coaching stock. This had led to an approach being made to the Admiralty and negotiations were eventually brought to a successful conclusion through the good offices of Sir Thomas, the W&L Chairman. Apart from the light railway systems in the then numerous Admiralty depots, few 2ft 6ins gauge lines had been built in Britain. The railway from which the W&L acquired rolling stock for re-opening lay at Upnor on the north bank of the River Medway opposite Chatham Dockyard in East Kent. The last scheduled service ran from Upnor to the terminus at Lodge Hill on 29th May 1961. Although it was sad for the Upnor line, this was the event which released the coaches so eagerly awaited at Welshpool.

Meanwhile, the W&L's two 0-6-0T Beyer Peacock locomotives were in Oswestry Works. A price of £654 (excluding movement) had been agreed for them with Western Region. Early efforts to raise the sum required from members met with an encouraging response boosted by a generous contribution from Midlands businessman John Wilkins (owner of the Fairbourne Railway) to cover the purchase price of *The Earl*. Overhaul of the locomotives went ahead at Oswestry and in April 1961, *The Earl* was steamed for the first time in four and a half years. Friday, 28th July 1961 was one of the most exciting and significant days in the new Company's history. On the previous day, *The Earl* had been dispatched for Welshpool on a BR flat wagon. At the same time, a set of 2ft 6ins gauge flat wagons and two semi-open coaches were being carried by rail from the Lodge Hill & Upnor Railway. A steam crane from Shrewsbury (Coleham Head) arrived at Welshpool on the morning of that Friday in July to find the new stock for the W&L waiting. The crane was propelled on to the Smithfield market siding. Alongside, a temporary extension of the 2ft 6ins gauge had recently been laid as the permanent way in the narrow gauge yard had already been recovered. The lifting of the rolling stock on to W&L metals was watched with exultation as first *The Earl*, then the coaches and lastly the wagons were pushed down the siding. Crowds cheered from the lineside at the brave sight of a steam engine in action again as the stock was moved through the town to reach the loop sidings at Golfa and Castle Caereinion.

A members' open weekend held two months later was celebrated by the first steam workings from Welshpool to Llanfair since closure, five years previously. Golfa bank proved difficult: much sanding was required and even with only two coaches and a brakevan, the help of the tiny diesel *Raven* was called on as a banker. Members commented on the smooth riding of the newly acquired coaches while photographers and tape recording enthusiasts made good use of one of the new flat wagons marshalled in the train. Later in the year, *The Earl* made several more trips through Welshpool hauling quantities

of ballast and sleepers transferred from BR wagons standing on the Smithfield siding. In November, the Shrewsbury steam crane made a return visit to Welshpool where seven more Upnor vehicles were ready to be lifted off the standard gauge bogie wagons on to W&L metals. Pride of this batch was the newer composite car. Again, the operation was performed by using the Smithfield market siding.

Only three months later, the arrival became imminent of yet another item of rolling stock, a 105bhp Planet diesel locomotive. This, too, was from the Admiralty's line in Kent, but this time the movement was by road. On a cold, misty, February morning, *Upnor Castle* as it was to become, was removed from the road lowloader by driving it over temporary track on to the narrow gauge stub in Welshpool yard.

The Countess was still in the workshops at Oswestry undergoing heavy repairs and money was being sought to meet the cost. Eventually, on an unusually sunny October day in 1962, within a few days of her ladyship's sixtieth birthday, *The Countess* returned home. Resplendent in her new coat of paint, W&L locomotive No. 2 travelled to Welshpool on a standard gauge wagon to be met by the Shrewsbury steam crane which once again had turned out to effect the transfer. After this was carefully and successfully accomplished, making use of the market siding, a start was made on raising steam in *The Countess*. *The Earl* then came to '*meet the wife*', as a wag put it at the time, before setting off for Llanfair hauling a special members' train. The engine was decorated with a flag of the Welsh dragon and a string of Union Jacks which, together with those hung out by the people of Welshpool, lent to the occasion a suitably festive air. After the special reached Llanfair, news came that *The Countess* had left Welshpool although it was reported from Golfa that the leading and trailing crank pin brasses were running hot. However, she ran on to Castle Caereinion where the returning special passed her. She ambled westwards, light, to Llanfair, making the first trip to Llanfair for over six years, while the special continued to Raven Square. Here the train was gravity shunted past the locomotive and propelled through the town. Dusk was gathering as the return journey began. Winding its way between the houses, *The Earl* left poised a path of languid smoke to complement the evening mist setting over the tumbled roofs of the town.

The Re-Opening

These were exciting days on the line. While the board was concerned about the mounting gap between available funds and the estimate of what was required, the Powis woods repeatedly resounded to the sounds of steam in action. Permanent way materials were collected from standard gauge wagons at Welshpool, and on at least one occasion double-heading was required, something never allowed in GWR days.

The Earl *and* The Countess *triumphantly cross Raven Square and head for Llanfair after the return of* The Countess *in 1962.*

W&LLR Pres. Co.

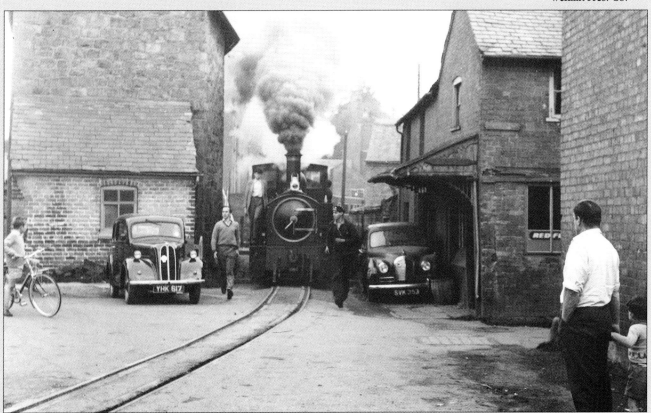

After The Earl *returned, steam hauled members' trains were possible. In Welshpool, obstacles on the track were often a hazard so this Special in October 1962 emerges cautiously from 'the Narrows'.*

Narrow Gauge Railway Society, E.K. Stretch collection

In the former narrow gauge goods yard at Welshpool, W&L track survived alongside the standard gauge market siding. After the Upnor wagons arrived in 1961, they were loaded with spent ballast bought cheaply from British Railways.

R. Johnson

Llanfair station in 1963, still retained its original layout. The three decrepit standard gauge van and coach bodies, installed by the GWR, clutter the platform. On the far left, The Countess stands on the coal road, soon to be lifted. The bank (and field) on the left are as yet largely undeveloped.

R. Johnson

Work was concentrated on the section between Llanfair and Castle Caereinion and the plan was for the first services to be restrictcd to this portion.

Just before Christmas 1962, special passenger-carrying trains were put on over this part of the line for Llanfair Fair, being the first advertised public service since 1931. The winter that followed was a hard one during which *The Earl* was derailed at Cyfronydd crossing when the rails were packed with ice. However, inclement weather did not prevent volunteers from carrying out sufficient repairs to the track to satisfy the Inspector from the Ministry of Transport when he visited the line on 26th March.

The great day for which everyone had worked for so long was Saturday, 6th April 1963, exactly sixty years after the first opening ceremony. As on the first occasion, the day dawned with threatening skies, but in contrast, and by way of a good omen, the weather later cleared and the sun appeared in time for the re-opening ceremony. Promptly at 11.00am, *The Earl* responded to the guard's whistle and set out manfully up the sharp incline from Welshpool narrow gauge yard, drawing two coaches conveying the Chairman's party.

The Chairman, Sir Thomas Salt, accompanied by the Earl of Powis, alighted at Llanfair at about 12.10pm and mounted a flat wagon, addressing the jostling crowd which had assembled in the yard. The Earl was due to go abroad and was having to change his arrangements slightly, little realising that sixty years before his predecessor had had to do something similar when he altered his plans and hurried back from overseas to preside at the official opening of the railway. The Earl contrasted his happy assignment with the gloomy news that had come that week of Dr. Beeching's report recommending the drastic pruning of the national railway system. Wishing the W&L prosperity, the Earl walked to No. 2 *The Countess* and drove the engine through the tape across the tracks before being presented with a memento of the occasion.

Following this ceremony, *The Countess* steamed out with the Chairman's train bearing the guests to Welshpool where, repeating history, they repaired to the Royal Oak Hotel for

Movement of the Preservation Company's newly acquired rolling stock through Welshpool often attracted much local interest. No.1 The Earl *emerges between the buildings and crosses Church Street shortly before the town section closed for good in 1963.*

The original goods shed at Llanfair station lost one of its awnings before closure and the other two were converted into a lean-to in which locomotive repairs were attempted in the first decade of preservation.

luncheon. Meanwhile, a second party was refreshed in the Public Institute at Llanfair before being conveyed on a special train to Castle Caereinion and back. This train, which left Llanfair at 1.30pm, turned out to be the first public service of the new regime's first season. The return working of the Chairman's special also carried fare-paying passengers, some of whom were allowed to ride from Welshpool to Castle, at their own risk, free of charge. This last train on a great day arrived at Llanfair terminus at 4.00pm precisely.

Sadly, the year that saw passenger services restarted also saw the end of the Welshpool town section. Only two days before the re-opening ceremony, Welshpool Borough Council completed the purchase of the railway from Raven Square eastwards, and soon afterwards the Council decided that the Company's trains would not be able to work over it after August of that year. On 17th August 1963 a genuine 'Last Train' ran through the town, spectacularly double-headed by *The Earl* and *The Countess*. Two days later, work on lifting the track commenced near the Church Street crossing. Few British railways have intermingled with road traffic or pushed past householders' back windows as this line had done in Welshpool. Now the fateful cut had finally come and not without causing bitterness on the part of some who believed it would bring more than just difficulties in transferring rail-borne materials. However, Welshpool's councillors were more concerned with the chance to extend the cattle market and car park and prepare for the construction of a 'bypass' along Brook Street. By November 1965, the recovery of the rail from the town section was all but complete.

That first summer of operation brought the first hint of major trouble to come. When divers from the Birmingham Sub-Aqua Club had discovered that one of the piers of the Banwy Bridge was being undermined, they had returned to underpin the pier with bagged concrete. It was then believed that the problem had been resolved. What drama a crystal ball could have revealed! Further help was provided when a military detachment came to undertake engineering work on the line in the spring of 1964. The work included restoring the siding at Sylfaen, and completing a short loop and a stop-block on the west of Raven Square.

Following the re-opening to the public of the Llanfair-Castle Caereinion section, services were run each weekend and on bank holidays, usually three workings each day. The 1964 timetable commenced at Easter and involved two weeks of daily running (one working). It also introduced trains extending to Sylfaen from 6th June of that year. With appropriate ceremony, these were inaugurated with a double-headed 'special'. The turn-round at Sylfaen required the use of the diesel locomotive *Upnor Castle* as there was a short siding but no loop. In August 1964 the state of the track beyond Castle Caereinion was causing such concern that during the last three weeks of the season services had to be terminated at Castle station.

A Disastrous Blow

Before the year was out, much more serious trouble was to arise. After only two years of operating, the courage and hopes of the pioneer supporters were to receive a severe jolt. Wet weather prevailed in mid-Wales towards the end of 1964,

Re-opening at last. This was the Chairman's train, with the 5th Earl of Powis aboard on 6th April 1963. No.1 The Earl started from the old goods yard beside Welshpool Smithfield.

Maurice Deane

Below: *The very last train through the town in August 1963, a double-headed members' special, crosses Union Street, near the site of the Seven Stars halt.*

Copyright: The Guardian

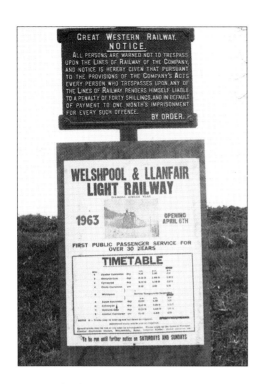

For the first time in years a passenger timetable is displayed on the Railway.

John Milner

not unusual for this area. As a result, the surging River Banwy at Llanfair Caereinion rose higher and higher until an inspection party found the menacing torrents flooding the track near Dolrhyd Mill. Alas, this was not all. On Sunday morning, 13th December 1964, it was discovered to everyone's utmost dismay that the bridge carrying the Railway over the river had sustained serious damage during the night. The northern stone-built pier had subsided and the girders dipped drunkenly above the swirling current.

The sad news spread and it began to be realised what a desperate position the Company was in. The damaged bridge prevented trains running further than Heniarth, just over a mile and a quarter from Llanfair Caereinion. This could only lead to lower passenger receipts and possibly the end of the Company in the form it had been established, unless some way of restoring the bridge could be found. But the Company had no capital reserves and considerable funds would be required for a job of this size. The weeks following saw a hectic series of discussions, Board meetings and consultations with civil engineering advisors. Soon an idea of the cost of rebuilding the bridge emerged. About £3,000 was estimated as the probable figure. This news was circulated to members together with details of the appeal fund which the Chairman had opened as soon as he heard of the disaster. Even if the fund succeeded beyond the dreams of the most optimistic, some way had to

Contemplation at Castle station. The members' 'Open Weekend', September 1961 saw the first steam hauled trains since closure. 4w diesel No. 3 Raven, *on the loop, had worked as banker on some trips up Golfa bank. The grounded cattle van awaits movement to the Festiniog Railway.*

H. Gunston

Disaster Strikes . . . .

On the night of the 12th December, 1964, the bridge over the River Banwy sustained serious damage due to heavy flooding. As can be seen, the northern pier has subsided.

John Milner

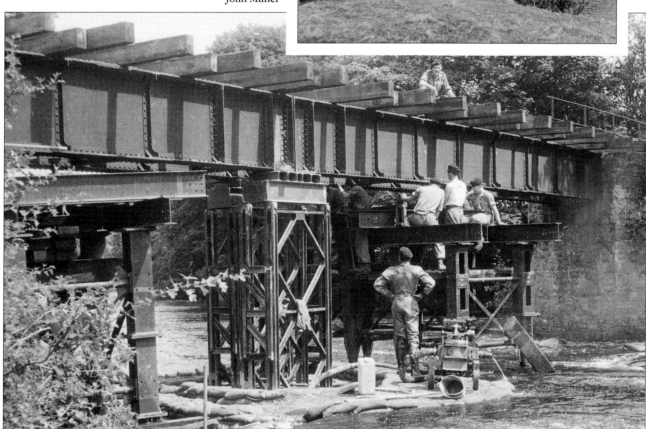

Following the near collapse of the bridge over the River Banwy, only help with the rebuilding from the Army's Royal Engineers (16th Railway Regiment) prevented the whole project being abandoned.

W&LLR Pres. Co.

be found of getting the work done quickly as well as cheaply. By a stroke of good fortune, it now appeared that behind the scenes the Chairman was arranging salvation in the form of a military exercise.

Although the appeal fund was still well short of the target, the response was so promising that the Board felt able to give the go ahead when the 16th Railway Regiment Royal Engineers finally agreed to do the work, having worked out realistic costings and a plan of action. Volunteers now set to work to remove the decking, track and timbers from the sagging girders. In April, a detachment of Royal Engineers arrived and set up

camp alongside the bridge. Light steel trestling was brought and lowered on to the river bed by crane on the Llanfair side and by rope from the locomotive *Upnor Castle* on the other side. Trestle frames were properly positioned and then the task of lifting the girders began by using jacks. This allowed the demolition of the leaning pier with the aid of pneumatic drills.

Work started next on a coffer dam intended to provide a dry area in which to build a new pier. Flooding and strong currents caused great difficulties and the Royal Engineers had to leave before the dam was completed. However, they returned at the end of July by which time the dam was finished and most of the remains of the old pier removed, despite continuing difficulties with water leaking through the coffer dam. By dint of various expedients it was possible to excavate the river bed and construct a base on which a new steel pier was to be erected. Lorries brought concrete to the bank on the Heniarth side and this was ferried in wheelbarrows over planks to secure the foundations. When the erection of the pier was completed, the girders were lowered on to it and the trestles removed. The soldiers followed this by expeditiously replacing the decking and track, and relaying the track from the bridge to Heniarth station where the loop was re-laid as two sidings. At 11.00am on Friday, 13th August, eight months after the floods, *Upnor Castle* crossed the bridge safely. On the following afternoon the first passenger train edged its way across as services to Castle Caereinion were resumed, subject to speed restrictions in the area of the bridge.

By a strange irony another disaster touched the Railway on the very next day, although of a personal nature. This was the death of the chairman, Sir Thomas Salt, who had led the Company through many adversities, not least the bridge calamity. Sir Thomas, who had had connections with the old

North Staffordshire Railway, had been Chairman of the Preservation Company since its formation. Members have recalled the way he inspired them in the days before public services started. Sometimes, when travelling the line on a members' 'special', Sir Thomas would stand up on one of the flat wagons to address the members present, outlining the problems to be faced and spurring them on to continued effort. In his last days, Sir Thomas had the satisfaction of knowing that what had seemed like an insuperable problem with regard to the river bridge had been overcome.

Keeping Going

While engineering works on the line were in progress in 1965, passenger trains ran only to Heniarth. When services were restored in August, two trains were run each day (three at weekends), though once again they terminated at Castle Caereinion. The pattern established for the ensuing years was a daily service in the high summer (July to mid-September), and services at weekends and bank holidays for the rest of the season. The daily three train service was gradually extended

The vertical boilered Sentinel Nutty *pauses at the old water tower on 6th June 1965. Its very occasional use on passenger trains was limited to the level mile to Heniarth while the bridge was being rebuilt. The water tower was disused after 1979.*

R.T. Russell

Heniarth was the terminus for passenger services from Llanfair during the rebuilding of the bridge. No. 4 Upnor Castle delivers permanent way materials and has probably assisted with the turn round of the train headed by The Earl.

R.T. Russell

Largely built by volunteers between 1967 and 1971, the first locomotive shed-cum-workshops was sited on the steeply sloping edge of Llanfair station.

Apart from the signs, Sylfaen looked much as it did in its heyday when the siding was restored in 1964. It was never a very busy spot!

Lens of Sutton

as the years passed. In 1967, five trains each day were introduced on the busiest days of the bank holidays. In addition, special trains for party bookings run at various times during the season, diesel-hauled on rare occasions. Sometimes they are photographic trips with extra stops for photography at picturesque spots and at one time with open accommodation on a flat wagon for tape recording devotees.

Although public services became so well established and although even the desperate problem of the Banwy Bridge was miraculously solved, the Railway continued to be plagued by grave difficulties, mainly financial. The Company had been desperately short of capital right from the start. Even before the flood damage of December 1964 at least five special appeals for money for the proper operation of the Railway went out to members, in addition to such appeals as that for saving *The Countess*. In 1961, £5,000 was being sought, and when only a fraction of this materialised winding-up was threatened. Nevertheless, with the overdraft soaring and the

decision taken to abandon running to Welshpool, services had opened and, promisingly, membership increased. In the year the river bridge collapsed, another appeal for funds had already been put out along with another threat of winding-up. The bridge appeal, when it came, had been on a public basis; this helps to explain the heartening response which produced sufficient money for restoration to go ahead. Meanwhile, membership subscriptions had to be raised to help reduce the overdraft. The closure of the bridge during rebuilding in the spring and summer of 1965 unfortunately delayed the hoped-for build-up of traffic revenue.

In the closing years of the 1960s progress was slower than many would have liked and even essential maintenance on track and locomotives was acutely hampered by lack of funds. Often, little cash was left over after running the services to buy supplies, although sometimes generous gifts in cash or kind prevented renovation from coming to a standstill. Volunteer labour, of course, was free, so pick and shovel methods were the order of the day. Despite these difficulties the rehabilitation proceeded of track which had deteriorated over many years. Each winter, with the cessation of passenger services, a new section was completely relaid with sound sleepers and fresh ballast. As each year passed the sections relaid became longer, and in the autumn of 1968 the first mechanisation was welcomed when an excavator was hired to clear the trackbed. The winter of 1969-70 saw further mechanisation. Not only was an excavator hired, but afterwards lorries lurched along the trackbed to deliver the ballast without transhipment. A power drill was used to prepare the sleepers for the spikes and powered tamping hammers helped with packing and consolidating the ballast. It was a boost to the morale of weekend permanent way workers.

Alterations to the track layout were also made as the demand and opportunity arose. A year after re-opening, the lifted siding at Sylfaen had been put back, while in 1967 a new siding was laid at Cyfronydd for wagon storage. The loop at Castle station had already been extended in the spring of 1966 to permit the turn-round of longer trains.

During the years which succeeded the re-opening ceremony, the question of running from Castle Caereinion to Welshpool continued to be raised. As the months passed, there was sobering realisation that membership numbers were not increasing significantly and that all funds were being swallowed for operating the Llanfair - Castle Caereinion section. As experience was accumulated, prospects of an early extension of services to Welshpool receded. Nevertheless, tentative plans were made. In the spring of 1966 a scheme was announced to run to Sylfaen the next year and to extend special workings to Welshpool in 1969. Soon after the announcement, locomotive No. 5 *Nutty* reached Raven Square on two occasions including a trip with weed-killing apparatus.

However, the year 1969 arrived without it having been possible to renovate the track between Castle Caereinion and Welshpool. In addition, there were difficulties (mainly financial) in providing the automatic braking on coaching stock which the MOT Inspector required for working public services on the dramatically graded Golfa bank. The short run-round loop and lack of station facilities at Raven Square were further handicaps. One proposal to overcome these problems envisaged a diesel-hauled shuttle service, with one or two coaches connecting with the steam-hauled trains at Castle or Sylfaen. Ingenious though this scheme was, it was not really a solution.

For the short-lived service to Sylfaen in 1964, tickets were sold from one of the original W&LLR brake vans. With no run-round loop, No.4 Upnor Castle *was used to manoeuvre the train for the return.*

R.T. Russell

Chapter 6

Getting to Welshpool

Events rousing particular excitement have been the arrival of further useful pieces of rolling stock as they became available. On 8th May 1966, the unconventional locomotive, *Monarch*, arrived by road and the diminutive *Nutty* struggled to haul the 28½ton articulated Bagnall on to W&L metals.

Early in 1968, the 0-6-0 Drewry diesel locomotive was secured, and the low-loader road vehicle which transported *Chattenden* from Cumberland left Llanfair conveying *Upnor Castle* for the Festiniog Railway and regauging. A momentous occasion soon afterwards was the coming of the Austrian coaching stock. Midlands businessman and W&L director Derek Mayman and others had helped to forge links including exchange visits with the busy narrow gauge Zillertal Railway in the Tyrol. It is intriguing that the Zillertalbahn and other Austrian (and eastern European) lines were built to the 760mm gauge and not 750mm which seems more logical but it has been fortunate for the W&L. Early in 1964 the transfer of some surplus passenger vehicles from the Zillertalbahn to the W&L was first mooted, but for four years financial and other considerations held up progress. However, as traffic mounted in Wales, the demand for more passenger accommodation became pressing at peak times. At last, the good news was received that on 25th March 1968 the transfer had started of four end-balcony saloon coaches. They were transported over the systems of the Austrian, German and Belgian railways to Ostend. Belgian Marine vessels ferried them to Dover where British Rail took over on 9th April. Two days later, a special train of four well-flats brought the continental saloons into Welshpool station where members had been awaiting their arrival throughout the day.

Although the dusk of evening was already gathering, two of the coaches, B24 and B16, were craned in turn on to a road vehicle and moved through the town to the level crossing at New Drive. This point, at the foot of Golfa bank, was easily accessible from the main road. A mobile crane gingerly lifted the new stock on to Welsh metals and the Drewry diesel locomotive drew them cautiously up to Golfa loop for the night. There was elation that the operation was going so well

and that the coaches appeared to run on the Welsh track better than anyone had dared to hope. Soon after first light the next day, a beautifully sunny morning, work began on moving the remaining two coaches in similar fashion. The diesel locomotive *Chattenden* inched the vehicles up to Golfa station where the whole rake was coupled up. For some months previously, members had been clearing overhanging vegetation in anticipation of the delivery of the 8ft (2.44m) wide saloons on to the unused section. Extreme caution was nevertheless observed as the train continued towards Llanfair Caereinion.

The arrival coincided with the start of the Easter holiday and the novelty of the new rolling stock helped to attract record numbers of Easter visitors. Many were carried in the Zillertalbahn saloons which, after hasty cleaning, had to be rushed into use on the day immediately after they reached Llanfair. Holiday times during the year continued to bring overwhelming crowds of visitors.

With the line's popularity growing, a search began for more motive power. It was realised that without reserve funds for major repairs to Nos. 1 and 2, and with the demise of the steam locomotive accelerating everywhere, it would be wise policy to obtain useful specimens in sound condition as the opportunity arose. As a result, another link was struck with Austria. This time, a visit was paid to the 760mm Steiermarkische Landesbahnen which threaded the picturesque Alpine valleys between Ratten and Weiz. About 20km from the valley resort of Graz an interesting 0-8-0T locomotive was for disposal which had been built for the German military authorities in World War II. Inspection confirmed that it was in very good shape overall and there was reason to believe that the all-important boiler condition was most promising. Arrangements went ahead swiftly and just after 6.00pm on Thursday, 11th December 1969, the locomotive was hauled on to the line in Llanfair Caereinion station yard. The mid-winter darkness had already descended and members' car headlights were pressed into service to illuminate the scene. Movement had started from Weiz eight days previously. A low-loading road trailer was used and, after traversing Germany and Holland, it travelled by ferry from

A delicate manoeuvre - coach B17 is re-railed at New Drive crossing. The first four Zillertalbahn coaches were moved by rail and arrived at Welshpool BR goods yard. They were then moved across the town by road, one by one.

With the river in placid mood, No. 2 The Countess with a busy train trundles eastward over the Banwy Bridge. The lattice steel pier built by the Army in 1965 contrasts with the stone pier.

Shabby but safely landed. Ex-Antigua Sugar Company No. 7 Joan *stands on Brocklebank Dock shortly after the 0-6-2 tank locomotive had arrived at Liverpool on 26th November 1971. It lacked a cab backsheet, while obtrusive steam feed pumps disfigured the front buffer beam and tank top.*

W&LLR Pres. Co.

Amsterdam to Immingham in Lincolnshire.

Plans to build up the motive power stock hardly envisaged movements half way across the world. However, an enthiusiastic member visiting the island of Antigua in the West Indies spotted the 0-6-2 tank locomotive *Joan* disused and rusting at the government sugar factory. Its specifications well suited it for work on the W&L. Purchasing was easy but then a number of daunting hurdles had to be overcome. These included the finding of a shipping company able to handle the load, movement to the wharf despite the branch line to the port being abandoned, a political furore on the island about the sale to 'imperialists' and the appearance of a rival bidder from the USA. Incredibly, the news came that *Joan* had been loaded on to the *Booker Valiance* on 20th October 1971, during the cool of the night. The ship sailed for a tour of Caribbean and South American ports and then crossed to Liverpool. At last, the Kerr Stuart was home!

Encouraging Developments

Welsh narrow gauge railways tend to provide idyllic scenery for passengers to enjoy at the 'country' terminus. Castle Caereinion was no exception. Invariably, in those days, the journey for passengers started from Llanfair, first threading the river banks and later rising up unbelievably steep grades. While the engine crew prepared to return, travellers were treated to the panorama of hill masses stretching towards Snowdon. But the track curved further uphill between high banks, beckoning eastwards. Unfortunately, a great deal of

work was required to make the next section fit for passenger trains again.

In the summer of 1970 with the financial position improving, plans were announced for rebuilding the line between Castle and Sylfaen. Volunteers toiled throughout that summer season lifting the disintegrating sleepers, digging out and clearing the track-bed and laying in sound sleepers. Within earshot of trains and tourists arriving and departing from Castle station below, members continued to drill and hammer and shovel as rails were spiked down and packed and ballasted. Scout groups and parties from schools lent a hand.

The following year the assault was transferred nearer to Sylfaen. Where the line parallels the Sylfaen Brook, foxgloves, brambles and bushes had taken over and trees spanned the railway. As clearing progressed, an engineering train pushed through to Pussy Bridge (as preservationists had christened it). Here, the watercourse passes obliquely below the line and reconstruction with a new concrete invert was essential. Another season of track building followed. The remaining section, the steep bank east of Coppice Lane crossing was tackled the next year by a dedicated group of members who devoted an early season holiday to an all out period of railway 'navvying'.

Finally, on 15th July 1972, Castle station was decked out with flags and bunting in readiness for a suitably elaborate re-opening ceremony. No. 10 *Sir Drefaldwyn*, appropriately decorated and piloting No. 1 *The Earl*, simmered while speeches were delivered. Then with the Mayor of Welshpool at the controls, the train broke a ceremonial tape and climbed

Overhauled and restored, W&L No. 12 Joan *makes a steamy approach as she climbs the bank to Coppice Lane.*

Hugh Ballantyne

With a Special on Dolarddyn Bank, No. 2 The Countess *and No. 14 (ex-SLR 85) climb the 1 in 32 incline towards Castle Caereinion.*

Hugh Ballantyne

towards Sylfaen.

At the new terminus, the wilderness of mud, nettles and brambles had given way to a new gravel platform 170ft (51.83m) long, constructed on the main line to the west of the siding reinstated in 1964. Space had never been provided for a loop line. The train engine therefore ran into a newly overhauled spur while a second locomotive, usually a diesel, drew the train past the points. After the train engine had backed on, the return to Llanfair could begin. A year after the re-opening, reconstruction of the main road alongside the station gave vastly improved access albeit sacrificing the hedgerows and attractive grassy banks.

The need to use a shunting engine spurred the Company to find a way of providing a run-round loop. When it became possible to acquire an adjoining if low-lying piece of land, planning permission was secured for alterations at Sylfaen. In October 1976, all the track through the station was lifted together with 400yd (366m) on the western approach, ready for levelling by excavator. A procession of lorries brought new ballast and large quantities of stone rubble to widen the trackbed on the north side of what had been the platform. Work began on realigning the main line over the widened formation. Tipping helped to provide the site on which a new platform was built and on the south side a 120yd (110m) loop line was laid. Within three weeks, the station was reopened for a charter train, an impressive achievement.

Of course Welshpool remained the ultimate goal. The tenth anniversary of the line's re-opening had given rise to the idea of special members' trains to Raven Square. These could be seen as a token of intent if something could be done about the jungle-like wilderness that had sprung up between Golfa

and Raven Square. A contractor with agricultural equipment was engaged to cut a way through, tunnel-like. Seeing a pipe dream evolving into reality, work parties turned out to undertake makeshift repairs to the track while arrangements were made for water to be supplied by the Montgomery Water Board from their hydrant at New Drive crossing.

The Earl with three coaches reached Welshpool at 12.25pm on 12th May 1973. The successful descent of the long and notorious Golfa incline was marked by exultant and sustained whistling from the veteran locomotive and as it arrived at Raven Square, it was watched by a great gallery of spectators massed along the main road. The Mayor of Welshpool and others welcomed the train. *The Earl* worked another special during the afternoon no less successfully. On the following day however, wet conditions for the third run taxed the crew's skill as the gallant machine slipped to a halt on the treacherously steep banks. Truly a memorable weekend, it inspired members, attracted publicity and underlined the Company's determination to reopen public services to Welshpool.

Few years seem to pass without a crisis of one kind or another. But with initiative, hard work and lucky breaks, the W&L has coped. Early on Monday 6th August 1973, the most disastrous floods for several years struck mid-Wales. Storms brought 4ins (10mm) of rain in 24 hours; the Banwy and the Vyrnwy burst their banks. At dawn, water was racing over the part of the line from the old water tower to Schoolmistress's Cottage near Heniarth and at the Banwy Bridge the torrent rose to within two feet of the cross girders. Luckily, fears for the safety of the bridge were not realised though a huge tree trunk was found wedged against the steel pier as the water

After Sylfaen Halt was reconstructed on a widened formation, the turn-round of trains was easier and later it provided a useful passing place. In this view, No. 2 The Countess, piloting Whipsnade Zoo visitor Superior, is ready to leave from the loop while No. 14 (ex-SLR 85) runs into the platform road.

No. 1 The Earl passes gingerly over Golfa crossing heading the crowded members' special in 1973. Utmost caution was used as the section with its long, steep incline, had not been used for so long.

In August 1975, four coaches from the Sierra Leone Railway were delivered, in convoy, to Castle Caereinion station for transfer to the W&LLR. At last, the railway had coaches with continuous brakes suitable for use on Golfa bank.

In 1973, the overgrown line was cleared just sufficiently for The Earl to reach Welshpool with the members' Special on 12th May to be welcomed by the Mayor. Here, on the west side of Raven Square, the line terminated in a short loop.

receded. Near Dolrhyd Mill, ballast had been carried away and discarded sleepers tossed about but no serious damage had been done. Services were suspended but they resumed on the following day.

Reference has been made to the advantageous terms which made possible the take-over of the line from British Railways. Nevertheless, the outright purchase of the Railway was a most desirable objective. It would safeguard the future beyond 1983 and provide more favourable conditions for major investment. The news that BR had offered to sell the line including all land and buildings came as a welcome 10th anniversary present. Negotiations on terms moved slowly but favourably and, on 12th March 1974, the Preservation Company became the owners of the Railway. The price was £8,000, which today seems an incredibly small sum. To meet what was even then a favourable figure an appeal was launched. A substantial contribution was made by the then Welshpool Borough Council while the Wales Tourist Board helped with a loan repayable over 15 years. At last, the preservationists seemed to be getting tangible support from outside the membership.

It had long been hoped to run with vacuum braked stock. The sharp changes of gradient on the western section of the line made this highly desirable while such provision was a prerequisite of operating public services to Welshpool. As most of the Upnor coaches were unsuited for fitting automatic brakes, sources of fully fitted stock were being investigated in 1974, mainly in the Isle of Man and Yugoslavia. Further afield, the Sierra Leone Railway was closing down and though the idea of extending the search to West Africa seemed ambitious, W&L representatives were sent out to Freetown. Shortly afterwards, negotiations were opened with the demolition contractor.

On 7th August 1975, a complete train was landed at Liverpool. It was a red letter day for the W&L: four modern high capacity coaches and a handsome prairie tank engine had been brought across the Atlantic despite competition from a West German scrap dealer, tenuous communications and a dock strike in West Africa. The 2-6-2 Hunslet tank locomotive reached Llanfair by road the same day while the remarkable procession of vehicles conveying the coaches halted near Sylfaen, continuing next day to Castle station. Here two mobile cranes accomplished the unloading in brilliant sunshine. In all, the operation cost over £14,000 met from an appeal fund, a much appreciated grant from the Wales Tourist Board and an interest-free loan from two members.

Another successful initiative at this time was the Railway Letter Service. In earlier times, the original W&L and the Cambrian Railways Co. had tried in vain to gain permission to carry mails. The Preservation Co. gained approval on its first application and the service began on 13th August 1975. The specially designed stamps and first day covers have since become much sought after and provide a useful source of revenue.

The 75th anniversary year of the Railway was marked by the organisation of special events on the weekend of 13th/14th May 1978. On each day, seven passenger services were operated using *Joan, Sir Drefaldwyn, Monarch* and the ex-Sierra Leone Railway locomotive in turn. Trains were crossed at Castle Caereinion. *The Earl* worked a freight train of original stock for photographic purposes and the former gasworks locomotive *Dougal* steamed along the line with some of the Upnor goods stock. Never before had so many engines been

The articulated Bagnall Monarch *negotiates the crossing at Coppice Lane summit with a Sylfaen to Llanfair train in August 1976.*

Above: *No. 11* Ferret *handled many of the engineering trains during the work on the extension to Welshpool. The mines diesel's low gears were an asset for duties on the steep incline. Crossing Cwm Lane at Golfa, the train will climb a 1 in 41 section to the summit.*

Above: *On Golfa bank, mechanical assistance was employed to widen the cutting and ease the sharp curves on the notoriously steep gradient.*

Left: *On Sylfaen bank in 1980, an access was made for lorries to deliver ballast directly to the trackbed after levelling with a JCB excavator. The view is towards the summit.*

In the workshops at Llanfair in 1972, volunteers work on No. 7 Chattenden. Monarch is under overhaul alongside while the ex-Upnor coach 199 was also receiving attention in the workshops.

in steam at once on the line. The Talyllyn Railway co-operated by arranging special events at Tywyn; joint rover tickets, joint publicity and a novel connecting bus service contributed to the success of the weekend.

Adapting Llanfair Station

Llanfair Caereinion terminus was not originally regarded as the ideal headquarters for the project. It is not as readily accessible as Welshpool and suffered from a number of other disadvantages. The cramped nature of the site hampered efforts to make it attractive to the visiting public. Car parking space was severely limited, especially as the premises were shared with a group of coal merchants until 1972. The area had to accommodate the Company's workshops, while the corrugated iron warehouse dating from the opening made access awkward for visitors entering the station. It served for a time after re-opening as a make-shift mess room and as an engineering store.

The south (coal road) siding was inconveniently situated and was therefore removed. A headshunt was then installed at the east end and a locomotive inspection pit afterwards added. During 1967 a modest brick-built signal box was brought into use, but not without having roused controversy among members regarding the necessity of signalling. The lever frame in it was salvaged from the main-line signal box at Llanbrynmair. In the south-east corner of the station was a steeply banked area, previously unused except for wartime vegetable growing. This was eventually chosen as the site for a two-road locomotive shed and carriage workshop. Excavations began in 1967, and over the next four years the building gradually took shape, largely constructed by volunteers. The steelwork was

secondhand and was only erected with the aid of considerable ingenuity. The north road came into use on 14th June 1970 and the second road during the following year.

Limited facilities at Llanfair had long meant that sidings at Heniarth and Cyfronydd had to be utilised for the storage of wagon stock and coaches. Eventually, the opportunity occurred to purchase an area of uneven, unused ground opposite the site of the old Tanllan timber dock, east of the station limits. Considerable earthmoving produced a suitable formation and the first of three carriage sidings was completed in August 1975. Beyond this point, the main line passed the picturesque old water tower by the river. Unfortunately, the supply from a nearby stream was becoming increasingly unreliable and in 1979 a new water tower was erected on brick piers in Llanfair station.

The old standard gauge coach bodies installed for storage by the GWR had been converted for use as volunteers' sleeping quarters when the line was taken over. The surviving coachbodies were dismantled in September 1969 to make way for a former Eastern Region 1st class sleeping car No. EI260E. Meanwhile, facilities for passengers were improved with the arrival of a mobile tea-bar in time for the 1967 season, and further with the erection, in March 1970, of a brick-built toilet block, this time by contractors. Subsequently, another mobile tea-bar and another sleeping car replaced the original ones.

As much of the traffic depended on visitors who arrived by car, adequate parking space was important. At Llanfair station, an improvement was achieved for the 1974 season by re-aligning the trackwork on a slightly more northerly alignment. But it was the purchase by Montgomery District Council of

The new terminus in prospect. A short loop on the edge of Raven Square was built when the line was truncated in 1964. The site chosen for the new Welshpool station was occupied by the stream and water meadows on the left.

In August 1977, volunteers begin re-laying at Golfa siding following the launch of the Welshpool Extension Scheme.

Most of the new sleepers needed were prepared at Castle station. There were over 6,000 of them, hardwoods imported from Australia.

No. 10 Sir Drefaldwyn *restarts from Golfa. Not an advertised halt and nowadays without even a siding, it is a convenient place to stop to get up steam.*

the meadows between Llanfair station and the River Banwy which made the biggest difference. This was for the construction of an approach road, several 'advance' factories and a site for the W&L to take (on a 10 year mortgage) and develop as coach and car parks. Though initiated as a scheme to help relieve mounting unemployment, it was good to have such local support. So the old entrance to Llanfair station disappeared and by Easter 1980, there was a decidedly superior access to the south side of the station and the new car park.

Raven Square at Last!

The surprising idea of the W&L taking on ten employees suddenly developed when the government-sponsored Manpower Services Commission offered a grant in 1976 to cover the wages for an initial period of six months. The W&L's project was accepted as part of the Job Creation Scheme which aimed to provide employment for young people. The project entailed one gang replacing fences west of Sylfaen and another gang clearing the scrub and trees on the Welshpool section. Though the work was important, it was difficult to accomplish

it with voluntary labour. The new grant-funded schemes were seen as a golden opportunity and when the first project ended, it was to be followed by a series of others including some devoted to specified work on rolling stock.

Hopes of running services to Welshpool never died and inspired sporadic efforts to improve the disused section although doubts were cast on the future of the existing run-round loop at Raven Square terminus with news of plans for trunk road improvement in the area. One troublespot lay at Hanged Man's Tree, half a mile down the incline below Golfa station. The track was shored up on timbers where the formation had subsided following a culvert collapse. In summer, new concrete culvert sections were obtained ready for rebuilding. Then, near New Drive crossing, lower down, the unwelcome discovery was made of a new washout. With collapse imminent, the track was promptly shored up until the embankment and the drainage could be rebuilt. The following year, the job of reconstructing the formation at Hanged Man's Tree was successfully completed.

The impetus was growing as was pressure from various quarters for properly devised and co-ordinated plans to reopen

Early in 1981, the formation was appearing at Raven Square and despite the wintry conditions, volunteers went ahead with track laying. Sleepers are in position for the new loop. The old line lies under grass by the hedge on the right.

No. 11 Chattenden *passes Golfa on 20th June, 1981, with the first train of passenger stock (empty), testing clearances on the line to the new Welshpool terminus.*

to Welshpool especially with the advent of vacuum braked stock. In August 1976, the board of the Company announced that a scheme had been adopted and costed; steps were being taken to apply for financial assistance and the submission was being made for the planning permission required for a new station at Raven Square. Welshpool Town Council was reported to be enthusiastic.

In May 1977, the plan was launched at a public meeting in Birmingham with the publication of a prospectus and an appeal for £63,000. The project involved rebuilding the whole line from Sylfaen to Welshpool, a distance of 2.62 miles (4.2km). This was to entail clearing the trees and bushes from fence to fence, lifting the old track, re-laying on new stone ballast with new sleepers and constructing a terminus of spacious dimensions. The purchase of another, more powerful, diesel locomotive for emergency use was envisaged (but not realised).

In due course land was leased alongside the old line near Raven Square and a safe access from the main road was eventually negotiated with the highway authority. It was intended to build a terminal layout with ample siding and platform space, full station facilities and a large car park. In all, this was to be the most costly and ambitious project the Preservation Co. had so far entertained; ultimately, costs were to rise well beyond the original estimate. However, the time was ripe for this initiative. Help was at hand in the shape of grants from the Manpower Services Commission for labour to carry out much of the clearance and trackwork. Meanwhile,

representations brought the W&L the most pleasurable embarrassment of simultaneous offers of funds from the Wales Tourist Board and the Development Board for Rural Wales. The latter body's offer of £20,000 was accepted while the struggle to find the balance involved raising donations, an interest-free loan scheme, sponsored walks and even the sale of the four Upnor coaches without vacuum brakes. An exhibition explaining the project and mounted in one of the Sierra Leone coaches at Llanfair station proved popular and raised more funds.

An ingenious idea was the attempt to import steel sleepers from the dismantled 2ft 6ins gauge Sierra Leone Railway. It was resolved to rebuild the line to high standards thus vastly reducing the need for expensive maintenance and replacement in the future. Unfortunately, political disputes and lack of co-operation in Sierra Leone defeated the W&L. With the project delayed, it was decided to buy 6,000 new hardwood sleepers from Australia.

At Raven Square, a great deal of work was needed to transform swampy meadows into the Welshpool terminal. Contractors with machinery helped. A new channel about 150yd (137m) long was excavated into which the Sylfaen Brook was diverted along the southern edge of the site. The original track descended on a grade of 1 in 58 along the other side but the new station had to be on the level. Vast quantities of material were tipped and after several months the old stream meanders had been filled in and the formation had risen, partly

At Raven Square in 1981, No. 12 Joan *and ex-SLR 85 take water from the wagon-mounted tank on the old formation.*

Re-opening . . . .

Above: *In May 1982, the work planned for Raven Square station was complete and this was marked with appropriate ceremony. No. 14 (SLR 85) and No. 12 Joan simmer sedately while guests on the newly built platform include the Mayor and Mayoress of Welshpool (wearing their chains of office) and the Earl of Powis, third from the left.*

Right: *The Mayor of Welshpool, Cllr. Tegwyn Evans, congratulates W&L Chairman Ken Fenton on the opening of the section to Welshpool in 1981.*

Left: *On 18th July 1981, Sir Drefaldwyn departs with the inaugural one-coach train from Raven Square station, which is still only partially completed.*

on embankment.

Meanwhile, a project supervisor was engaged charged with organising the extension works and overseeing the labour provided under the Manpower Services Commission schemes. Removal of the old track began at Golfa prior to work on the drainage and the excavation of cuttings to ease the tightest curves. Lorries arriving with the new ballast were directed along the trackbed. Meanwhile, a base was established at Castle station for drilling the new sleepers and as they were hauled to the railhead on Golfa incline, re-laying proceeded rapidly. The sections below New Drive crossing and west of Golfa were similarly dealt with in turn.

The year 1981 brought an all-out effort by volunteers. A search for suitable rail at an affordable price located a cancelled order for West Africa and even the Zillertalbahn contributed material. Now, at Welshpool, new rail laid on brand new formation linked the old route with the new station layout. Here, pointwork, tracklaying, the provision of passenger access and water had all to be undertaken. Meanwhile, trainees on a government scheme were re-laying Sylfaen bank. It was a race against time.

Nevertheless, on 4 July, *Sir Drefaldwyn*, on crew training, became the first steam locomotive to reach the new station. Shortly afterwards, after a final inspection, the Department of Transport sanctioned the re-opening of the Welshpool section on a 'one engine in steam' basis for the time being.

The great day so many had awaited for so long was 18 July 1981. *Sir Drefaldwyn* entered Raven Square station about midday, the triumphant and prolonged whistling echoing in welcome from the tree clad slopes tilting skywards all round. Jubilant crowds were addressed by Welshpool's Mayor and Company Chairman, Ken Fenton, before the train left, its single Sierra Leone coach filled with contributors to the Appeal Fund. At 3.05pm, the first public train from Welshpool to Llanfair was packed and necessitated double heading. With no buildings, van 213 served as a ticket office. The short, temporary, sleeper-edged platform and the wagon-mounted 800 gallon tank for water supplies were all signs of the improvisation which had ensured the target date was met.

Financial constraints prevented the full implementation of the plan for the Welshpool terminus but work went ahead to construct a substantial platform, and a permanent water tower. A former L&NWR lever frame from the Caernarvon-Afon Wen line installed in the open was soon housed in a signal box ingeniously designed to incorporate a ticket office. This was in use when the official re-opening ceremony was performed by the Earl of Powis on 16th May, 1982.

The Golfa incline proved a fearsome challenge for footplate crews and aficionados revelled in the sound of vintage locomotives blasting up the climb of 300ft (91.45m) in only a mile. Over fifty years after the GWR had closed passenger services, trains ran regularly again between Welshpool and Llanfair.

A month after the extension opened in 1981, No. 14 waits beside the temporary platform and a van, derailed, serves as a booking office. A tank on a wagon did duty as a temporary water tower. The bay platform is not yet built.

Chapter 7

Modern Times

Although trains now worked the whole length of the line, passenger numbers did not expand as hoped. As years passed, more and more special events were introduced into the timetable and these helped significantly to improve normal traffic levels. An augmented service for a local Festival of Transport became an annual event, for a time, attended by numerous vintage road vehicles. Some of these occasions saw every serviceable coach in use and four locomotives. Once staff and ticket working was extended to Welshpool, in 1984, using a black, hexagonal staff, trains could pass at Sylfaen where a blockman was stationed. For four years, trains crossed here as a regular feature of the high season timetable but in 1988, the normal service reverted to operation with one train only. However, the period of operation was extended to match changing tourist trends.

Another innovation at Christmas 1987 was the line's first ever Santa trains, both profitable and jolly. For years some had said it wouldn't work, voicing objections that trains from Welshpool would have difficulty on Golfa bank in winter, that the usual winter track re-laying would prevent trains running and that the locomotives would be at risk from frost damage. New thinking in 1986 came up with a plan to run to Castle and to construct Santa's grotto in the wooden building that was there then but soon a scheme emerged to run round at Cyfronydd, sporting '*Toyland*' signs. Santa was to be picked up from a caravan-cum-grotto en route to distribute presents during the journey. Now Llanfair seemed the only practical starting point as all the necessary facilities were there.

Work went ahead to refine the details. Investigations began into sources of mince pies, sherry, costumes, mailbags, heaters, a caravan cover ... and ready wrapped, unisex, all-age gift packages. Members offered to make outfits for ticket elves and station staff and others agreed to bring cartoon costumes. To provide 'seasonal refreshments', the kitchen of the volunteers' caravan restroom pwas commandeered for a sherry bar. With no steam heating then on the train, the SLR coaches had to be warmed at Llanfair with electric heaters though in fact body heat proved more effective!

When December arrived, all went well, to everyone's relief.

Children (and grown-ups) came from miles around and filled the trains; Santa felt exhausted by the mere thought of all those chimneys he promised to descend!

Despite the possibility of wintry conditions, members volunteered for duties. There were just enough on some days and on others more than sufficient. In the Loco. Shed, the stove was kept burning to prevent water freezing in the locomotive in between its stints in service while, in the yard, the Railway's patrons warmed themselves around burning braziers as they sipped free tots of sherry and munched hot dogs (and even ice cream!). Fifteen gallons of sherry were dispensed together with 1,600 mince pies. Meanwhile, the platform was a remarkable sight, seething with expectant, excited children being shepherded by indulgent grannies into coaches vacated by radiantly smiling youngsters delighted with the visit from Santa (complete with reindeer and good fairy) during the trip to '*Toyland*' and back. A little girl with a be-kind-to-dumb-animals look voiced the only complaint: the reindeer refused to eat the sticky mess she had held under its nose! Few changes were made to the Santa operation until a longer trip was introduced in 2000 when Castle Caereinion became the terminus.

But running trains in winter was not always troublefree. Saturday 21st December 1991 brought samples of problems which might have turned out to be serious — but didn't! As the morning moved towards the 12.00pm departure time, the rain sweeping Llanfair station seemed to drive ever harder and the Christmas tree and bunting looked ever more bedraggled. Had anyone seen Santa? Where was the ticket elf? In fact, they were on their way but difficult travelling conditions resulted in a 'just in time' appearance. Another little local difficulty was the absence of the back half of Rudolph the Reindeer! What's more, there was now speculation about the behaviour of the River Banwy and how close it was getting to the track.

With a goodly number of passengers determined to have their trip with Santa, *Sir Drefaldwyn* steamed out as scheduled with the first train, now steam heated to feel less wintry. And still it rained . . . and rained. Some twenty minutes or so later, an agitated controller deserted his telephone and emerged

As No. 14 (ex-SLR 85) drifts into Llanfair station with a train from Welshpool, the single line staff is handed in to the volunteer signalman.

The Drewry diesel waits for the 'right away' from Castle station. In the 1980s, No.7 Chattenden *frequently deputised on passenger trains either when the regular steam locomotive was indisposed or on extra services.*

For many years, volunteers have used power tools to help with track renewals. In support here is the compressor unit which was mounted on the frames of a Hunslet mines diesel. It was in use until 1999.

The ex-Admiralty Hunslet mines diesel locomotive No. 11 Ferret *arrives at Castle Caereinion station on a permanent way train.*

from Llanfair signal box to report that the train was waiting at Cyfronydd with *Sir Drefaldwyn* having been unable to run round until a problem with the pointwork was resolved. Trains were then '*subject to delay*' but as the afternoon wore on, the Llanfair High School Band arrived and, despite the deluge, struck up with a watery rendering of *0 Come All Ye Faithful* etcetera as a welcome diversion for passengers bravely waiting. The efforts of the band - damp but undaunted - were appreciated not least by the rainswept audience who, after struggling through floods which had appeared on the main road, found themselves enduring a somewhat extended wait for the last train.

When it eventually arrived from '*Toyland*', the reason for the delay caused a flurry of consternation. The river had spilled over the track at Dolrhyd Mill. Santa's train had just escaped being marooned near 'North Pole' (alias Heniarth) but had gingerly negotiated the Mill curves with water lapping around the carriage steps. Further back, furious torrents were seething under the Banwy Bridge girders.

A hasty conference was held. Then, the diesel *Chattenden* was attached to the rear of the train and the footplate crew of *Sir Drefaldwyn* was instructed to run as far as it was safe to do, not forgetting to collect Santa (whose base had now moved to Tanllan). Edging past the old water tower, a halt was made where the rails disappeared beneath the floodwaters. After allowing Santa to complete his all important mission, the train returned safely, leaving unresolved the problem of what to do with heavily booked trains the next day. In complete contrast, Sunday dawned bright and fine! The river had retreated and an early inspection showed little damage to the track or, as far

as could be seen, to the Banwy Bridge. Judging by the spate of telephoned enquiries, some would-be passengers thought the line had been washed away. But all was well and all trains ran as scheduled; in fact the day's operations '*went like clockwork*' as someone remarked.

Memorable Weekends

Another first, in summer 1989, was a weekend for children based on Thomas the Tank Engine stories, with amazing results. The event was planned jointly with Welshpool library who promoted the famous stories about Thomas and his friends during the week before the event and held story readings in an ex-SLR coach based at Raven Square during the weekend. It was thought that what would be needed would be a tank engine (as *Thomas*), two coaches (*Annie* and *Clarabel*) operating a short, frequent journey, and a Fat Controller. An enhanced train service between Welshpool and Sylfaen would suit this formula. Although originally *Sir Drefaldwyn* was to have been *Thomas* for the weekend, a protracted overhaul resulted in the more accurate appearance of *Joan* being converted into *Thomas the Tank Engine*. Sponsorship was obtained for the repaint in light blue and for modifications to the chimney from No. 14 (SLR 85) to fit *Joan*. Painted faces were constructed from papier mâché which was liberally varnished.

Unfortunately, just prior to the chosen weekend, a stormburst struck mid-Wales. When Saturday 8th July 1989 dawned, it was wet, but one of the few wet days that summer. Conditions were difficult and *Thomas* slipped so badly on its

At Raven Square station, No.12 Joan, *masquerading as Thomas the Tank Engine, captures the attention of the younger generation. The chimney was borrowed from No.14 (SLR 85).*

Gasworks engine Dougal *seems to be in control as it marshals the 'Troublesome Trucks' during the 'Thomas' event in July 1997.*

To publicise the Santa operation of 1992, the Mayor of Welshpool, Cllr. John Corfield, and the Mayoress, Mrs. Jan. Mason, were invited to Llanfair. A lively Santa Claus 'played to the (press) gallery'. The Fairy Queen and entertainers were also present. No. 14 (SLR '85') carries a Santa Special headboard for the event.

first trip from Llanfair to Welshpool that one coach had to be abandoned at Castle Caereinion causing delays to the departure of the 11.00am service train from Llanfair behind *The Countess*. On the return journey to Sylfaen, diesel powered assistance was provided by *Chattenden* but despite this, the train slipped to a standstill in the rain on Golfa Bank and disrupted the timetable for the rest of the day. Meanwhile, at Raven Square, crowds far larger than anyone had anticipated were gathering to travel behind '*Thomas*' and the Booking Office had to start issuing Control Tickets to guarantee seats in trains two or three hours later! While *Thomas* was scheduled to operate an hourly service from Welshpool to Sylfaen and back, *The Countess* maintained the normal advertised service to Llanfair. A free service of vintage buses was provided between Raven Square station, Welshpool town centre, the BR station and the Festival of Transport at the Powis Castle Showground. Although the problems at the beginning of the day had resulted in the cancellation of two trains, the revenue from Raven Square booking office alone was higher than ever before for the whole Railway on one day.

In contrast, Sunday was dry and sunny bringing even larger crowds. However, the timetable was operated smoothly and extra trains were provided. At 12.30pm, *The Countess* was ready

Left: *At Raven Square station, No. 10* Sir Drefaldwyn *fills up at the first water tower, which was superseded in 2001.*

Welshpool (Raven Square) station shortly after the erection of the 1873 station building from Eardisley (left) and the attached building with an ex-North Staffordshire Railway roof.

Tanllan sidings: an impressive line-up in August 1994. From the left: Joan, Sir Drefaldwyn *(on the main line),* The Countess, The Earl,
No 14 and a guest, Bredgar's Siam. *Behind is the capacious shed which accommodates the carriage stock and the wagon workshops.*

David Moseley

to depart from the bay platform at Raven Square with two SLR coaches full of 110 passengers for Llanfair as *Thomas* and *Chattenden* arrived at the main platform with 200 passengers aboard one SLR and four Ziller coaches whilst another 200 passengers waited to take their places. The story reading coach in the bay platform had to be added to *Thomas's* extended train early in the day to help carry the waiting passengers and Thomas stories were told en-route. This volume of passengers continued all day and the previous day's ticket revenue was doubled.

Such was the success that the event became a firm annual fixture. At the year end, traffic figures were the best for ten years. And on a glorious June evening the previous year, specialist caterers had served a fine meal on board a train of vintage Zillertalbahn saloons waiting at scenic Castle Caereinion station. The '*Champagne Dining Train*' (the Railway's first ever) was one way of celebrating the Railway's 25th anniversary of re-opening. Another experiment, a little

later, was an end-of-season weekend featuring Postman Pat, famed in children's stories. It became an established success but after ten years, it was abruptly killed off by bureaucracy. Another wheeze, started more recently, is enjoyed (typically) by husbands and dads. This consists of instruction and a day's driving experience (under supervision) on the line with a locomotive and a couple of coaches, which earns useful income.

Although the nineties dawned with a period of economic recession, traffic income became buoyant. A regular late season event for narrow gauge modelling enthusiasts was turned into a Gala event in 1991, which has become an annual fixture. Every available locomotive is in service on the day and the timetable usually includes mixed trains and demonstration goods trains. At Llanfair, an ex-Aberystwyth RDC road roller and a Garrett showman's tractor regularly appear, simmering gently in company with a splendidly restored Sentinel wagon. The wagon occasionally makes forays to Welshpool nimbly

Providing a secure base for the troublesome western pier of the Banwy Bridge proved a bigger job than expected in 1999 - even for the experts.

Andy Carey

enough to startle quite a few motorists. Chester City Transport's No. 1 bus (a 1953 Guy Arab) has been on hand, too, while Newtown Model Engineering Club usually provides rides on their miniature track and in the workshops various superb examples of model engineering and several working layouts go on display. A special attraction for some years was a visiting locomotive, despite the rarity of other 2ft 6ins gauge machines in Britain. The most unusual visitors were two flywheel-powered Parry mini-trams which shuttled along a temporary siding at Raven Square in 1994.

Crowds arrive each year and the intensive service of trains is often hard pressed to cope. The event is a tremendous feat of organisation and as the years have passed the number of trains run has increased hugely with as many as twenty five return workings in the weekend, not to mention a flood-lit evening steam-up. It is somewhat daunting to think of what all this means in terms of finding locomotive crews, guards, blockmen for passing places, booking clerks, and sales staff, not to mention the staffing of displays in the workshops and on the main stations.

One of the most unusual episodes was the conversion of Castle Caereinion station into a border post in Ruritania. In May 1984, BBC film makers arrived with an army of technicians and set erectors. Within a week they turned the station into Zenda in the 1890s. The W&L had been chosen as the location for making scenes for an episode in the first television version of the classic novel *The Prisoner of Zenda*. The signal box received a new exterior while on the car park the (plywood) facade of a large building sprang up. This was to feature as the Customs House when filming began. Surprised passengers on

the line's normal services could have been forgiven if they had felt somewhat disorientated as trains paused at 'Zenda'!

Coachloads of actors and 'extras', vans full of equipment, mobile canteens and restrooms squeezed into the narrow roads around Castle station. The star attraction of the filming was No. 10 *Sir Drefaldwyn* with a train of Zillertalbahn coaches. No. 12 *Joan* with some of the freight stock stood (in steam) on the loop in the background.

Several film sequences were made including numerous runs down the bank from the Welshpool direction into Castle to simulate night-time arrivals at Zenda. Leading characters in the story were the King of Ruritania and his double Rudolph (the Englishman), both played by Malcolm Sinclair and Princess Flavia played by Victoria Wicks. On the footplate, volunteers played their parts convincingly as did the guard who shared his job with one of the actors.

Saturday 16th August 1986 was the day the Railway celebrated the return of No. 2 *The Countess* after sixteen years out of service. It was one of those rare days that summer when the sun shone. The first train of the day into Welshpool was doubleheaded by *The Countess* piloting No. 14 (SLR 85). The train was divided and the Hunslet then departed with the 12.15pm service train while No. 2 took water and backed on to Ziller coaches 14, 24 and 17 to form the special train. Looking especially smart after being meticulously cleaned for the occasion, the saloons had also been transformed internally with specially fitted tables, attractive table covers and floral decorations. Meanwhile, the star of the day, *The Countess*, simmered gently, brasswork polished, paintwork gleaming, adorned with colourful posies and draped with the Welsh flag.

The arrival of the Countess of Powis was the signal for the ceremony to begin. Chairman Ken Fenton welcomed the 96 year old dowager, whose predecessor saw her son cut the first sod for the line. He outlined the history of the slightly younger locomotive emphasising the part played by the group of volunteers who had striven to restore it to running order. Her Ladyship responded by referring to her awe of the occasion and her delight at seeing the locomotive working again. Lady Powis then drew aside the Welsh standard covering the nameplate to the applause of the crowd of well wishers. A bouquet was graciously accepted and then the Countess stepped up into the cab of her namesake, first to pose for photographers and then to quiz the crew on the working of their machine. Eventually, the Countess took her place in the train accompanied by the directors, officers and guests who included the Mayor of Welshpool, the Deputy Chairman of Powys County Council, the Chief Executive of Montgomery District Council, the Chairman of Llanfair Parish Council, the Manager of the Midland Bank, Llanfair, and their wives. Leaving Raven Square at 2.07pm, the special stormed up Golfa Bank and stopped at Sylfaen to exchange staffs and pass the service train from Llanfair. After arriving at Castle station, the train was shunted into the loop and afternoon tea was served aboard. Her Ladyship left the train after enjoying the tea party and the special departed for Welshpool arriving at 4. 0pm. It was shunted into the bay until the arrival of the service train when a doubleheaded formation was made up. Onlookers were treated to the magnificent spectacle of *The Countess* and No. 14 (SLR 85) attacking the 1 in 35 bank out of Raven Square with the double bark of their exhausts reverberating from the steep hills which flank the line.

Managing the Railway

These were years of steadily rising membership with a welcome boost in 1991 when the Vale of Rheidol Railway Supporters Association dissolved, merging its members and funds with the W&L following the sale of the Rheidol line into private ownership. A vital ingredient in the success of the W&L is the involvement of its members. Services are operated entirely with all-volunteer crews despite the expansion of the timetable over the years. This involves the training of personnel from a wide variety of callings in their normal everyday life and arrangements have to be made for a nucleus of such members to attend on the large number of days that the services operate. Many people in the early years were sceptical

Resplendent in Glasgow Corporation Gasworks livery, No. 8 Dougal *does a stint of shunting in Llanfair yard.*

about the viability of such a scheme, but it ensured the Railway's success and is now common elsewhere. Continuity of control has been achieved since 1962 by the engagement of a general manager on a full-time basis. In chronological order, Michael Polglaze, Ralph Russell and Andrew Carey held the post for long periods. Latterly, new 'broom' Terence Turner arrived from the bus industry. Deputies have also been employed for many years.

The Company is organised by means of several departments with volunteers in charge. Each department (or subsidiary company in the case of sales) is responsible for activities within its sphere such as locomotive maintenance, carriage and wagon work, operating duties and publicity. Progress reports are included in a magazine circulated quarterly to all members. In this way, support has been retained and stimulated. Financial control and overall strategy is the responsibility of the board of directors elected directly by members at annual general meetings. Board (and Company) Chairman Ken Fenton has maintained a fatherly lead here since 1970, a commendably long stint in such a crucial position.

Maintenance work and a rehabilitation programme have continued each year winter and summer alike, largely dependent on volunteers' efforts. As well as the support given by members, from time to time, the splendid scenery and novel or challenging tasks have attracted help from youth groups of various kinds. Amongst these have been some from the services, scouts, students, Duke of Edinburgh Award scheme participants and even international groups. When regular work parties for a Young Members' Group take place (frustrating regulations notwithstanding), hope is fanned for the future ranks of adult members.

The winter months have been earmarked for major trackwork to avoid interrupting summer services. Following a successful venture in October 1974, when volunteers turned out in force for a week, every winter since has seen similar weeks designated for the complete rebuilding of a section of line, frequently as much as quarter of a mile. Such flurries of activity were possible as a result of a substantial team of members arranging to spend a working 'holiday' together on the Railway.

A smaller yet wholly admirable project was that to rebuild the Railway's permanent way huts. The Preservation Company inherited six such huts and from these, gangers went out to maintain a section of track, and in them they stored their tools, brewed tea, and sheltered from the weather. They were built of sawn discarded sleepers on three sides and a brick wall and chimney on the fourth. The roofs were of corrugated iron. Over the years two had collapsed completely. The others were in a very dilapidated state, overgrown, with rotten cladding and fallen chimneys. The problem was not so much wilful neglect or even lack of interest but simple shortage of money.

Towards the end of 1997, two working members decided to take on the restoration of the huts as their personal project. During 1998 work was completed on the hut just east of Cyfronydd which involved clearing back overgrowing trees and shrubs, replacing the cladding on two walls and rebuilding the chimney. The roof was still sound.

Next, they tackled the hut on Sylfaen Bank, once nicknamed 'Keyse Cottage' because Stanley H. Keyse, founding father of the Preservation Company, used to sleep here at nights when working on the line. His ashes, at his own request, were scattered nearby. Again, the chimney was in a bad state and had to be taken down to the ground and completely rebuilt. All the cladding had to be replaced. Once again, the roof was sound. Gradual progress was made on the others though at Heniarth, only a firegrate remained and here new walls, chimney and roof were built from scratch. Although not features crucial to the running of the Railway, the restoration of the huts to their original condition is part of the effort to preserve the Railway's heritage.

Mixed Fortunes

The success in financing and completing the project to rebuild the Railway to a new terminus at Welshpool was an achievement not lost on the Company. However, it was in the nineties that a transition became evident. The early years of enforced frugality with 'make-do-and-mend' methods now gave way to an era of ambitious projects with heartening results in the search for funds. While much remained dependent on the work and support of loyal volunteers, increasingly it became possible to make use of contractors.

The last years of the century brought significant developments not least in the provision of buildings the line needed for its modern role. A long felt need was cover for the coaching fleet. At length, a shed was planned for the site at Tanllan sidings, just east of Llanfair station. By mid-summer 1989, the carriage shed was complete, being 105ft (32m) long and with four roads. At last, the vintage stock could be protected from the harsh winter weather. Meanwhile, at Llanfair station, an extension to the locomotive shed was erected (fitted with salvaged nineteenth century cast iron windows) to house the workshop machines.

Whilst these achievements brought pleasure, there were occasional setbacks to withstand. There was a double tragedy when Ralph T. Russell, General Manager 1973-87, died after a period of illness followed within weeks by founding father Stanley H. Keyse. Their pioneering efforts will be gratefully remembered and their generous bequests which the Railway was to receive. Maximum benefit was secured as, in 1990, after considerable agonising, the Company was registered as

Running as GWR No.823 Countess, *the veteran Beyer Peacock tank makes a fine sight as it lifts a train of original Pickering freight stock up the 1 in 35 bank out of Raven Square station. Such photographic specials operate as chartered workings from time to time.*

Phil Waterfield

a charity. The move proved to be extremely advantageous for the Railway's finances.

A tragedy of a different kind, also in 1989, occurred when the only intact survivor of the line's original pair of brakevans was largely destroyed by fire. Hoping for restoration of other original goods vehicles which were in poor condition, an appeal was made for members to 'adopt a wagon'; at first without success. Sadly, the state of the historic wagons was going from bad to worse. Fortunately, a few months after the fire, a volunteer came forward to start the rebuild of brakevan No. 1 while others helped to renovate the GWR cattle van. And within a decade, interest in work on the Pickering stock was to be revived, inspired by the availability of funds from a new source.

Meanwhile, after almost ninety years in service, the wooden bodied end balcony Ziller coaches, always great favourites, were rapidly approaching the end of their life. Rebuilding by a contractor would have been prohibitively expensive. Then, fortuitously, a training organisation for would-be shipyard apprentices was found which could help. Plans were drawn up for rebuilding and, one by one, the two in worst condition were sent away to Birkenhead with the third similarly rebuilt when funds permitted, eight years later. Another challenge was that of finding suitable coal for the locomotives. Changes in the coal industry meant that Welsh steam coal was no longer available and it took time to locate a suitable if less than ideal, alternative (in England).

Despite the line's several open crossings, it is very fortunate that so seldom have they been the cause of a mishap. However, in June 1983, a works train headed by No. 11 *Ferret* was involved in a collision. The accident took place when an Austin Mini pickup failed to stop as the train ran on to Dolarddyn crossing. The pickup was pushed down the line and into the culvert on the Llanfair side of the crossing. The Manpower Services Commission workers who were travelling from Raven Square to Cyfronydd pulled the 69-year old woman driver out of the wreckage of her vehicle. The unfortunate lady was taken to hospital suffering from facial and leg injuries. The diesel was undamaged and no one on the train was hurt.

On Saturday 22th April 1987, a special was arranged to take members to Llanfair after an evening in Welshpool. Leaving Raven Square at 10.00pm, the train was climbing towards Golfa when it was in collision with a Vauxhall car at New Drive crossing. Luckily, no one was seriously hurt although the car was wrecked. The train was headed by No. 14 with headlight blazing and, of course had right of way. The 21-ton locomotive was undamaged: the volunteer driver commented afterwards: '*I never felt a thing!*' The incident produced banner headlines in the local press and the details, which emerged, showed that the motorist was on her way from Leominster to Paris. Perhaps, only on the W&L would a train be raced for a crossing by a

motorist who had travelled 50 miles in the wrong direction!

A little earlier, in 1984, there was a derailment of a passenger train west of the Brynelin Viaduct, close to the river. On 1st August, No. 12 *Joan* was heading for Llanfair with the 12.15pm train from Welshpool. As the train was descending the bank, the front four driving wheels of the locomotive and the rear pony truck left the rails.

Prompt action by the footplate crew stopped the train quickly using the vacuum and hand brakes. No other stock left the track and no one was hurt. The train was protected with red flags while the trainee fireman walked to the public callbox at Cyfronydd to report the mishap. As No. 7 *Chattenden* was waiting at Raven Square after working the 12.00pm from Llanfair, it was dispatched to Cyfronydd with No. 11 *Ferret* and the works train. *Chattenden* then took the passenger train back to Welshpool while a few passengers who wished to alight at Llanfair were taken on by members' cars.

The works train was moved to the site of the derailment and work began on rerailing No. 12 *Joan*. The locomotive eventually returned to Llanfair at 8.15pm. Earlier, the diesel *Chattenden* had operated a passenger service from Welshpool to Castle and back. No. 10 *Sir Drefaldwyn* replaced *Joan* on services for the rest of the week. An examination of *Joan* in the workshop revealed that the most likely cause of the derailment was a broken spring. Curiously, during a period when major accidents were being reported on the country's main lines, many passengers on the 12.15pm from Welshpool seemed quite amused by the incident and were pleased to have an entertaining story to tell on returning home.

Welshpool Station Completed

Now thoughts turned to Raven Square station where, ingeniously, a portion of the signal box had served as the booking office since 1982. A modernistic design for a station building was submitted by Powys County Council. It was a generous move but it started a controversy not completely settled even when traditional designs were selected from entries in a members' competition. Then, by a stroke of luck, one of the winners discovered a 'readymade' station building of character in the English/Welsh border country. It had served as the main station building at Eardisley on the Hereford, Hay & Brecon Railway which opened in 1863.

The building was supplied (apparently, 'off-the-peg') by timber contractors Eassie & Co. Ltd of Gloucester, whose staple products were wooden huts of standard design for military and colonial use including some for the Crimean campaign. Curiously, the section housing the booking office was apparently not designed with the idea of being joined to the other section where the waiting rooms were situated.

Following the closure of the line in 1964, the building

An unusual event in 1990 was a 'Jazz train', hauled by No.12 Joan*. Waiting at Castle station, the band is sitting on the flat wagon, entertaining passengers.*

became private property and was reduced to serving as a humble garden store and hen hut. Now dilapidated but available gratis, this station seemed to settle the debate over what style the Railway should adopt, provided that restoration was possible. It was to be an expensive project. However, after investigation and some heart searching, plans were agreed with the local building control and the Welsh Office. Exacting specifications were then provided for firms who offered to tender for the work of dismantling, transporting it piece by piece and rebuilding.

At Eardisley, the accommodation consisted of four rooms including two waiting rooms with corner fireplaces and a booking office with an iron stove and pipe chimney. A clock, outside the booking office, faced the platform on a wall which was replanked at Welshpool as a result of damage from a long forgotten assailant's gunshot pellets. The Eardisley building's tall windows with four horizontal glazing bars and the plain barge boards on the end of the roof gable were characteristic of the Eassie design. Inside, it was originally lined with hessian overlaid with wallpaper though later this was covered with matchboarding. Dismantling revealed traces of Victorian wallpaper and a Midland Railway poster advertising

excursions in 1875.

Careful control of the restoration work at Welshpool ensured that all the woodwork was scrupulously examined, replaced as necessary and comprehensively treated to ensure long life. Inside, the two small waiting rooms were combined to provide enough space for the shop while outside the ornate chimneys, attractive paving, traditional wooden fencing and new pathways provided pleasing finishing touches for Raven Square station. The design for a separate building housing toilets, built with modern materials but externally clad with matchboarding, successfully achieved complete harmony with the HH&BR construction. The toilets incorporate doors and roof slates from Horninglow on the North Staffordshire Railway's Uttoxeter-Burton line. An appropriate touch was the erection between the buildings of a pair of ex-GWR iron gates salvaged from Yardley Wood station.

Putting in sewers and power from beneath the main road provided unexpected problems but, in April 1992, the building was proudly opened to passengers by the Mayor of Welshpool while W&L President the Earl of Powis officiated at a second ceremony. The widespread admiration and three awards since opening confirmed the building as the right choice.

Handsomely painted in chocolate and cream, the buildings were ready to serve for another 130 years!

Rising Standards

On the track, the earlier practice of laying half length ex-BR softwood sleepers had given way to the use of brand new purpose cut jarrah sleepers imported from Australia. Even more substantial sleepers were acquired in 1993 when a large quantity of high quality concrete sleepers was located. Supplied to the NATO depot at Broughton Moor, Cumberland, most had never been used. Their considerable weight meant that new handling techniques had to be devised. At the same time, the overgrown site of the one time timber works at Tanllan near Llanfair station was converted into a storage yard with a ballast loading dock and the siding, believed last used about 1930, was reinstated for use of the permanent way department.

The summer season in 1993 had been unusually wet and -west of Cyfronydd, by the river, ground movement had damaged the formation. At this persistent trouble-spot, once again the line threatened to slide towards the river and action had to be taken to stabilise it. This involved digging deep drains and the tipping of large quantities of stone. Another battle was that against vegetation constantly encroaching on the line. In response to this problem, a well wagon was built from spare materials and went into service just before the 1993 season carrying a tractor-mounted mechanical flail. This was an example of how jobs done laboriously for many years gradually became mechanised as funds or opportunities permitted.

By far the most revolutionary of such moves was the import of a sophisticated 2ft 6ins gauge Plasser tamping machine in November 1999. This was found in South Africa having been little used but transport costs made it hugely expensive. Its acquisition was made possible by an unexpected and very generous bequest. Track renewals could now be finished with far fewer aching muscles.

In the whole of the line's history, no accident is known causing hurt to any passenger. But concern arose that in the event of an incident occurring, it was only possible to summon assistance from a limited number of points along the line.

West of Brynelin Viaduct, the formation has several times subsided towards the River Banwy (on the right). A major effort in 1993 aimed to stabilize it by installing substantial new drains.

Equipment was therefore introduced in 1994 to permit radio communication between train crews and Llanfair control with signals from any point relayed via a base station at Castle Caereinion. And here, at last, the disused signal box was restored to pristine condition after years of neglect. This was fitting treatment for the last one remaining in the British Isles of those built by Tyer & Co. Ltd of Carlisle. Nor was the nearby waiting shelter forgotten.

Llanfair Station Upgraded

With an oft praised station of considerable charm at Welshpool, attention turned to Llanfair where the hotch-potch of buildings was hardly impressive. A plan emerged giving heritage considerations high priority. With the cost estimated at £270,000, an Appeal Fund was launched (as always!) and the search began for grant aid. The allocation of substantial funds from the European Regional Development Fund and further assistance from other sources was the signal for work to begin in autumn 1993.

The original goods shed (the sombre all-black 'Long Shed'), long used for stores, was to be rebuilt to provide a new booking office, shop and station buffet. It needed new foundation timbers, a new floor, internal linings and renewal of much of the corrugated iron cladding. A canopy was restored over the siding complementing an attractive portico to face arriving visitors. Other canopies on the opposite side covered an ingenious removable pedestrian bridge forming the entrance to the former cattle dock and the platform. An extension in mellow yellow hand made brick provided a tea-room with a period look and cream paint overall was reminiscent of Cambrian days. Passengers started to use the new facilities in December that year.

Meanwhile, work began on a new raised platform, faced with blue bricks, the edgings surfaced with a diamond pattern, all very laboriously recovered for the purpose from several disused Cambrian stations. Rebuilding the 1903 booking office-cum-waiting room with its condemned chimney and deteriorating corrugated iron restored the building to its original (cream-painted) condition with canopy, though now to serve as offices.

Meanwhile, progress was being made with the Railway's grandest building yet on the edge of the car park. To be named '*Keyse Cottage*' in memory of benefactor and founder member Stanley Keyse, this was to provide overnight accommodation for volunteers in twelve bunk rooms on the ground floor with kitchens, dining, lounge and other facilities on the first floor. And what an elegant building it was! Beneath a roof of Welsh slate, the brickwork (laid in Flemish bond) included corbelled details to the eaves and gables and a band of dog tooth construction at half height. All in traditional style, sash windows, window arches and an embellished chimney also helped the building to appear much as a nineteenth century railwaymen's lodging house. This was the end for the grounded standard gauge sleeping car and was a welcome Christmas present for volunteers who came to operate 1994's Santa trains. With such extensive and tasteful construction and reconstruction at both termini, the award of publisher Ian Allan's '*Most Improved Railway of the Year*' for 1995 seemed well deserved.

Cruel Blows!

Ever since its reconstruction in 1965 by Army engineers, regular inspections of the Banwy Bridge were regarded as essential. As the years passed, low water levels tended to reveal the concrete base of the lattice steel pier in increasingly ragged condition and by 1994, underwater inspections were showing that protective work had become necessary. The next year, contractors were engaged to cast a new concrete block around the base of the steelwork. It turned out to be a rather irregular structure of poor quality.

But only two years later came the startling and unwelcome news that the pier had been undermined. This unexpected revelation was the result of a diving expedition by General Manager Andy Carey. Concern was such that the bridge was immediately closed to passenger services. In the last few days of the 1997 season, trains from Welshpool terminated at Castle Caereinion with a vintage bus link to Llanfair station. Meanwhile, remedial work was quickly put in hand to prevent collapse.

Once again, the bridge was threatened. Expert advice was sought and the recommendations were to rebuild the pier, or possibly the whole bridge. The estimated cost was enormous. Thoughts turned to the possibility of grant aid and as investigations proceeded, the temporary repair, by bridge contractors who regularly worked for Railtrack Plc, allowed train services to cross the bridge once again. The Company bravely decided to go ahead with rebuilding but in the end it was a sudden, generous and substantial bequest from a previously unknown sympathiser which funded the work on the pier.

A temporary roadway to the site was constructed for plant and materials. Then, when work began, the staggering discovery was made that the bridge builders of 1902 had sited the pier on inclined strata so that only one tip of the base rested on stable material. An attempt was made to reach hard rock with rock anchors but failed. Meanwhile, contractors fought a constant battle with the turbulent Banwy necessitating repeated rebuilding of the coffer dam. Eventually, sheet steel piling was driven down to solid rock which was some thirteen feet (4 metres) below in places. For a time, five huge centrifugal

Llanfair station's passenger facilities in 1994. The dilapidated goods shed was transformed into a shop, booking office and tea-room. The awning is reminiscent of those under which farm supplies were once unloaded.

pumps were needed to keep the site dry. Concrete, with reinforcing, was poured to fill the void and support a new base and rock armour in the form of massive boulders was deposited in the river bed around the pier to prevent erosion.

To complete the reconstruction, the steelwork was fully encased in concrete and faced with stonework to match the existing original pier. Above this, the girders were renovated and all the timbers and decking replaced. When the work was finished in 1999, aesthetically as well as structurally, the bridge was in better condition than it had been for almost half a century, even perhaps since it was built.

Alas, troubles seem often not to come singly. This was a period during which the Railway had to contend with several changes of permanent staff. Then, even before the bridge crisis was resolved, another disaster struck. Late on an April evening in 1998, a blaze broke out at Llanfair station.

As flames were seen leaping skywards, nearby residents alerted the Llanfair fire brigade. Sadly, the eastern end of the shop and booking office newly converted from the old goods shed was largely destroyed and the tea-room beyond was damaged by smoke. Furthermore, much of the Pickering-built van No. 6 had gone, too, having been displayed under the canopy. Miraculously, No. 12 *Joan* also on display there escaped with scorched paintwork. Saddened but undeterred, the Company set up facilities in temporary premises on the

car park until the insurers had arranged restitution of the building. The work was soon under way and was completed towards the end of the season.

Towards the Centenary

All through these latest difficulties, spirits were buoyed by preparations for the centenary which had been given a tremendous boost when support from the Heritage Lottery Fund was announced in 1997. For an ambitious five year programme costed at £786,000, the W&L secured 65% in grant aid, a magnificent award. In fact, this was the biggest ever grant to the W&L (and the biggest then to any railway from Lottery funds). The value of volunteer labour counted towards part of the remaining anticipated cost. And another appeal to members was launched to raise some of the additional funds needed. There were a number of aspects to the plan. Paramount, was the rebuilding of the two original locomotives with new boilers and the erection of a shed for them close to Llanfair station. With a single road 90ft (27.4m) long, the new shed incorporates a smoke vent cowl along the roof ridge and a 50ft (15.2m) pit.

Then there was the restoration of one of the wooden Ziller coaches and the unused *ex*-Sierra Leone Railways coach (eventually abandoned) and an extension of the carriage shed.

One of the original brake vans and several wooden Pickering-built wagons were to be restored in a new carpenters' shop which was to be erected at Tanllan. Other items in the programme were the extensive renovation of the girders and decking of the river bridge, the provision of new toilets at Llanfair station and the acquisition and laying of new rail. The search for rail extended to South Africa where suitable stocks were found and imported.

This was a very demanding but inspiring schedule and members showed their support both by turning out to help in the workshops and on the track and by generously contributing to the Appeal Fund. It might be remarked that prior to this, there had been a series of appeals for funds for the carriage shed, development of the two main stations, for the Tubize locomotive and even for new rail. Yet almost every one raised more than its predecessor and the Centenary Appeal seemed likely to break all records. This demonstrates how, in modern times, those who love the line are willing to try to ensure that it has funds to achieve its aims.

With an eye on future coaching needs, news was welcomed that some surplus high capacity bogie vehicles were available from a 760mm gauge line in Hungary. It was the W&L's links with the 760mm gauge Jindrichuv Hradec Railway in the Czech Republic which made negotiations possible. The coaches were eventually inspected after movement to the Ciernohronska Forestry Railway in Slovakia. Although negotiations had been going on for some months, problems with transport made delivery dates unpredictable. Permission was needed to exceed normal load heights in Germany and Belgium and the coaches were held up at the JHR for four weeks. A four-day journey by road and cross-Channel ferry preceded their arrival at Llanfair station on 26th July 1999 for unloading the next day.

For the volunteers who keep the line running, these have been exciting times. The beginning of a new century brings the sight of *The Earl* and *The Countess* in service together and finds heavier trains being regularly taken, at last, by 'the big Finn', the 2-6-2 Tubize tank locomotive *Orion*, all three having completed heavy overhauls. Refurbishment of the Hungarian State Railways coaches should see two splendid substantial bogie vehicles in service, probably outshopped with end balconies. And who knows, perhaps a scheme may also emerge for the building of a replica of the original coaches. In marked contrast to earlier days, a flow of funding has emerged for increasingly expensive capital projects and a pool of expertise is available for their proper management. So much has been achieved so far that no dream should be lightly dismissed. The future is certain: the efforts and financial support of many dedicated volunteers will ensure that.

On a charter working in May 1994, No. 2 The Countess *lifts a mixed train towards Coppice Lane crossing. Curiously, the headlamp code signifies a light engine movement!*

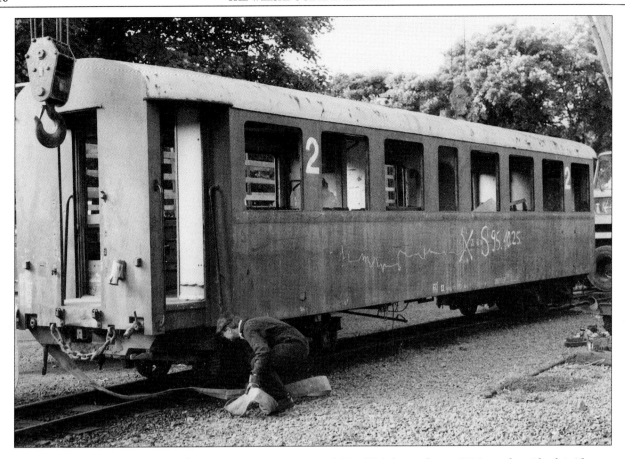

At the end of a long road journey from eastern Europe, MAV coach No. 428 is lowered on to W&L metals at Llanfair. The acquisition of two coaches from Hungary was timely. Later, the authorities there forbad the movement abroad of surplus narrow gauge stock.

At Raven Square station, on 21st June, 2001, locomotive No. 14 takes water at the newly commissioned ex-Cambrian Railways water tower. It was originally installed at Pwllheli in 1909.

Chapter 8

Infrastructure and Working Procedures

The original rail is flat bottomed, 45lb/yd (22kg/m) and was laid mainly in 30ft lengths with staggered joints. It was intended to use 75lb (37kg/m) to the yard grooved rail for the crossings in Welshpool but Collin gained approval of the Board of Trade for the use of the same rail as elsewhere. The Railway was constructed with 6ft sleepers of creosoted Baltic fir, 9ins by 4¹/₂ins, laid at 3ft intervals and ballasted with river gravel and broken stone about 5ins deep. In many places check rails were laid on sharp curves, on bridges and on the steep Golfa Bank. Some have since been lifted. Metal ties were also introduced at intervals on curves as required by the Order.

Dog spikes were used to secure the rails, with base plates only at the joints. In between, the rails were spiked direct to the sleepers. On the mixed gauge section in Welshpool, chaired track was laid. The sharpest curve was 3 chains radius (60.4m), out of Welshpool terminus. In modern times, the sharpest curves are 3.3 chains (65.2m) radius, west of Sylfaen and 3.4 chains (68.6m) radius at Dolrhyd Mill. The contract provided for oak gradient posts to be installed in appropriate locations.

When they took over, the GWR seem to have completely resleepered the line, using their standard creosoted Baltic fir sleepers cut to 6ft in length with a cross section of approximately 9ins x 4¹/₂ins. Four-hole base plates were installed on all the sleepers. Sylfaen bank was re-laid some time after 1926 with 56lb (28kg/m) rail allegedly cascaded from the nearby Tanat Valley Light Railway. New timber distance posts on a metal stanchion (pieces of broad gauge bridge rail) were installed by the GWR on the north side of the line, replacing the original simple, white-painted oak posts. Distances were indicated every quarter of a mile from the passenger terminus at Welshpool. The post and wire fencing from Welshpool to the Banwy bridge was also renewed, using concrete uprights.

Under British Railways, re-laying in patches took place at various times with standard gauge softwood sleepers cut in half and the Preservation Company continued this practice until 1978. Then, the first jarrah (hardwood) sleepers were installed west of Cyfronydd. These were acquired from London Transport and though second-hand they proved satisfactory for over twenty years despite their large 7ft 6ins x 12ins (or 14ins) x 5ins measurements. The first new sleepers in modern times arrived in 1980 for the rebuilding of the Sylfaen-Welshpool section when new jarrah sleepers were bought from Australia. These were 5ft 3ins long with a 9ins x 4¹/₂ins cross section and were generally used here without base plates, though later some were found necessary. The use of imported jarrah sleepers has continued although the one-off opportunity occurred in the 1990s to acquire a large quantity of new or nearly new concrete sleepers from a closing NATO depot. They are 5ft 3ins long with an 8ins x 7¹/₂ins cross-section.

Remarkably, much of the line is still laid with the original 1901/02 rail, including that recovered from the town section. On straight sections, parallel joints are now usual. New 60lb (30kg/m) rail was used in 1980 for the incline out of the station when the terminus was constructed at Raven Square. A quarter mile of the main line west of Dolarddyn was re-laid in 1995 with sound ex-military 75lb (37kg/m) rail and in 1997 enough good 60lb rail was imported from South Africa to re-lay almost a mile between Cyfronydd and Heniarth. Formerly laid on the Donnybrook Railway, this came in 60ft lengths recently re-worked from (mostly) German rail circa 1930. In modern times, the Preservation Company has introduced a variety of fixings including elastic spikes, Pandrol clips and coach screws.

Quarter milepost. The post at 3¹/₂ miles is GWR pattern.

Operating

Under the Light Railway Order of 8th September 1899, the maximum speed permitted was 20mph. Lower speed limits were required to be imposed in various places. Where the gradient was steeper than 1 in 50, the limit was 15mph; on curves sharper than 5 chains (100m) radius and where the line was unfenced between Welshpool terminus and Raven Square, it was 10 mph except that, in Welshpool, a lower limit could be imposed by direction of Welshpool Corporation.

Numerous speed restriction boards were erected along the nine miles of the line. In the Up direction, Cambrian drivers had to watch for nine 10mph boards, two 5mph boards and three 4mph boards. The GWR introduced 15mph boards, too, and instructed drivers not to exceed 5mph over crossings within approximately a mile of Welshpool station or 10mph over public level crossings.

By 1911, the overall speed limit had been raised to 25mph as the appendix to the Cambrian Railways Working Time Book for 1st June of that year shows. The date of the actual raising of the speed limit was probably earlier; it may be significant that journey times were reduced by 15 minutes in 1905. On 11th August 1927, an Extra Traffic Notice was published by the GWR which included an apparently new amendment to the instructions regarding the overall speed: it was reduced to 20mph. In 1939, the speed limit was further reduced to 15 mph. This prevailed until closure in 1956 and was reimposed when the line was opened again in 1963.

Special regulations were in force with regard to timber trains. Under the GWR, speeds were not to exceed 10mph. A match truck was required when round timber overhung two wagons, although if it was no longer than three wagons' length, two wagons were to be used connected by a drag chain attached at intervals to the timber.

WELSHPOOL AND LLANFAIR BRANCH - PUBLIC LEVEL CROSSINGS

Church Street Level Crossing (0m. 29ch.)

Up Trains.

Owing to motor and other vehicles having to pass along the Welshpool and Llanfair line in order to gain access to the Bakery premises near Church Street Level Crossing, Welshpool, a Stop Board lettered "STOP" has been erected at 0m.30$\frac{1}{4}$ch. and Drivers of all Up-trains must bring their train to a stand at the Stop Board and satisfy themselves that the line is clear before proceeding.

The Level Crossing Gates must be opened by the Fireman who must signal the Driver to cross over the roadway after first satisfying himself that all is clear.

Down Trains.

Each train requiring to pass over the crossing must be brought to a stand and the gates opened by the Fireman who must satisfy himself that the line is clear over the roadway and beyond the Bakery premises before handsignalling the Driver to cross over the roadway.

Up and Down Trains.

No Train must pass over the Crossing until the Driver receives a handsignal from the Fireman to do so.
The gates must be closed after the passage of the train over the crossing by the Guard.
In the case of light engines the gates must be opened and closed by the Fireman.

Castle Caereinion Level Crossing (4m. 64$\frac{1}{2}$ch.).

Each train requiring to pass over the crossing must be brought to a stand and the gates opened by the Fireman who must signal the Driver to cross over the roadway, after first satisfying himself that all is clear. No train must be allowed to pass over the crossing until the Driver receives a handsignal from the Fireman to do so. The gates must be closed after the passage of a train over the crossing by the Guard.
In the case of light engines the gates must be opened and closed by the Fireman.

Extract from the GWR Appendix to No.16 Section of the Service Timetables, March 1943 (and until further notice), p.108.

Permanent way hut near Sylfaen, restored to original condition

The maximum loading height was 12ft (3.66m). Owing to the steep gradients, regulations required shunting on the Standard Quarry siding and the Tanllan corner timber siding near Llanfair to be carried out with the locomotive at the Welshpool end. Eventually, regulations necessitated the collection of Down traffic from the Standard Quarry to be taken to the yard *before* the morning train left the Welshpool terminus, to be formed into the train. Drivers were enjoined to *'freely ring the engine bell'* when approaching level crossings in Welshpool and to whistle when approaching all other crossings.

When the Railway opened, all sidings were worked by ground frames from the Isca Foundry and were opened by Annett's key attached to the train staff. At Castle Caereinion, points were worked from the signal box at times following its installation in 1907; curiously, the ground frames here seem to have been retained and were used when the signal box was not operational. Existing frames are from Tyer and Co. Ltd. The loops at intermediate stations were used as sidings with catchpoints to protect the main line. In modern times, catchpoints are not required at Sylfaen or Cyfronydd where the loops are intended only for passing trains.

For the one-engine-in-steam system when the line opened, a round wooden staff painted red was used. New regulations in 1907 specified that the line was to be worked by train staff and telephone. Passing was to be allowed at Castle Caereinion only, with separate staffs for the two sections which were locked up when operating on the one-engine-in-steam system and vice versa. By 1921, a T-shaped staff was in use. The regulations introduced in 1907 stipulated that if a train was

All part of the job for the (BR) guard - working the ground frame at Welshpool.

W&LLR Pres Co.

Castle Caereinion signal box. This is a picturesque relic of the 1907 signalling scheme that was never regularly utilised and was eventually abandoned.

assisted by a second engine, it was to be attached at the rear and the staff was to be carried by the engine at the rear. Similarly, the GWR did not permit the working of two engines coupled together.

The Preservation Company operates a divisible staff system. The staffs consist of painted metal bars each marked with the names of the two stations at the ends of the appropriate section. Possession of the staff permits a train or light engine to move in *either* direction within that section. Two tickets, which are also metal bars, are attached to each staff, one for each direction within the section. A ticket is used when a blockman requires a train to move away from the staff after first showing the driver the complete staff. A second train with the staff and the ticket attached for the opposite direction can then follow when the first train has cleared the section. For ease of handling, metal hoops are provided with the staffs and tickets. Annett keys, painted yellow, are slotted into the carrying loop for the staff. There are block posts at Castle Caereinion and, since 1967, at Cyfronydd, while Sylfaen was introduced after running was extended to Welshpool. Instead of block instruments and bells, trains were signalled by telephone until 1994. Telephones at intermediate points were then removed and radio communication is used instead.

Until 1956, all points at each terminii were worked by ground frames. Now, at Llanfair, within station limits, movements are controlled by a two-arm bracket signal and a starting signal operated from the signal box. There are also shunting signals and ground levers. The Preservation Company first installed an eight-lever frame from Buttington crossing (in 1963) opposite and just beyond the site of the present-day

signal box. It was superseded four years later when the box was erected, equiped with a Dutton-made 17-lever frame from Llanbrynmair on the Cambrian main line to Machynlleth.

Welshpool (Raven Square) is protected by a Home signal in the form of an unusual splitting colour light authorising entry to the main platform road or the bay platform. The signal box was built in 1982 round an LNWR 18-lever tappet-locking frame of 1911 vintage with nine levers in use. It was installed the previous year, having previously served at Groeslon on the Caernarvon-Afon Wen line. A main platform starter, bay platform starter and an advanced starter are provided and a shunting signal. However, the signal box here is normally unmanned when one-engine-in-steam operations are in force. The colour light signal is then unlit. 'U' boards are displayed here and on the starter signals to indicate that the train can proceed with caution.

Fares

Tickets exist showing the single third class (parliamentary) fare from Welshpool to Llanfair as 9d (3³/₄p) which seems to have lasted until revised during World War 1. The first class fare then from Seven Stars to Llanfair was 1s 3d (6¹/₄p). There were also market ticket arrangements: in Cambrian days cheap third class returns to Llanfair were offered on Saturdays from Welshpool and all intermediate stations; and from stations along the line to Welshpool on Mondays. For the full distance, the return excursion fare was 1s 3d (6p) for many years and in 1903 even half-day returns were offered, at 1s (5p), on Wednesdays and Thursdays. Through tickets were offered to

Courtesy: National Railway Museum

Tickets

Edmondson card tickets were issued by the Cambrian Railways and the GWR from booking offices. Guards issued tramway style tickets.

Courtesy: National Railway Museum

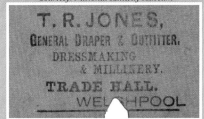

Reverse side

Reverse side

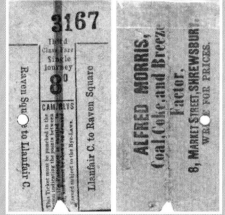

Reverse side

Courtesy: Mike Lister

Ticket issued for a Special on 27th October 1956.

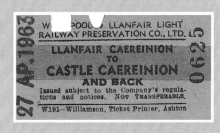

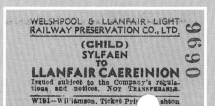

and from some main line stations; at times this arrangement included cheap third class return market tickets to Llanfair on Saturdays and from Llanfair to Oswestry on Wednesdays (3s 5d - 17p), to Newtown on Tuesdays (3s 3d - 16p) and to Wrexham on Mondays (5s 5d - 27p).

Season tickets were offered at standard Cambrian rates when that Company was operating the line. For example a third class twelve monthly season ticket from Welshpool to Llanfair cost £5.6s.0d (£5.30) in 1905. By 1922 it cost £5.3s. 6d (£5.17$\frac{1}{2}$) for a third class six monthly season ticket. After 1931, special excursions on the line were usually charged at 2s 6d (12$\frac{1}{2}$p) return. The final trip before closure cost 3s 2d (16p). The Preservation Company's charges for the return journey from Llanfair to Castle were 2s 6d (12$\frac{1}{2}$p) in 1963 and, in 1981, for the return journey between Llanfair and Welshpool, £2.50. Over the years since, they have been revised in line with inflation.

Tickets

During the early years of passenger services, tickets were issued from the booking office at the passenger terminus in Welshpool and at Llanfair Caereinion, but later the booking office at Llanfair was closed. These tickets were standard Edmondsons similar to the operating company's main-line tickets. In fact the W & L Company's name did not appear but instead that of the Cambrian Railways (abbreviated to CAM RYS) and later GWR.

Guards' duties included both the issue and collection of tickets. At some stage, the Cambrian Railways introduced punch-type, tramway style tickets for issue en route which seem to have been peculiar to the line. These tram-type tickets were divided into three columns. In the centre column was printed the fare, class, single or return, name of the operating company

and the conditions of issue. The left hand column showed the stage (or stages). On the 9d single, this was Welshpool Seven Stars to Llanfair C., on the 1$\frac{1}{2}$d single it was Heniarth Gate to Llanfair C. and on the 1d single the stages were:

> Welshpool - Raven Square
> Golfa - Sylfaen Farm
> Sylfaen Farm - Castle Caereinion
> Cyfronydd - Heniarth Gate

On the right hand side the stages were reversed. The tickets were punched to show the points between which the passenger was entitled to travel: on the back was carried an advertisement of a local trader. By 1917, the tickets were marked 'Revised Fare'. It has been recorded that 1d tickets were white and 11d tickets were blue with a red bar down the centre. Card dog and bicycle tickets were also issued by the guard, and were 'To any station on Welshpool & Llanfair Line'. Bicycle tickets were orange and cost 6d, becoming cream when the rate was increased to 9d. Tickets were later needed for enthusiasts who were carried on special trips after the cessation of passenger services. In BR days single or double coupon special issues were used.

Under the present administration, Edmondson card tickets are issued at the booking offices. They bear the Preservation Company's name, and show the destination but not the fare. In earlier years, they were printed by Williamson's of Ashton. Return tickets are marked 'and back' and half-fare tickets 'Child'. There are other special categories. Various colours have been used from time to time and commemorative tickets have been issued for special events. Guards issue tickets to passengers joining at intermediate stations and for many years used a travelling ticket rack. In recent times, paper tickets have been issued by guards and booking offices for journeys to or from intermediate stations.

For further details, see *Welshpool & Llanfair Light Railway - A Century of Tickets* by Mike Lister, to be published by the Transport Ticket Society (2003).

The
Welshpool & Llanfair
in Colour . . . . .

PHOTO: David Moseley

In Welshpool narrow gauge yard, No. 823 Countess *has made up a train of coal and general merchandise on a gloomy day in 1954. The line's steep gradients and sharp curves limited trains to a maximum of eleven wagons and vans of general merchandise.*

Jim Jarvis

Although closure is imminent, Llanfair yard is busy in October 1956. No.822 The Earl *waits with a line of empties while a lorry from the local farmers' co-operative collects supplies. On the right are the standard gauge coach bodies installed for storage.*

T.B. Owen/Colour-Rail
BRW 1299

Llanfair bound trains crossed Raven Square roundabout against the flow of traffic. In the 1950s, this gave a growing number of motorists quite a surprise. No. 823 (now without nameplates) is remarkably clean.

Jim Jarvis

The watering point at Welshpool was on the road into the loco shed and next to the carriage shed, seen behind The Earl. There was an outside pit, just to the right of the loco. In 1951, the nameplates of No. 822 were removed. Two years later, it has probably just returned with a train from Llanfair.

John Milner

Welshpool bound, the crew had to be vigilant even with a train of empties as the track snakes down Golfa's 1 in 29 bank. Except in the sheep season, there was now little traffic in this direction.

John Milner

The old passenger terminus in the standard gauge coal yard at Welshpool was still useful in BR days for making up the daily freight for Llanfair. This train is about to depart over Smithfield Road crossing. The road lay behind the line of coal wagons. A roundabout now occupies this site.

John Milner

Following the withdrawal of No. 823 on 16th March 1956 to store in Oswestry Works, No. 822 had to carry on alone. Here, departure from Llanfair station seems imminent. Then, the station was flanked only by sheep pastures. Curiously, the timeworn paintwork of the leading wagon has assumed an unusual shade.

John Milner

The end of an era. Great crowds gathered at the terminus near Welshpool BR station for the Last Train on 3rd November 1956. Newtown Silver Band is preparing a musical farewell.

Ivo Peters

Raven Square had never before seen so many people crammed into the little wagons as the Last Train steamed out of the town. Cars with astonished occupants waited as the train headed for Golfa bank.

New beginnings . . . . . .

On Re-Opening Day, 6th April 1963, the inaugural working calls at Castle Caereinion. The chairman rode in the comfort of the 'Combination Car' whilst others enjoyed an invigorating trip in the semi-open toastrack.

Sylfaen was re-opened with a ceremonial train on 6th June 1964. The siding just installed by a squadron of Royal Engineers accommodates The Countess *leading* The Earl *as* Upnor Castle *shunts the train past them. But the re-opening was to be short lived.*

D.J. Mitchell

A pre-season working in March 1964. No.1 The Earl *passes Heniarth with the 'Combination Car'. The loop siding was still in place.*

J.D. How

No. 1 The Earl *ambles towards Cyfronydd with coach B24 on a wintry morning in March 1977. Here, where the line follows close beside the River Banwy, gradients are erratic and the formation occasionally unstable.*

The ex-Admiralty diesel Chattenden *shunts an ex-Upnor toastrack in Llanfair yard. The original drab green livery of the coach has given way to a smarter livery and doors have been fitted. In 1976, Chattenden was in its original condition.*

After Raven Square station was opened in 1981, trains faced a fierce 1 in 35 grade as they departed. No. 2 The Countess storms away ready for an even steeper mile ahead.

Train operations are controlled from the signal box at Llanfair. The one in the picture was to be replaced in 2002. The single line staff is handed in as No. 10 Sir Drefaldwyn *returns with the morning service.* The Countess *stands on the headshunt.*

Far from its Austrian origins, the one-time tender locomotive Sir Drefaldwyn crosses the Banwy Bridge with a typical mix of Zillertalbahn and Sierra Leone Railways stock. For over thirty years, the lattice steel pier erected in 1965 was considered solidly based.

No. 6 Monarch *approaches Sylfaen in August 1976 when this was the eastern terminus. Different circumstances in later times might have spared the articulated Bagnall its fate. The variegated liveries of the coaching stock reflect the vehicles' different origins.*

Golfa incline, arboreous and tortuous, in 1989. No. 12 Joan *had just exchanged a stylish crimson livery for a rather garish blue livery which, coincidentally, was the house colour of the Staffordshire Building Society who sponsored the repaint. Note the conventional chimney (from No. 14) replacing the original.*

D. Tambling

Crossing the Banwy Bridge, No. 2 The Countess *leads 0-6-2T* Superior *from the Great Whipsnade Railway. The Kerr Stuart, built in 1920, was visiting for the Gala event in September 1992.*

Hugh Ballantyne

No.14 (ex-SLR 85) restarts from the former Golfa Halt. In 1992, the Hunslet 2-6-2 tank had just received its new red livery but was awaiting the double box lining which later enhanced it.

No. 8 Dougal *is most frequently used on demonstration civil engineer's trains during the Gala events. Waiting on the loop at Cyfronydd, the driver on the open footplate was doubtless pleased to have a fine day.*

Above: *Stomping up the 1 in 29 Golfa bank with its notorious reverse curves, No. 2* The Countess *pilots No. 14 (ex-SLR 85). It carries a 90th Anniversary headboard.*   Below: *Built in Belgium,* Orion *worked as Finland's Jokioisten Railway No. 5 for only fifteen years. It then languished in the UK for almost 30 years before being overhauled and returned to service. In August 2000, the massive 2-6-2 tank pauses at Castle Caereinion.*

Visitors . . .

0-6-0 side/well tank Siam *was rescued from a sugar factory in Thailand by the Bredgar & Wormshill Light Railway. The Henschel, built in 1956, visited the W&L in 1994.*

The first 'guest' locomotive was 0-6-2T Chevallier *from Whipsnade Zoo in 1991. This ex-Admiralty locomotive, waiting here at Cyfronydd with freight stock, also double-headed on passenger trains.*

In August 1993, Hoboken Steelworks No. 6 has just returned from Castle Caereinion on its first run in the UK. This visiting engine was built in 1929 by SA Des Ateliers De La Meuse in Belgium for work in Antwerp. Eventually, it passed to the Bredgar & Wormshill Light Railway.

A brave sight. Ex-GWR No. 823 Countess *climbs towards New Drive Crossing, at the foot of the Golfa incline. In 2002, the locomotive was ready to celebrate its centenary (in GWR livery) after being completely rebuilt, new boiler included.*

Above: *Running as GWR No 823 Countess, the Beyer Peacock heads a train for Welshpool over the rebuilt Banwy Bridge in September 1999. For the first time in almost a hundred years, the pier is located on genuinely solid rock, over 13ft below the bed of the river.*

Left: *Just returned to service in April 2000, The Earl crosses Brynelin viaduct. The unlined black livery represented the locomotive's appearance in the British Railways era.*

Chapter 9

Motive Power

Two identical locomotives were designed by Mr. S. E. Garratt, of Beyer Peacock & Co. Ltd, Gorton Foundry, Manchester, and supplied for the opening of the line. After seeing a preliminary design, a larger boiler was chosen and, in June 1901, the order was placed for two locomotives at £1,630 each (equivalent to just over £100,000 today).

Nos. 1 & 2 *The Earl* & *The Countess*

No. 1 *The Earl* 0-6-0 side tank, Beyer Peacock & Co. Ltd, 3496/1902, supplied new 2nd September 1902. Renumbered GWR 822 in 1923. Withdrawn 1956. To Preservation Co. 1961.
No. 2 *The Countess*, Beyer Peacock & Co. Ltd, 3497/1902, supplied new 30th September 1902. Renumbered GWR 823 in 1923. Renamed *Countess* ca.1923. Withdrawn 1956. To Preservation Co. 1962.

Beyer Peacock were not light railway specialists and their design for the W&L is not without interest. The specification was for locomotives which could take a 40 ton load up four miles of a 1 in 30 incline at 10mph. The difficult gradients made it necessary to have a short boiler to minimise the risk of uncovering the crown of the firebox. And to obtain maximum adhesion an 0-6-0 wheel arrangement was adopted which resulted in a very long rigid wheelbase (10ft 0ins/3.04m) considering the severe curvatures on the line. Almost certainly a light railway specialist would have favoured an 0-6-2 type with short rigid wheelbase, even at the expense of higher total weight. The engines had a tractive effort of 8,175lb at 85% working pressure, were built with outside frames, outside cylinders and valve chests with Walschaerts valve gear. Although this was new to the limited British narrow gauge light railway scene, British manufacturers had been supplying this arrangement for several years on narrow gauge locomotives for colonial light railways and for industrial service at home.

The numbers 3496/7 are carried on the motion but not on the builders' plates. They are re-issues of numbers originally allocated in 1892 to 4-4-2 tanks for the Buenos Aires Great

Southern Railway which were never built.

Vacuum and handbrakes were fitted, acting on all wheels. In order to clear the ashpan the trailing wheel brakeblocks acted from the rear end, the other blocks acting from the front end. Steam assisted sanding was fitted, the sandboxes being tucked between the boiler and the tank sides. Ramsbottom safety valves were mounted over the firebox. A small bell mounted on the cab roof was intended to act as a warning at road crossings and over the Welshpool town section. Traverser jacks were usually carried on the footplating over the valve chests. Both engines survived the Cambrian era without major modification but it seems that the boilers were not very free steamers and an inordinately long wait was often necessary to raise steam from cold.

Early in 1925, each loco in turn was out of service for some weeks undergoing a heavy overhaul. On completion, the Great Western influence was evident with the fitting of huge safety valve casings of the familiar Swindon brass 'trumpet' pattern. More important was the fitting of steam heating equipment to warm up the long suffering customers. Probably this coincided with replacement of the original tiny rectangular front buffer beam by a deeper version recessed top and bottom, as this would have facilitated attachment of the extra piping. This steam heating piping was removed from No. 1 by 1956 but remained on No. 2 until 1964.

By the late 1920s the original boilers were due for renewal and in 1929 *The Earl* was sent away for an extensive overhaul in the GWR's former Cambrian Workshops at Oswestry, not at Swindon as once thought. However, Swindon Works designed and built the new boilers. They incorporated copper fireboxes and made the following changes in specifications:

	As built	As in 1929/1930
Tubes	119	136
diameter	$1^3/_4$ins	$1^5/_8$ins
length	7ft 6ins	7ft $3^1/_4$ins
Total heating surface	433sq ft	457sq ft

The external appearance of the locomotive was greatly

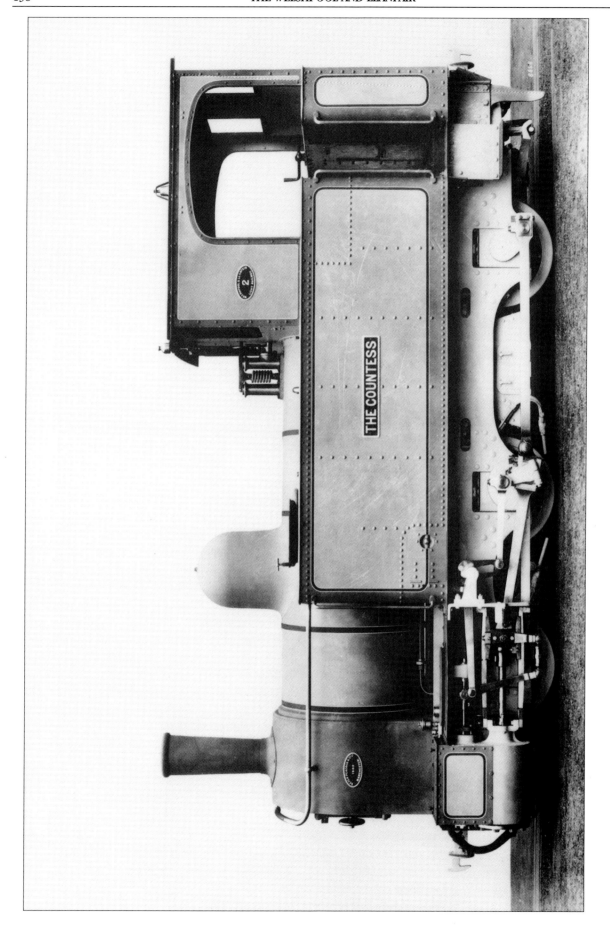

The Countess in lined works grey at the Gorton Works of Beyer Peacock & Co. Ltd., 1902.

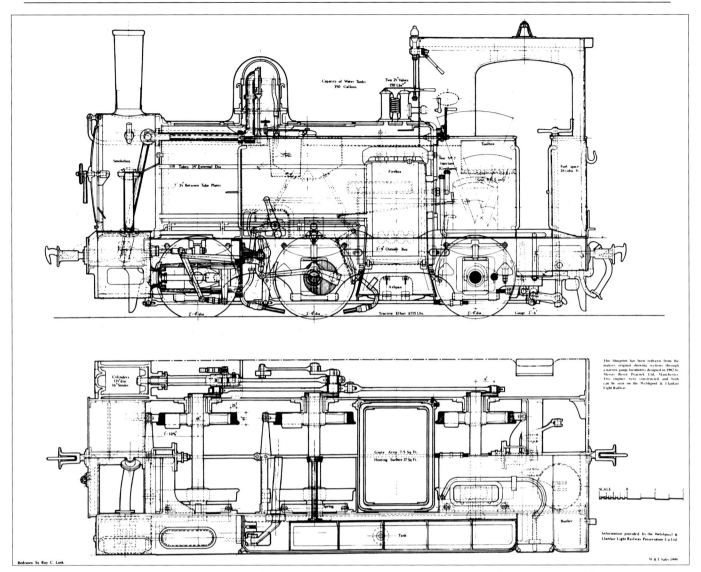

*General Arrangement drawing: Original locomotives (*The Earl *and* The Countess*) as built by Beyer, Peacock Ltd, 1902.*

Copyright Roy C. Link - NG&IRM Review

Beyer Peacock Design Specification for *The Earl* and *The Countess*

Cylinders,	diameter	11¹⁄₂ins	Wheels,	Leading	2ft 9ins
	stroke	16ins		Driving	2ft 9ins
Boiler,	Barrel	7ft 0ins		Trailing	2ft 9ins
	Outside Dia.	3ft 5¹⁄₈ins	Water capacity of tanks		350 gallons
Firebox,	Outside	2ft 9in x 3ft 10¹⁄₂ins	Working Pressure		150 lb/sq ins
	Inside	2ft 3in x 3ft 4¹⁄₂ins	Tractive effort (85%)		8,175 lb
	Height	3ft 7¹⁄₄ins	Weight,	full	19 tons 18 cwt
Tubes,	No.	119		empty	17 tons
	Diameter	1³⁄₄ins	Coal capacity		28 cub ft
	Length	7ft 6ins	Maximum load per axle		7 tons
Heating Surface:			Minimum curves at sidings		3 chains (198 ft)
	Tubes	396.0 sq ft	Maximum speed		25 mph
	Firebox	37.0 sq ft	Specification load behind engine:		
	Total	433.0 sq ft			40 tons up 1 in 30 incline at 10 mph
Area of Firegrate		7.5 sq ft	Brakes		Auto Vac and Hand Screw

The Earl at Llanfair during the Cambrian era. It was a long-lived practice to run with an open cover over the motion.

Collection: R.W. Miller

changed by standard GWR boiler fittings, including a parallel chimney topped by a copper cap (replacing the original tapered stovepipe), top feed apparatus, a very large steam dome and, inevitably, the safety valve 'trumpet'. Twin whistles, incorporating the deep 'emergency' whistle, were also fitted. It was perhaps fortunate that all the incongruous fittings on the rebuilt *Earl* added up to a most pleasing effect. Certainly in the affectionate attitude which was to surround the narrow gauge after the 1939-45 war, the chunky and slightly preposterous proportions of the W&L engines were to have an appeal all their own.

Following the return of No. 822 to traffic on 3rd April 1930, No. 823 was sent to Oswestry in July of that year for similar treatment and was returned to traffic on 10th October 1930. No further major modifications were carried out by the GWR, but extremely ugly deflectors were fitted to throw smoke and steam from the safety valves clear of the cab windows. This problem had been aggravated when the cab was extended forward to enclose the whistle valves.

During the 1939-45 war the engines received only minimum maintenance, though for No. 822, a general overhaul was completed in March 1942, this time at Swindon. But within weeks, it was sent to Oswestry for further work and returned

to service on 19th May. By the end of 1946 both were in very poor condition, with badly corroded fireboxes, worn tyres and generally run down mechanical condition. Of the two, No. 823 was in the worst state with 77,000 miles since last overhaul, and on 10th December 1946 she was declared unfit for further service. Consequently No. 822 had to soldier on alone, reduced to the indignity of a monthly boiler inspection, until the intended closure of the line could be effected. In the event this was not possible and major repairs could be delayed no longer.

On 28th November 1947, No. 823 was sent to Swindon for a major overhaul including much work on the firebox. Unfortunately the strain was too much for No. 822, which failed completely on 28th November 1947 so stopping all services. As a result of very efficient mobilising of resources, a remarkable amount of work was carried out at the Welshpool shed between 30th November and 4th December 1947, including removal of all wheels for tyre turning at Oswestry Works, refitting of axleboxes, overhaul of motion, repairs to brake gear, and replacement of several boiler tubes, stays and flange rivets. The engine was ready to resume services on 5th December 1947, an effort which earned a congratulatory letter from Swindon; the authorities had estimated fourteen days for the work. This is a good example of how the W&L was able, with main line facilities on call, to survive with only two locomotives. There is evidence that an attempt was made to locate another locomotive for the line in 1947, apparently without success.

No. 823 returned from Swindon on 13th February 1948 and No. 822 was sent away two weeks later, returning on 24th June 1948. Thus the line was then provided with two locomotives put into first class order at considerable cost, and this influenced decisions to continue services for several years. However, for over five weeks in 1953, No. 823 was out of service this time being in the hands of Oswestry Works and on its return, No. 822 was stopped. With a decision pending on the line's future, no repairs were made for three years. By February 1956, however, No. 823 was also unserviceable and no services were possible for six weeks. At Oswestry, work started on No. 822 including retubing and tyre turning and the locomotive returned on 15th March. No. 823 was destined never to run again under BR auspices. She was sent to Oswestry for storage on 16th March 1956. This left No. 822 to operate the final months and to clear the line of wagons and equipment after closure in November 1956. After this No. 822 languished in the Welshpool shed until sent to join No. 823 in Oswestry

Works on 7th May 1958.

They stood side by side in the wheel turning bay off rails and without name or numberplates. In 1960, they were offered to the Preservation Company for £654, but it was not until 28th July 1961 that No. 1 was unloaded from a well wagon in Welshpool yard by the Salop steam crane.

No. 822 was in quite good general condition when purchased and handled its share of traffic until 1978 when it became apparent that major repairs were needed, including new firebox crown stays. Then an offer from the National Railway Museum, York, to house and display the locomotive seemed a better alternative than open storage in Llanfair yard. After a move in 1987 to the Birmingham Railway Museum, it was exhibited at the Great Western Steam Centre at Didcot before eventually returning home in 1991.

In 1996, the locomotive was dismantled and examination of the boiler showed that the time had come for its renewal. It was indeed fortunate that the Heritage Lottery grant made this possible. Work started on a heavy overhaul which even included repairs to the frames. It was a complete rebuild, a tremendous feat for volunteers. Contractors cast and machined new cylinders (to the original specification), re-tyred the wheels and supplied new tanks, which were welded but with dummy

No. 1 The Earl *(right) alongside No.2* The Countess *at Llanfair in 1995. They are substantially as rebuilt by the GWR.*

rivets. The new boiler with a welded steel firebox was made by Israel Newton in Bradford and allowed a higher working pressure (160lb/in^2) than before. A Lempor exhaust was fitted to further enhance performance and reduce fuel consumption. In December 1999, *The Earl* started running in on some of the Llanfair - Cyfronydd Santa trains and then, in BR unlined black livery, it successfully re-entered service on the run between Llanfair and Welshpool in April 2000, performing better than ever before.

As stored at Oswestry, No. 823 was in a run down state. Before it left Oswestry to join No. 822, various repairs were effected including re-tubing the boiler. The livery of No. 823 was Cambrian black, rather prominently lined straw and it made a brave sight when unloaded at Welshpool yard on 6th October 1962. After eight years' trojan service, *The Countess* was withdrawn in need of a heavy overhaul. This started in 1978 and gradually fittings and plating throughout were refurbished and renewed where necessary.

The biggest problem lay with the firebox. Funds were raised and in 1985 the boiler was moved to specialist contractors at Warrington to have new crown stays fitted and wasted rivets replaced as well as being retubed. At last, in July 1986, the locomotive returned to service and ran very successfully for over twelve months. Disappointingly, the locomotive then unexpectedly failed with leaking firebox seams. However, the remedial work was successfully undertaken at Llanfair and *The Countess* returned to service in May 1988. The locomotive continued in regular service acquiring a modified 4-nozzle blastpipe, blower ring and ejector in 1994 which enhanced its performance. The next year it was turned out much as it appeared in Great Western days, a livery that was widely welcomed. Then, with funding available for a heavy overhaul,

it was dismantled at the end of the 1999 season and an extensive rebuild began. New tanks, cylinders, bunker and tyres were ordered while all else (including frames) was overhauled. A new boiler was built in Bradford to the same specifications as that for *The Earl*. Re-assembly started in 2001 with the aim of returning *The Countess* to service in good time for its centenary.

Liveries

When turned out new both engines were in the standard Cambrian Railways gloss black livery of the period, lined middle chrome yellow with a fine lining of signal red on each side of the yellow band. After 1910 the broad lining of the W&L locomotives is reputed to have been changed to pale straw (or off-white). Brass nameplates with red painted background were centrally mounted on the tank sides and oval plates carrying the running number and the full light railway title were affixed to the upper cab sidesheets.

The makers' plates were mounted on the side of the smokebox. During the latter part of the 1914-18 war, there was an austerity livery of plain grey according to old employees. Under Great Western ownership both engines soon acquired Swindon green, unlined. The W&L company numberplates were removed and the nameplates transferred to the cab sidesheets. Because of the restricted space available the nameplates of *The Countess* were abbreviated to *Countess* by the simple expedient of hacking out the offending letters and brazing the remainder together again! Full size cast iron Swindon numberplates, including the magic initials GWR, were put at the centre of the sidetanks and 'G W' transfers were applied, one letter each side of the numberplate. The lettering

No. 3 Raven, at Llanfair, In September 1962. In 1961, three days after arrival, Raven ventured to Welshpool and thus became the first true locomotive to be operated by the new regime.

Industrial Railway Society,
Brian Webb collection

No. 4 Upnor Castle *at Llanfair in 1962. Unfortunately, the four-coupled arrangement caused such movement of this 13-ton machine that it proved to have a detrimental effect on the W&L's poor track.*

was in yellow shaded black and vermilion. Buffer plate numbers were in yellow shaded black. In the 1939-45 war both engines became unlined black, but after nationalisation *Countess* reverted to unlined green. The letters 'G W' were erased from both locomotives and a small 'w' appeared over the 823 numberplates to emphasize Western Region ownership. A curious nonsense was the Oswestry (89A) shedplate affixed low down on each smokebox door. Following an alarming increase in the activities of souvenir hunters the nameplates were removed and sent to Swindon for safe keeping in March 1951, but the numberplates were carried until after closure, being sent to Swindon in January 1957.

As received by the Preservation Company from Oswestry, *The Earl* was in grey undercoat but later in 1961 a plain black livery was applied. This lasted until summer 1966 when a change was made to fully lined GWR green. Both Nos. 822 and 823 reverted to their original titles as under Cambrian Railways operation with *The Earl* and *The Countess* nameplates centrally sited on the sidetanks and replicas of the W&L Nos. 1 and 2 plates on the upper cab sidesheets. At times these numbers have also appeared on the buffer beams. From 1995, No. 2 ran as GWR No. 823 *Countess* in unlined green and in 2000 *The Earl* entered service in all over black with full size 822 numberplates.

No. 3 *Raven*

4-wheeled diesel. Builder: Ruston & Hornsby Ltd.
No. 170374/1934. Acquired 1961.

This was a standard 16/20hp cabless locomotive, built in 1934 for the Mid Lincolnshire Ironstone Company at Greetwell, Lincs. It was transferred to Nettleton Top mines, near Claxby, Lincs., in 1935. In 1944, John Lysaght Scunthorpe Works Ltd. took over and eventually donated the locomotive to the Preservation Company. Delivery was made by road to the line on 28th March 1961. One brass nameplate was fitted on each side of the bonnet together with W&L No. 3 plates.

This robust little engine proved invaluable for maintenance work at a critical time in the railway's development. The condition of the track was such that a somewhat modest motive power unit was best for the necessary clearance work to proceed while the steep gradients precluded hand-pushing of loaded wagons. However, after 1964 its use was limited by driving sprocket wear. In December 1966, the wheels and balance weights from Ruston 191680 built in 1938 arrived from Nettleton Top and were transferred to *Raven*. In 1969/70, *Raven* was completely rebuilt incorporating a reconditioned engine from Belton Brickworks, Lincs. Despite renovation, however, this elderly diesel was of limited use in view of its low weight and on 26th October 1974, it was sold to W. Free of Frampton-on-Severn.

No. 4 *Upnor Castle*

4-wheeled diesel. Builder: F. C. Hibberd & Co. Ltd.
No. 3687/1954. Acquired 1962. Sold 1968.

Built to the makers' 'Planet' design, this was delivered to

No. 5
'Nutty'

The Sentinel locomotive Nutty *arrives at Llanfair in 1964 from the Narrow Gauge Railway Museum, Tywyn, complete with spare boilers.*

John Milner

Nutty on test without its bodywork, showing the vertical boiler unit with its off-set chimney, the engine unit, chain drive and horizontal water tank.

John Milner

No. 5 Nutty *is seen here on a permanent way train, circa 1965. When new, sliding doors to the engine compartment gave it a very neat appearance.*

R. Johnson

the Admiralty, Lodge Hill and Upnor Railway, Kent, numbered *Yard No. 44*. The frame was of H-section girders and each axle was chain driven. A Type FD6 Foden engine was fitted developing 126bhp at 2,000rpm but derated to 105bhp at 1,800rpm.

Following the closure of the Upnor line, the W&L were able to purchase the engine which arrived at Welshpool by road on 21st February 1962. The name was then suggested by the Admiralty. The dark green livery, fully lined in white, was not altered while the loco was at Llanfair. No. 4 performed a most valuable function as principal motive power for the maintenance trains from 1962 to 1968, but its short wheelbase led to rough riding.

In 1968, the opportunity arose to obtain the six-coupled diesel formerly on the Upnor line, and to finance the purchase of this locomotive (which became No. 7), *Upnor Castle* was sold to the Festiniog Railway and left Llanfair for Porthmadog on 13th February 1968.

No. 5 *Nutty*

4-wheeled over tank, vertical boiler. Builder: Sentinel Ltd.
No. 7701/1929. Arrived 1964. Relocated 1971.

The London Brick Company Limited had 2ft 11ins gauge lines in the Fletton district of Huntingdonshire, some equipped with geared steam locomotives of special design to work within a six foot loading gauge in the brickworks. The last survivor of these was *Nutty*, built by the Sentinel Waggon Works Limited, at Shrewsbury, and employed at Hicks No. 1 Works alongside the Great Northern main line until 1964. It was then moved to Llanfair by road by arrangement with the Narrow Gauge Railway Museum Trust at Tywyn. *Nutty* has the usual Sentinel features with a vertical water-tube boiler, chain drive and twin cylinders. In this case, the cylinders are mounted horizontally to reduce height clearance with the tank above. During the 1964/5 winter the locomotive was overhauled and regauged to 2ft 6ins at Llanfair. The unlined bright yellow livery was continued. After steam tests on 8th February 1965 it was used primarily as a maintenance train engine, having insufficient braking power for passenger working over the heavier grades, though it was seen on occasional turns to Heniarth in 1965 during the emergency period following the Banwy Bridge collapse.

While *Nutty* proved to be a reliable machine, the very cramped cab was hardly suitable for double manning. The gauge glasses, for instance, are but a few inches from the fireman's face. After 1966 it was used less frequently and on 23rd October, 1971, it was dispatched back to the Narrow Gauge Railway Museum Trust at Tywyn, now in Gwynedd, before moving elsewhere.

No. 6 *Monarch*

0-4-4-0 side tank. Builder: W. G. Bagnall Limited.
No. 3024/1953. Acquired: 1966. Sold 1992.

Built in Stafford, this locomotive was the last narrow gauge steam engine to be built for industrial service in the British Isles. Messrs Bagnall were the established supplier of steam motive power to the extensive 2ft 6ins gauge system of Bowaters Lloyd Pulp and Paper Mills Limited at Sittingbourne, Kent, and this articulated side tank design offered considerable advantage in weight distribution on the line's long viaduct. Several of this design which dated back to 1936, were supplied for service in Natal. No. 3024 cost £10,092 and was delivered on 31th July 1953, painted in the then standard Bowaters livery of medium green lined red, with black frames and brass nameplates *Monarch*, appropriately commemorating the Coronation of Queen Elizabeth II in that year.

Monarch is a modern version of the Meyer type. It has power bogies in the reversed position, that is with the cylinders at the inner end and both bogies are free to swivel. The mainframes are of rolled steel channel. Unconventionally, the superheated boiler has a steel marine (i.e. circular) firebox, no less than 5ft 9ins (1.75m) long! This had the big advantage of giving adequate clearance under the rear bogie for pipework and the like with the added bonus of very cheap construction.

It cannot be said that *Monarch* was a great success at Sittingbourne. However, after renewal of the firebox in 1961, the engine worked well until taken out of service in May 1965, as first stage of economy measures which were ultimately to close the commercial operation of the Bowaters line in 1969.

The W&L was able to purchase the engine with funds donated by a member while the Preservation Company was recovering from the financial setback resulting from the Banwy Bridge collapse. After a repaint it left Kemsley Mill by road on 6th May 1966, arriving at Llanfair two days later. Standard W&L *No. 6* plates were fitted on 21st May 1966.

Monarch ran on trial later that summer but did not see passenger service until August 1973, after a major overhaul which included retubing, new wheels and the fitting of a stovepipe chimney to replace the original large spark arrester type.

Various problems made it necessary to undertake further modifications to improve its steaming performance. *Monarch* worked again in 1976 and spasmodically until autumn 1978 when it failed with a recurrence of weeping tubes and defective superheater flues. It had then covered less than 5,000 miles in service on the W&L. Repair work began yet again including the installation of vacuum brake equipment but in due course it was decided that resources could not be spared for this problematic locomotive and that it was not suitable for the

0-4-4-0T No. 6 Monarch *with its original spark arrester chimney soon after arrival at Llanfair.*

W&L's steep and undulating gradients. On 24th February 1992, No. 6 *Monarch* departed for Porthmadog under new ownership.

No. 7 *Chattenden*

0-6-0 diesel. Builder: E. E. Baguley Limited, Burton on Trent. No. 2263/1949. Acquired: 1968.

Supplied by the Drewry Car Company Limited of London, this locomotive was delivered new to the Admiralty, Lodge Hill and Upnor Railway, Kent in November 1949, and was originally titled *Yard No. 107*. There were later number changes.

In contrast to the Planet locomotive (W&L No. 4), it has plate frames, six wheels with outside coupling rods and jackshaft drive to the rear pair of wheels. Drive is transmitted via a fluid coupling to a 4-speed epicyclic gearbox with self-changing gears, final drive to the jackshaft being through a David Brown spiral bevel. Flameproof equipment on delivery included 12v lighting and an exhaust gas scrubber.

When the Upnor line closed the locomotive was moved to Ernsettle Depot, near the Saltash Bridge, Devon, and in 1965 was transferred to Broughton Moor Depot, Cumberland. At neither site did it do much work, the wheelbase being too long for the sharp curves in the depots. When the engine was declared surplus in 1968 it was purchased by the W&L, arriving at Llanfair by road from Broughton Moor on 13th February. The nameplates *Chattenden* fitted in May 1968 recall the earlier title of the Upnor line, the Chattenden and Upnor Railway. In 1980, a Gardner 6LXB Guy lorry engine was fitted derated to 150bhp, with a maximum governed speed of 15mph. Vacuum gear for working passenger and ballast trains was installed. Other work included alterations to the cab, providing rear access with steps from each side. The original side doorways were plated up.

As the years passed, the locomotive received new tyres, had the gearbox rebuilt (twice) and was fitted with a freewheel. By 1996, a new engine block and pistons were needed. *Chattenden* continues to be a most useful and reliable machine, capable of taking in emergency a five coach passenger train and yet having well designed controls for shunting work.

Baguley-Drewry diesel No. 7 Chattenden *after alterations to the cab had provided a rear entrance.*

W&LLR Pres Co.

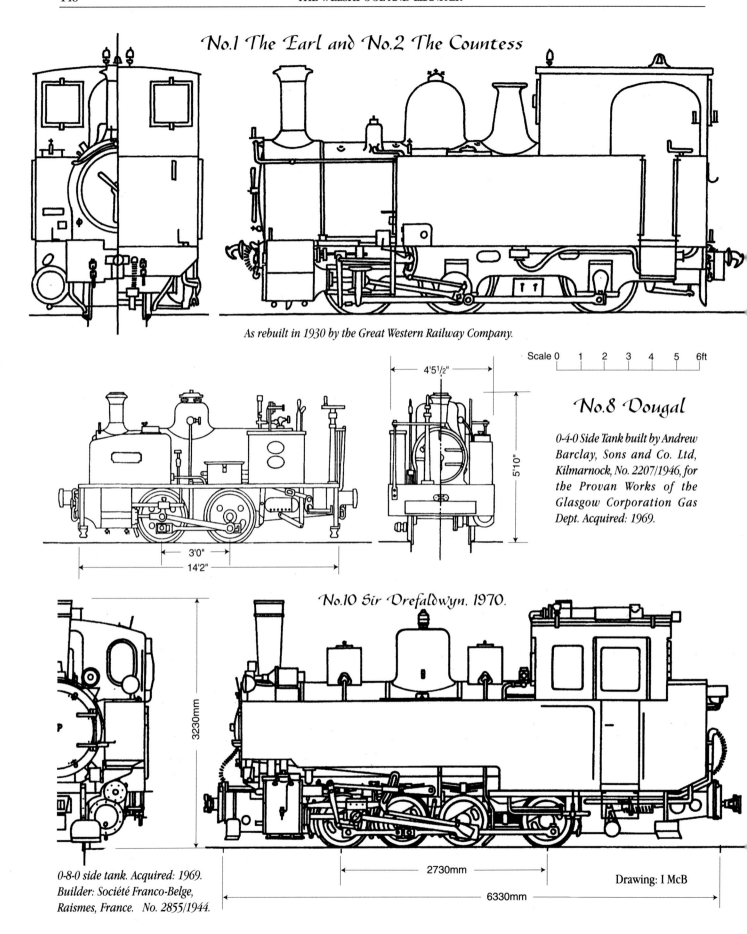

No.1 The Earl and No.2 The Countess

As rebuilt in 1930 by the Great Western Railway Company.

Scale 0 1 2 3 4 5 6ft

4'5½"

5'10"

3'0"

14'2"

No.8 Dougal

0-4-0 Side Tank built by Andrew Barclay, Sons and Co. Ltd, Kilmarnock, No. 2207/1946, for the Provan Works of the Glasgow Corporation Gas Dept. Acquired: 1969.

No.10 Sir Drefaldwyn, 1970.

3230mm

2730mm

6330mm

0-8-0 side tank. Acquired: 1969. Builder: Société Franco-Belge, Raismes, France.   No. 2855/1944.

Drawing: I McB

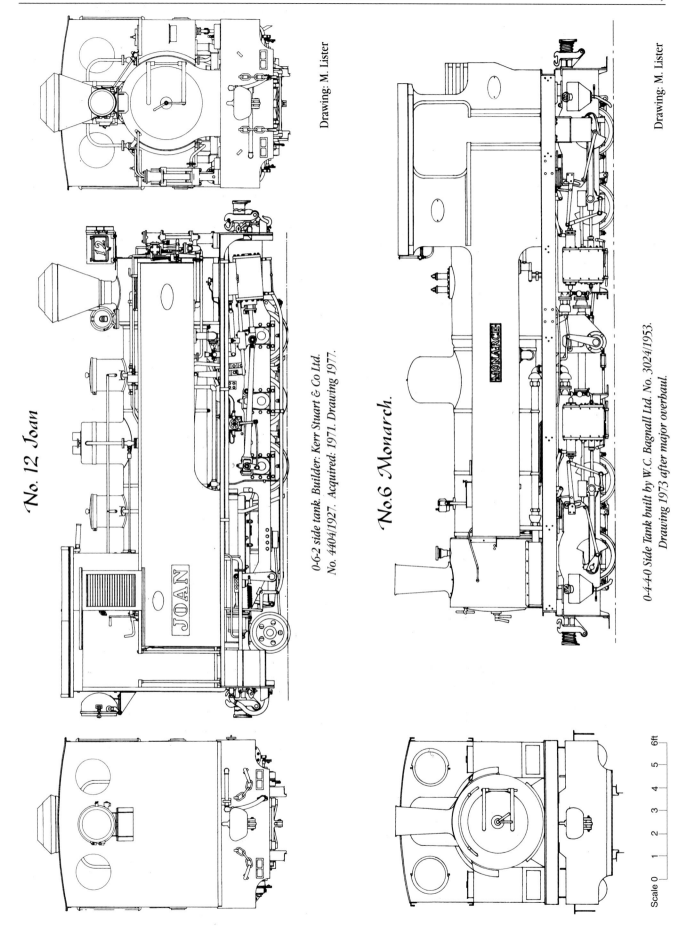

No. 12 Joan

0-6-2 side tank. Builder: Kerr Stuart & Co Ltd.
No. 4404/1927. Acquired: 1971. Drawing 1977.

Drawing: M. Lister

No.6 Monarch.

0-4-0 Side Tank built by W.C. Bagnall Ltd. No. 3024/1953.
Drawing 1973 after major overhaul.

Drawing: M. Lister

Scale 0 1 2 3 4 5 6ft

No. 8 Dougal *restored for service in plain maroon livery in 1976.*

No. 8 *Dougal*

0-4-0 side tank. Builder: Andrew Barclay, Sons and Co. Ltd, Kilmarnock, No. 2207/1946. Acquired: 1969.

This locomotive was delivered new to the Provan Works of Glasgow Corporation Gas Department. The design dates back to 1903 when six engines of the type were supplied to the newly opened Provan Works. The use of miniscule steam locomotives has distinguished many Scottish city gasworks, but only the relatively modern Provan site used the 2ft 6ins gauge. The squat appearance was due to the very limited confines of the gasworks retort house. Barclay No. 2207 was operated for most of its working life at Provan with its brake gear completely removed!

The Provan system closed on 25th May 1958. Barclay No. 2207 was rescued for preservation by the Railway Enthusiasts' Club at Farnborough, Hants, leaving Glasgow by rail on 23rd March 1962 and later it was sold to two W&L members in a partly dismantled condition for eventual service at Llanfair. On 18th November 1967 it left Farnborough for Oldbury, Worcs., for overhaul, where it remained until moved by road on 8th November 1969 to Llanfair where it was fully restored. Necessary alterations to enable the engine to work on the W&L included larger water tanks, increasing capacity from forty to eighty gallons, and fitting new handbrake gear to the original

design. No. 8 was first steamed at Llanfair on 19th December 1975 and occasionally worked in Llanfair yard or on demonstration freight trains.

Then, in 1983, it was stopped in need of work on the boiler which was sent away first to one contractor and then another. After four years, it returned with the firebox crown stays replaced, the tubeplate built up and some of the tubes replaced and was quickly restored to working order. However, in 1992, the tubeplate was found to be defective again together with the boiler barrel and No. 8 was withdrawn from service. It seemed likely to remain in store as no funds could be allocated for repairs. Very fortunately, however, a benefactor appeared willing to underwrite the cost and in 1996, the boiler was lifted and sent to boilersmiths in Sheffield for repairs and replacement of the barrel. The motion and valve gear were overhauled and a vacuum ejector was fitted for working passenger stock. When *Dougal* returned to service in March 1997, it appeared in the livery of Glasgow Corporation Gasworks Department. It seemed to gain a new lease of life, causing some merriment by occasionally working two-coach passenger trains. It also proved useful for Driver Experience Courses.

When turned out new, Barclay No. 2207 was painted standard Barclay olive green, with painted title *Provan Works No. 1* and the full Glasgow coat of arms surmounted by the letters G.C.G.D., all on the little coal bunkers. From 1969 to

0-6-0 diesel No. 9 Wynnstay, circa 1970. Originally destined for East Africa, it was discovered by the W&L in South Wales. On arrival at Llanfair in 1971, an overhaul extending over eighteen months included the fitting of reprofiled wheels and reconditioned axleboxes. But it eventually proved unsuitable for the line.

1996, maroon livery was applied. Standard W&L *No. 8* plates and *Dougal* nameplates are now fitted. The name has no profound significance - just a doggy cartoon character with a similar low chassis to the Barclay.

No. 9 *Wynnstay*

0-6-0 diesel. Builder: John Fowler & Company (Leeds) Ltd. No. 4160005/1951. Acquired: 1969. Sold 1972.

This machine briefly provided a link between the W&L and the exotic railways of East Africa. Not only was it structurally almost identical to the East African Railways 8000 class, apart from gauge, but No. 9 itself was built for the ill-fated Groundnuts Scheme. After the collapse of the groundnuts project it remained on the builder's hands until sold about 1954, with two similar locomotives, to the British Portland Cement Manufacturers Limited at Lower Penarth Works, Glamorgan, becoming their No. 5. The 2ft 6ins gauge system here was abandoned in 1968, and in 1969 the W&L purchased No. 5, the most complete survivor, with many spares, including the engine unit and a set of wheels of No. 3 (Fowler 4160006). The locomotive was moved by road via Brecon and Newtown on 9th August 1969. Livery became Iona green (BS6/074), darker than at Penarth, with yellow lining. W&L No. 9 was named *Wynnstay* in 1971 after a popular Llanfair hostelry.

W&L No. 9 had a McLaren type M4 four-cylinder engine developing 100bhp at 1100rpm. A heavy-duty dry plate clutch transmitted the drive to an integral 4-speed and directional gearbox. The jackshaft drove the middle pair of wheels by a lengthy connecting rod. Unfortunately, the rather inflexible engine, manual clutch and gearbox made the locomotive unsuitable for passenger operation over the severe grades. On 18th March 1972, it moved to the railway at Whipsnade Zoo.

No. 10. *Sir Drefaldwyn* (ex-StMLB No. 699.01)

0-8-0 side tank. Builder: Société Franco-Belge, Raismes, France. No. 2855/1944. Acquired: 1969.

Though of modern construction, few British locomotives of any age have such an interesting history as this continental machine. As supplied to the German Military Railways in March 1944, it was an 0-8-0 tender locomotive with short auxiliary side tanks, Feldbahn type KDL 11. Many of these locomotives were built for use on the war fronts, particularly the Eastern Front. The original design was German, and the drawings surviving for this locomotive are by Berliner Maschinenbau A.G. at their Kleinbahn Works, Berlin.

It appears that it was at the Feldbahn stores depot at Mittersill, near Zell-am-See, Austria, when this fell into the hands of the American Occupation Forces at the end of hostilities. On 6th January 1946 it was loaned to the Salkzkammergut Lokalbahn, near Salzburg. Built to German standard 750mm gauge, trouble soon ensued on pointwork and adjustment to correct 760mm gauge was carried out. The SKGLB purchased the engine as from 1st April 1950, working it on the picturesque Salzburg-Bad Ischl line as No. 19 until July 1955 when it was sold to the Steiermärkische Landesbahnen (Styrian Provincial Railways) near Graz, Austria,

No. 10 Sir Drefaldwyn *in 1971, sporting the county coat of arms.*

for use on the 42km line from Weiz to Ratten.

It was rebuilt in 1957 with full-length side tanks and a coal bunker to replace the tender, the result being an increase in adhesive weight from 22 to 27 tons in working order. The bunker is built on an extension of the frames with the original buffer beam left in position. The engine was numbered 699.01, probably because its original tender form was identical to the Austrian State Railways 699 class, resulting in two locomotives numbered 699.01 in Austria. In 1961, the original steel firebox was replaced by copper and 699.01 worked regularly from 1962 to late 1965, when steam working on all the Steiermark lines was much reduced.

In general design this engine gives an insight into modern continental narrow gauge practice. The boiler has the quite high working pressure of 200lbs/sq in, and is fitted with a 3-row 16-element superheater supplying steam through piston valves to cylinders of 'oversquare' proportions. Perhaps the chassis is the most novel feature to British observers. The four axles are arranged to give a total wheelbase of only 8ft 10^{1}/$_{2}$ ins (2.73m) compared with 10ft 0ins (3.04m) for the *three* axles of *The Earl*. In addition the front axle had an arrangement to allow lateral movement on curves and the third pair of wheels is flangeless, the net result being a very compact unit capable of negotiating sharp curves with ease.

The nominal tractive effort (at 85 per cent working pressure) is 13,535lb, which makes it one of the most powerful engines of its size to work in Britain. Steam, vacuum and handbrakes are fitted, the vacuum equipment operating on the train only, not on the locomotive wheels. A steam turbogenerator is mounted alongside the chimney, powering twin headlamps at front and rear and maintenance lights beneath the side-tanks.

No. 699.01 left Weiz depot on 4th December 1969 and arrived at Llanfair on 11th December. The cost of the project was £1,200, entirely met by members' donations. Following a trial run on 1st May 1970, the new acquisition made its debut on special trains for members on Saturday 2nd May 1970, the first occasion in the Railway's 67 year history that *The Earl* and *The Countess* had been supplanted by another steam locomotive on the Llanfair line.

Since coming to Wales, the Steiermark livery has been adopted, i.e. black, lined red. As the result of a ballot of members, the company chose the name *Sir Drefaldwyn* (Welsh: Montgomeryshire) and the official naming ceremony was held on 5th September 1971. A cast of the Montgomeryshire crest is mounted above the nameplate. No. 10 went into regular service very soon after arrival, proving a very economical machine which steams well on slack coal - a fuel which Nos. 1 and 2 are very loath to digest. The heaviest trains, and the fierce grades on Golfa bank, were tackled in spirited style.

By 1985, a heavy overhaul was needed. It took five years for volunteers to complete a thorough refurbishment of the locomotive during which an intriguing discovery emerged. Cardboard shims were found in the axleboxes giving rise to theories about wartime sabotage! The overhaul also included work on the front tubeplate by hired boilersmiths. The opportunity was taken of slightly reducing the backplate of the bunker (an aesthetic improvement) and to fit steam heating equipment. *Sir Drefaldwyn* returned to traffic in 1990.

A decade of service followed during which a modified blastpipe with a four-nozzle top was fitted to improve an already fine performance. In May 2000, with its boiler certificate expired, *Sir Drefaldwyn* was stopped to await its next heavy overhaul.

No. 11 *Ferret*

0-4-0 diesel. Builder: Hunslet Engine Co. Ltd., Leeds. No. 2251/1940. Acquired: 1971.

This was one of the earliest flameproof mines diesels built by the Hunslet company. Arguably, its ancestry lies in the range of small diesel locomotives taken over by the company in 1930 following the collapse of the Kerr, Stuart concern. The dry, multi-plate clutch, constant mesh gearbox activated by compressed air and jackshaft drive were characteristic Hunslet developments. Its four wheels have outside coupling rods and jackshaft drive to the leading pair of wheels. With an overall height of only 5ft, a deep well in the cab provides accommodation for the crew.

In 1939, Hunslet supplied the first certificated flame-proof machine to work in a coal mine and also supplied one of this

Ex-Admiralty mines diesel No. 11 Ferret *soon after arrival. With the cab doors removed, one of the two cylindrical air cylinders can be seen inside.*

type, a 2ft 6ins gauge machine, for service at a Royal Naval Armaments Depot. The 'Manrider' (or Mines type) was offered as a 50hp machine using a Gardner 4L2 four-cylinder engine from the beginning of 1940. With the war effort in full swing, many of these, all 2ft 6ins gauge, were ordered by the Director of Naval Contracts. A batch of seven ordered in 1940 and dispatched at intervals during the following year to RNAD West Dean in Wiltshire included, on 9th July 1941, HE 2251, designated *Yard No 86* which was to become W&L No.11. With delivery apparently behind schedule, the makers' plates made earlier, were now misleading.

To fit it for underground work, it had an exhaust conditioner with a water chamber to clean the exhaust gas. Brakes, gear changing and whistle are operated by compressed air. The 4-speed gearbox provides an ultra low ratio bottom gear. It was designed to start and haul in first gear a load of 76 tons on a 1 in 50 gradient, or 286 tons on the level and to negotiate curves as sharp as 30 feet (9 metres) radius. Such capabilities made *Ferret* a valuable acquisition for a line like the W&L.

By about 1965, HE 2251 was no longer needed by the Admiralty and was sold, reaching the W&L on 11th July 1971. On arrival, the paintwork of No. 11 was a shade of bright green though this was quickly replaced with an overall olive green livery. *Ferret* was then given a smart crimson lake livery and for a few years the cab was attractively lined out in yellow. As the locomotive now spent its working life in the open air, an early modification was the removal of the exhaust water scrubber and the fitting instead of an expansion chamber for the exhaust. While *Chattenden* handled heavy ballast trains, No. 11 *Ferret* provided useful motive power for many lighter permanent way works trains and for shunting at Llanfair. During its first five years on the line, the locomotive even had a period of glory involving limited working of passenger trains, serving at Sylfaen as the shunting engine assisting with the turn-round of trains when there was a siding but no loop.

Although the doors to the cab removed earlier had recently been refitted, it was ironical that, in 1978, vandals were able to let it run away near Welshpool with disastrous results. Serious damage was sustained, notably to the engine mountings. It transpired that spares for this design of the Gardner engine were no longer being made so a search began for a new engine. Luckily, the National Coal Board was able to help, offering two Gardner 4L2 engines, recently overhauled, one in Scotland and one in Yorkshire.

Building and fitting a replacement engine with parts from both together with other jobs went on for over a year. Various modifications were incorporated including fitting additional covers and locks to protect accessories from tampering. It was also decided to move the two cylindrical air reservoirs to the outside of the backsheet of the cab to improve conditions

inside for the driver. Grondana (ex-SLR) screw-link couplings were fitted and by January 1979, the work was completed, including repainting.

Ferret then served successfully on engineering trains except for a period in 1985 when problems were experienced with the gear changing. Around this time, the locomotive's funnel-shaped chimney was exchanged for a straight exhaust while its green livery was restored, enhanced by red buffer beams, wheels and motion. Service on permanent way trains continued until 1994 when No. 16 *Scooby* came into service and *Ferret* was able to 'retire'. In 1996, it was repainted in crimson lake livery and was put into store.

Ferret survives as an early representative of a pioneering class of underground motive power which proved invaluable in war service and whose longevity is a tribute to the practicality of the design and to those W&L members whose efforts have overcome the problems of wear and misfortune.

No. 12 *Joan*

0-6-2 side tank. Builder: Kerr Stuart & Co. Ltd.
No. 4404/1927. Acquired: 1971.

With its large balloon style chimney, this is a very good example of the colonial estate machine, once a major feature of the British locomotive industry. *Joan* was exported from the maker's California Works in Stoke-on-Trent on 24th September 1927 to the Antigua Sugar Co., British West Indies, where it became No. 7. The engine worked in Antigua until 1956 after which it was rarely used due to dieselisation of the system. In 1971, it was purchased by the W&L from the Antiguan Government Estates and Development Board and shipped via Georgetown, Guyana, to Liverpool, completing its journey of over 4,000 miles to Llanfair on 27th November.

Kerr Stuart No. 4404 was the maker's standard Matary class chassis, modified to take a larger than standard Huxley class boiler, presumably to give more steam for the heavily graded 'main lines' of the sugar system in Antigua. As built, the working pressure was 160lb/sq in giving a tractive effort of 7,555lb at 85%. The original water tanks carried 420 gallons. Over the years, the large firebox has been used to burn a variety of fuels. At first oil was used but during the 1939-45 war a shortage of oil led to the use of coal or sugar cane waste (bagasse). In 1949-51, the engine was extensively renewed above footplate level, with a new boiler now working at 170lb/sq in, steel firebox, full length side tanks, all from the Hunslet Engine Co., Leeds. The engine returned to service in 1951 for only a few years before being put in store.

After arrival in Wales, No. 12, as it was to become, was stripped down for a detailed examination and minor modification to suit operation on the W&L. Originally, two

The Matary (or Barretto) design produced by Kerr, Stuart & Co.; Joan was a modified version.

Courtesy: Hunslet Holdings Ltd.

0-6-2T No.12 Joan *at Llanfair, 1987, The name was bestowed in Antigua in honour of the wife of the General Manager of the sugar mill.*

Sierra Leone Government Railways No. 84 at the makers in 1954. Nos. 84 and 85 were identical.

Courtesy Hunslet Holdings Ltd.

Mumford vertical steam feedpumps had been fitted on each side of the front footplating. However, by 1971 the left hand pump had been replaced by a large horizontal pump on top of the sidetank. This pump was removed in favour of a standard injector, and in 1983, the right hand pump was similarly replaced. Ross Pop safety valves were fitted at this time. Other work carried out included retubing, conversion of the left hand oil bunker for coal, fitting of vacuum brake equipment, removal of various buffer beam girder appendages used in Antigua to carry tools (and personnel!), fitting of Grondana couplings, adding safety chains and an extensive rebuild of the cab with a closed back. A steam turbogenerator was fitted in Antigua to

power typical American Baldwin searchlights but the closed back of the new cab necessitated a change to a Sierra Leone Railway searchlight at the rear.

The engine entered service on 10th April 1977 painted unlined Midland Red. The large nameplate *Joan* was retained. For the next decade, *Joan* was a regular performer even showing how it could run on old wood during a coal shortage. A brand new outside framed pony truck was fitted as recently as 1990 and modification to the detail design of the Stephenson valve gear considerably improved its ability to run well notched up in both directions of travel. Appearing in a new blue livery in 1989, No. 12 *Joan* proved popular with children but by

W&L No. 14 (formerly SLGR No 85) in 1979.

then it was spending periods out of service for repairs to cracks which were appearing in the firebox. Eventually, at the end of the 1991 season, having run almost 24,000 miles in service on the line, *Joan* was withdrawn from service to await the time when it will be possible to undertake boiler repairs including replacement of the firebox.

No. 14 Sierra Leone Railway No. 85

2-6-2 side tank. Builder: Hunslet Engine Co., Leeds.
No. 3815/1954. Acquired: 1975.

This was the last of 32 similar engines built by the Hunslet Engine Co. for the Sierra Leone Railway between 1898 and 1954. These engines were developed for quite long journeys (the SLR main line was over 200 miles long), and in later years they banked trains from the Water Street terminus through the main streets of Freetown.

The last order for two of the class was placed in May 1952 by the Crown Agents for the Colonies. These became SLGR 84 and 85 and cost £21,273 for the two. They were sent whole from Leeds on 8th October 1954 to Liverpool for shipment to Freetown. They had outside frames, Walschaerts valve gear, a flush roundtop firebox, Ross pop safety valves and 5mm Gresham & Craven combination injectors mounted on the firebox backplate. Steam and handbrakes applied to the engine

with a vacuum ejector to operate the train brakes. Sandboxes fitted between the tanks and the boiler (like *The Earl* and *The Countess*) and, uniquely to these two locomotives, Timken roller bearings were fitted to the pony trucks. By 1975, No. 85 had lost the rear roller bearing pony truck in a swap of trucks.

The locomotive arrived at Llanfair via Liverpool on 7th August 1975 having been shipped with the four coaches acquired by the W&L. Not surprisingly, considering the complete abandonment of the SLR, the machine was in a rather rundown condition and a thorough overhaul was necessary. After complete dismantling, it was evident that much replating was required including rear pony truck support plates, damaged in some long forgotten mishap. The extra coal-boxes fitted forward on top of the sidetanks were removed, greatly to the benefit of the engine's appearance. After reassembly, a mid-green livery was used, being a former livery of the SLR and a *No. 14* plate affixed. The oval *SLR 85 1954* plate was retained on the tank sides. The engine therefore then appeared much as a 2-6-2 tank working in Sierra Leone before the 1939-45 war.

No. 14 entered regular service at Easter 1979 and has proved to be a reliable performer. By 1991, the locomotive needed a heavy overhaul and in 1991 its boiler was sent away to a contractor for an extensive (and very expensive) rebuild including the fitting of a new firebox. It returned to service in a double lined crimson lake livery. Another boiler lift became

2-6-2T Orion, ex-Jokioisten Railway No. 5, at Llanfair in 2000. The name Orion was chosen for this locomotive by a ballot of members although nameplates were not provided during its first season in service.

necessary at the end of the 1999 season for renewal of firebox stays. The locomotive continues to be popular with the volunteer crews, giving a smooth ride and with free steaming characteristics and economy of fuel. It has proved to be a favourite for *driver experience* days. Certainly it is a testimony to a long-lived design.

(No. 15) *Orion* - Ex-Jokioistenrautatie No. 5

2-6-2 side tank. Builder: Atelliers Metallurgiques (Tubize Div.). No. 2369/1948. Acquired: 1983.

The original home of this locomotive was the 750mm gauge Jokioisten Railway (Jokioistenrautatie) in southern Finland. This 14 mile line, opened in 1898, ran through gently rolling farmland to the industrial town of Forssa. At the end of World War II, a shortage of motive power was highlighted when the JR lost a 2-6-2 Henschel tank locomotive to the USSR as part of Finland's reparations. There were only two established locomotive builders in Finland and they were occupied in building 0-8-0T forestry engines for the Russians as reparations. So the hunt was on for replacements with post war European locomotive builders facing full order books. One builder approached was the Tubize division of the Société Anonyme Les Ateliers Metallurgiques at Nivelles in Belgium. The Tubize concern had built up a considerable export trade in locomotives, staple products being large 2-6-2 tanks and 4-8-0 tender locomotives with full length tanks using standard patterns where possible.

Here, in 1947, the JR found some capacity and a 2-6-2 tank, No. 2365, possibly partially erected. It is believed it was an unfulfilled order for a 3ft gauge line in Java in the Dutch East Indies. However, civil war in the region was preventing resumption of normal commercial activities. It was therefore agreed that Tubize would supply No. 2365 to the Jokioisten Railway. It was completed to 750mm gauge in autumn 1947 and in the following year, twin No. 2369 was also supplied. They became JR Nos. 4 and 5 and were put to work on heavy trains of transporter wagons, timber and passenger traffic on the JR's undulating line.

The closure of the JR to passengers in 1954 saw No. 5 confined to freight duties and then, after a working life of only fifteen years, it was withdrawn with the firebox needing major repairs, never to run again in Finland. The end almost came in 1972 when closure of the line was imminent and No. 5 was offered for sale for scrap. However, by a stroke of luck, English enthusiast Malcolm Knight had spotted it the previous year, discarded down the line in an old wooden shed. Now, Malcolm promptly telegraphed a ridiculously low bid for it.

Being unexpectedly successful, he then faced the daunting task of collecting his prize, which he had not even inspected!

Malcolm tells how he hastened to make an examination which was carried out in the old shed by dint of peering into the smokebox, through the cab windows and by lying on his back in the long grass. Deciding that it really was worth saving, movement (at considerable cost) was arranged. The journey to the ferry was beset with minor crises but eventually the locomotive was landed at Harwich on 5th September 1972. There followed a decade when it languished in store in East Anglia. Then, in 1983, it was purchased by the W&L and delivered by road to Llanfair on 28th September.

Although this move ensured the continued preservation of an impressive example of continental locomotive building, for many years full restoration and operation remained a low priority task. Work was limited to external renovation, mainly involving painting in an attractive livery of mid-green, lined in red. It was referred to as No. 15 but did not carry this number.

After many years on display at Llanfair station, dismantling started in 1993, ready for a major overhaul. While the frames were cleaned and repainted and the axleboxes refurbished, the wheels were sent away for re-tyring and adjusting to 2ft 6ins gauge.

Work on the cylinders, fitting of a Hardy vacuum ejector and provision of a new smokebox and chimney followed. A quaint touch was the making of the chimney cap from the wheelsets of the old Austin trolley. The mechanical lubricator which was inside the cab to keep the oil from excessive thickening in Finnish winters, was repositioned to the motion plate and the drive taken from the expansion link, a much more accessible arrangement for W&L conditions. The boiler was sent to a contractor in Bradford for a new firebox and some remedial work on the barrel. The work made possible a working pressure higher than that originally permitted. The safety valves were relocated on top of the dome and the water gauge frame lengthened for reliable negotiation of the line's severe gradient changes.

Following re-assembly and running-in trials, the locomotive entered service at last in June 2000. Turned out in unlined green livery, the numberplates proudly carried were the originals from the Jokioisten Railway. The particularly large driving wheels are powered by cylinders of massive proportions for the narrow gauge ($12^1/2$ in x $17^3/4$ins). With 527sq ft of heating surface enhanced by 161sq ft of superheating elements, it boasts boiler power superior to that of any other locomotive on the W&L.

No. 16 *Scooby/Scwbi*

0-4-0 diesel. Builder: Hunslet Engine Co Ltd., Leeds. No. 2400/1941. Acquired: 1992.

Scooby (Welsh: Scwbi) is another Hunslet 50hp mines type

No. 14 Sierra Leone Railway No. 85

2-6-2 side tank. Builder: Hunslet Engine Co., Leeds.
No. 3815/1954. Acquired: 1975.

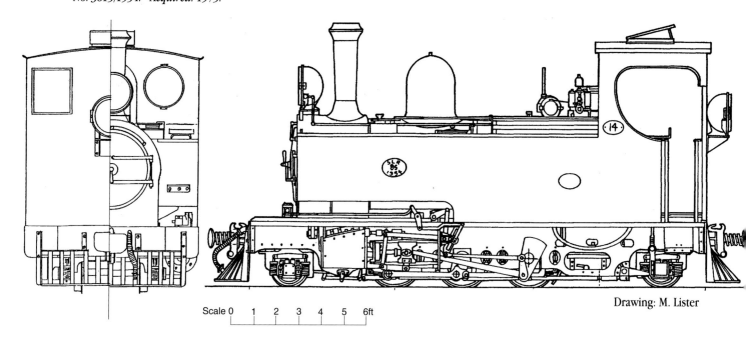

Scale 0 1 2 3 4 5 6ft

Drawing: M. Lister

(No. 15) Orion. – Ex-Jokioistenrautatie No. 5

2-6-2 side tank. Builder: Atelliers Metallurgiques (Tubize
Div.). No. 2369/1948. Acquired: 1983.

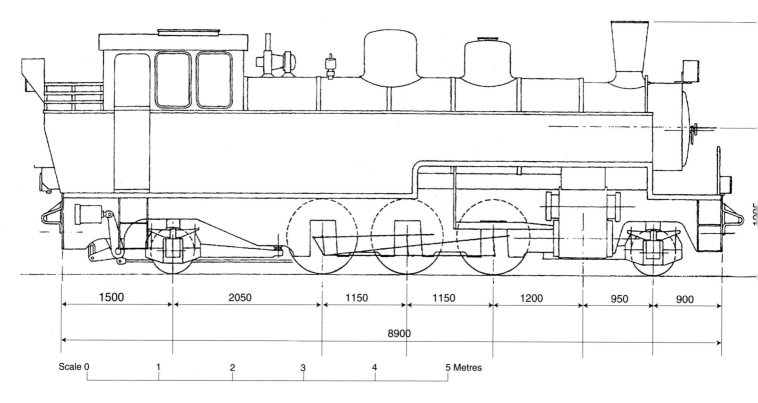

| 1500 | 2050 | 1150 | 1150 | 1200 | 950 | 900 |

8900

Scale 0   1   2   3   4   5 Metres

Above: *Loco line-up at Llanfair station. On the left, No. 14 (SLR 85) has arrived with the service train. On the loop, No. 2* The Countess *is marshalling coaching stock while to the right, ex-JR No. 5* Orion *is on display.*

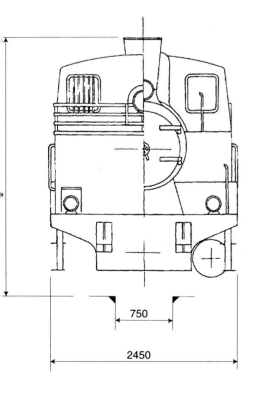

No. 16 Scooby/Scwbi, *rebuilt from a Hunslet mines diesel. On arrival it was identical with No. 11* Ferret *but underwent a transformation in the workshops at Llanfair.*

750

2450

diesel though no longer recognisable as such. It was built for the Director of Navy Contracts and dispatched to the Royal Naval Armaments Department, Trecwn, in Pembrokeshire, as *Yard No. B21* on 11th May 1942 (the previous year appearing on the builder's plate).

These 8½ ton 50hp flameproof machines, fitted with Gardner 4L2 four cylinder engines, served the depot well during World War II and after; at least fourteen were supplied and were the mainstay of the fleet at Trecwn for many years, eventually being supplanted by more modern types.

In 1984, HE 2400 was overhauled and repainted but in the same year it was moved to the Ministry of Defence NATO Ammunition Depot at Broughton Moor in Cumbria (gaining a *ND3062* numberplate). Its lease of life here was cut short, however, with the announcement of the closure of the depot and bids were invited for much of the railway equipment.

The locomotive (a 'peace dividend') was delivered to Llanfair on 17th June 1992. It was in mostly sound condition (the wheelsets excepted), but being intended for underground work, the design had certain disadvantages for the W&L. In achieving a low overall height of 5ft (1.52m), the location of the (rather cramped) cab limited the driver's view and necessitated the use of compressed air to actuate the 4-speed gearbox.

Modifications were therefore undertaken at Llanfair which involved moving the radiator and building a new full height cab above the frames over the jackshaft drive. Direct mechanical levers are now utilised for gear changing with a foot-operated clutch. The conversion made use of surplus materials already in stock (including two mines type cabs) and the locomotive was turned out in November 1993, sporting plates with its new name in English and Welsh. The livery was mid-blue changed to unlined mid-green in 1998. Having 'come home' to Wales, No. 16 *Scooby*, in converted guise, has proved to be a considerable asset for permanent way trains.

The Wickham Trolley (GWR No. PWM 1906)

On 3rd December 1940 Messrs D. Wickham & Co. Ltd, of Ware, Hants, supplied a new four-wheeled inspection trolley to the line. A small shed in Welshpool yard, off the main line, was used to house the machine. The trolley was Wickham No. 2904, type 8S, and seated four persons on back to back seats. These seats folded down to facilitate loading on to the train

No.14 (SLR 85) is completing a heavy overhaul in the workshops at Llanfair. Remarkably ambitious overhauls have been undertaken by volunteers with components sent away for specialist attention by contractors as necessary.

should this be necessary. It was used by the gang responsible for spot sleepering, mending fences and cutting the grass and hedges. The trolley became BR No. 109W and survived to be taken over by the Preservation Society and was subsequently transferred to the Preservation Company.

A 350cc blower-cooled J.A.P. engine was fitted, power being transmitted through a cone type clutch. As built, its length overall was 5ft 3ins (1.62m), its width overall was 3ft 7ins (1.1m) and it had 1ft 6ins (462mm) diameter wheels.

When acquired in 1959 the J.A.P. engine then fitted was worn out but a suitable 350 cc J.A.P. engine was found and fitted. In 1967-8 and again in 1984-90, the trolley was completely rebuilt without major structural alterations and is now used occasionally for demonstration purposes. The two motor trolleys were allocated numbers in the wagon series, the Wickham being No. 12 while No. 13 was a hand trolley. It is however doubtful if these numbers were actually carried, certainly the Wickham bore only its small *PWM 1906* plate by 1964.

The Austin Trolley (No. 14)

In an attempt to provide much needed motive power, a four-wheeled trolley was constructed by members of the Company in 1959. The basis of this vehicle was a derelict hand pump trolley in Welshpool yard. From the appearance of the axles this had originally been a standard gauge vehicle probably adapted for use on the W&L in 1931 by the GWR. A frame was constructed of steel angle and a 10hp Austin engine mounted

to drive the wheels through the chain drive of the pump trolley. It was soon evident that the chain drive was inadequate and alterations were made by Hudson Engineering Co. Ltd., of Welshpool, the trolley being returned complete on 11th March 1961. Two gearboxes were fitted, each with four speeds and reverse, but one box could only be operated by prior removal of the driver's seat! At first this vehicle was a definite asset though the complete absence of springs gave a very sporty ride, particularly as the speedy nature of the trolley was completely at variance with the sharp curves on the line. On two occasions the leading axle fractured, the second time being in early 1962 when the trolley was in full flight down Golfa Bank and its unfortunate crew were projected into the nearby ditch. After this wiser councils prevailed and the trolley was never used again, being cut up at Heniarth in September 1966.

The Ballast Tamper

The acquisition of this piece of modern plant was something the early preservationists could not even dream of! Built by Plasserail (Plasser Railway Machinery, South Africa Pty. Ltd.) circa 1986 for contract hire, the machine had been sent to a gold mine near Johannesburg but was returned to the makers after only a few hours work and then put into store. It arrived at Llanfair on 10th November 1999, the purchase having been made possible by a generous bequest. Powered by an air-cooled Deutz engine, Plasser *UGM No. 9* is designed for single sleeper ballast packing and also has a laser sighting system for aligning and levelling the track.

Note: Unlike the arrangements on some other preservation schemes, all the locomotives described above and the rolling stock now on the line are the property of the W&L Preservation Company Limited.

Above: *The Wickham trolley after restoration in 1990. The trolley is capable of a remarkable turn of speed and its soft springing gives a tendency to heel over on sharp curves—this is not transport for the fainthearted!*

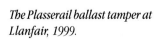

The Plasserail ballast tamper at Llanfair, 1999.

Left: *The boiler of the Sierra Leone prairie tank was sent away for rebuilding in 1991. Rivets are being removed from the smokebox which was separated prior to dispatch.*

David Mark

Parry mini-tram No. 7 on demonstration at Raven Square during the Gala in 1994. It was powered by a horizontal underfloor flywheel, accelerated by an electric motor picking up current at the end of the siding. A larger version of the tram later ran trials on the Llanfair-Heniarth section.

David Moseley

Track maintenance continuing near Sylfaen in March 1956. Afterwards, the Wickham trolley would have provided a lively experience on the return to Welshpool down Golfa Bank.

Hugh Ballantyne

Outside the workshops at Llanfair, the reassembling of No. 8 Dougal is continiuing after a heavy overhaul including boiler work by a contractor.

No. 10 Sir Drefaldwyn *waits at Raven Square station. The crew must be prepared for the 1 in 35 bank as soon as the train departs.*

On the scenic switchback section between Cyfronydd and Heniarth, the articulated Bagnall No. 6 Monarch *proceeds with care as it heads for Llanfair. The locomotive was in service on the line for only five years, and then rather spasmodically.*

Chapter 10

The Passenger Stock

Three coaches were ordered from R. Y. Pickering & Co. Ltd., Wishaw, Lanarkshire in October 1901 and arrived several months before the opening of the line. They were the only passenger stock operated on the W&L for the period of public passenger services 1903-1931.

W&L No.	GWR No.	Type	Class	Date Built
1	6338	Bogie Composite	1st/Brake/3rd	1902
2	6466	Bogie Composite	1st/Brake/3rd	1902
3	4154	Bogie Saloon	all 3rd	1902

All were impressive vacuum fitted vehicles with steel frames and 30ft (9.1m) long saloon bodies of oak and mahogany riding on bogies of 'American' pattern with disc wheels. The covered balconies at each end had lattice gates and two wooden steps for easy access as there were no raised station platforms on the line. The guard could pass from coach to coach via gates and fallplates arranged to span between the balconies, but passengers were not permitted to use these or, indeed, to travel on the balconies at all while the train was in motion. Having regard to the grossly inadequate accommodation reported on some fair days, however, one can imagine that here was one rule that was occasionally stretched. The third class seats were lathed, only the first class having simple mat 'upholstery' and the luxury of floor-mats.

The narrow design of 6ft 6ins (1.98m) was probably an asset on the town section but limited seating capacity. Coaches 1 and 2 were composites having a small first class compartment for 10 persons, a guard's compartment near the middle (fitted with a brake wheel) and a third class compartment for 26 persons, a few of whom could have squeezed into a tiny 'smoking' sanctum. The compartments were separated by sliding doors with glazed upper panels. Infiltration of the first class by third class passengers was no doubt inhibited by the presence of the guard in his den between them! The provision for luggage and 'smalls' traffic was minimal and it was soon evident that the goods brake van had to be attached to all passenger trains to supplement the space for this traffic. A rejected alternative design for the composite coaches had a distinct section for luggage. Coach 3 was an all-third class saloon seating 46 persons, only 16 of these being accommodated in the 'smoking' section.

The coaches were originally fitted with oil lamps. Photographs of the coaches in service show that, very early on, new lamp housings were fitted along the centre roof line. In 1913, the Cambrian proposed to convert the oil lamps to acetylene gas but the W&L, who would have had to pay for this, would not agree. However, in October 1923 all three coaches are believed to have been fitted by the GWR with their incandescent gas equipment. The Cambrian management were notorious devotees of the metal footwarmer, filled with hot water at the start of the journey, and it was left to the GWR to bring the delights of steam heated coaches to the W&L.

With the cessation of passenger services in 1931 the coaches were railed to Swindon Works and stored off bogies in the paint shop until scrapped in 1936. This delay has been said to be due to thoughts of using the bodies on the Vale of Rheidol section of the GWR. There is a strange sequel to this tale as there still exists a Swindon drawing dated 1931 which infers that the bogies were to be modified for use in the '*River Dee Bridge reconstruction*'!

Liveries

The full Cambrian Railways livery was applied to the new coaches. The lower body panels were bronze-green, the upper panels and waistline white (varnished off-white), with mouldings picked out in red and yellow. The underframe was black, edged with a fine red line. The coach number appeared within a garter emblem all in gilt and centrally placed below the waistline, with the W&L Company's monogram displayed at the same level towards each end. From early photographs it seems that this monogram was not repeated when the coaches were repainted. The class was boldly lettered along the waistline in gilt. Unfortunately this splendid livery was short-lived, as in 1909 economies included the adoption of an all

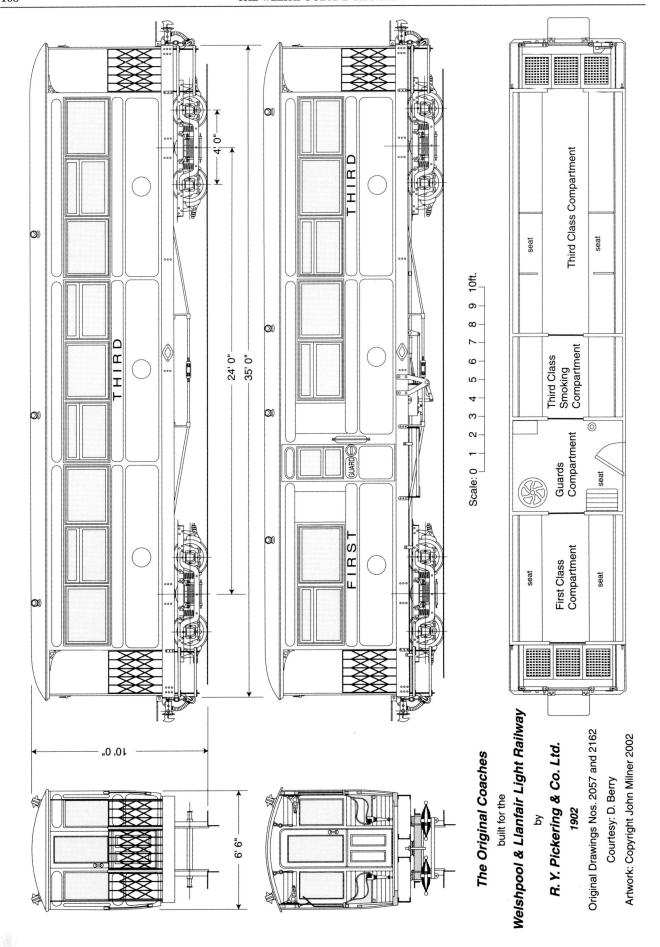

THIRD

THIRD

FIRST

GUARD

4' 0"

24' 0"

35' 0"

10' 0"

6' 6"

Scale: 0 1 2 3 4 5 6 7 8 9 10ft.

Third Class Compartment

seat

seat

Third Class Smoking Compartment

Guards Compartment

seat

First Class Compartment

seat

seat

The Original Coaches

built for the

Welshpool & Llanfair Light Railway

by

R. Y. Pickering & Co. Ltd.

1902

Original Drawings Nos. 2057 and 2162

Courtesy: D. Berry

Artwork: Copyright John Milner 2002

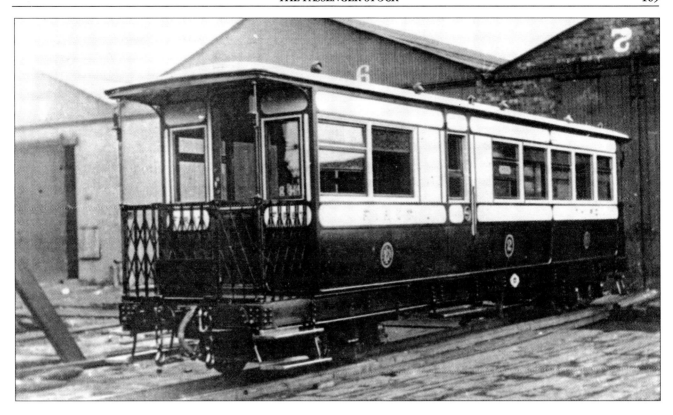

Bogie composite saloon No. 2 at the makers' works, Lanarkshire, in 1902.

over bronze-green coach livery for the Cambrian Railways. In due course this drab guise was applied to the W&L coaches.

Soon after the GWR took control, the lower and upper panels were painted in the familiar chocolate and cream colours of that railway, the GWR monogram taking the place of the gartered number at the centre of the lower panels. The GWR number was painted in a conventional position at the end of the waistline and the letters GWR were placed at the centre of the waistline immediately over the monogram.

Coaching Stock of the Preservation Company

The Admiralty Coaches (Lodge Hill & Upnor Railway)

Upnor & W&L No.	Type	Date built	Date of arrival
196*	Toastrack Bogie Coach	1941	28th July 1961
199*	- do -	1941	- do -
200*	- do -	1941	24th Nov. 1961
204*	- do -	1941	- do -
(214)**	bogie closed coach (combination car)	1957	- do -

*Built by Cravens Ltd, Sheffield.
**Built by D. Wickham & Co. Ltd., Ware, No. 7372

With its objective of running a public passenger service from Welshpool to Llanfair, the problems of the new Preservation Company were formidable. Though the two original locomotives were mercifully stored at Oswestry Works, the only other stock available consisted of old W&L freight wagons and vans lying almost derelict in Welshpool yard. There was no other public passenger line in Britain of 2ft 6ins gauge from which equipment could have been sought and the line had no repair facilities to enable extensive rebuilding or regauging to be contemplated. The presentation to the Preservation Company of the Admiralty stock was indeed timely and a stroke of good fortune. The arrival of the first batch of these vehicles coincided with the return of *The Earl* to the line in July 1961. The 30 ton Salop MPD steam crane was used to transfer both batches to W&L metals in Welshpool yard.

The **Toastrack Coaches** had transverse slatted seats for forty persons in five doorless 'compartments'. They had wooden bodies on steel frames with roofs of curved corrugated iron and were carried on bogies of simple construction having manganese steel wheels with no separate tyres. Excepting coach 199, there was separate brakegear on each bogie, with brakelevers each side. Outside brake-handles were provided. Two toastracks were reconstructed as closed coaches using old GWR corridor doors for coach 204 and new steel panelling and door pillars for coach 199 which was given a centre brake compartment. Coach 196 was eventually given simple half doors. However, being unsuitable for vacuum brake conversion, in November and December 1978, all four toastrack coaches were transferred to the Sittingbourne & Kemsley Light Railway.

The **Combination Car**, to use its official Admiralty title, was in railway terms a first/second/guard's coach, and was formerly used to convey officers and NCOs. When received by the W&L it had no running number and was designated No. 214 in 1968. It was painted a darker green than the toastracks with white window frames; in the centre of the sides was the badge of the Royal Naval Armament Supply Department with '*Upnor-Lodge Hill Railway*' under it. In contrast to the spartan toastracks this was a rather splendid vehicle, with an all-steel flush panelled body with a reinforced floor, full-length doors, sliding windows and upholstered seats in the small compartment. At one end was a well-equipped guard's compartment with sanding gear, electric light controls, Klaxon horn and brake wheel. The passenger accommodation comprised a compartment for six and a saloon for fourteen persons. The Preservation Company fitted upholstered seats throughout and a supplement of one shilling (5p) was charged per single trip in this coach, this practice being discontinued from the 1968 season. The coach was carried on heavy bogies fitted with coil springs and dampers giving a very smooth ride. The body was transferred to the South Tynedale Railway on 14th April 1989, later being bought by the Welsh Highland Railway. The bogies remained at Llanfair for further use.

Ex-Zillertalbahn Passenger Stock

W&L & ZB No.	Type	Date of arrival
B14	4-wheel saloon	12th April 1968
B16	-do-	11th April 1968
B17	-do-	12th April 1968
B24	-do-	11th April 1968
B27	-do-	18th Sept. 1975

Built by Grazer Waggon und Maschinen Fabriks A.G., of Graz, Austria.

These coaches were donated to the Preservation Company by the Zillertalbahn in Austria, as a culmination of several years of friendly relations.

The first four were moved by rail and were delivered to the W&L at New Drive crossing near Welshpool. Coaches B14, B16 and B17 are original ZB wooden bodied vehicles, weighing $4\frac{1}{4}$ tons as built. Coach B24 is a wooden framed coach with steel panelling built new for the Salzkammergut Lokalbahn (SKGLB). Historically these coaches are significant as being typical of many coaches of both types constructed by the Grazer

Ex-Admiralty toast-rack bogie coach in original semi-open condition, at Llanfair, 1967.

J.D. How

Ex-Zillertalbahn coach B16 at Llanfair, 1992. During the 1989/90 rebuilding, the balcony end was replaced in slightly modified form and without a central gate. Double doors into the saloon were provided to help wheelchair users. The weight of the coach increased to 5 ½ tons.

W&L staff are seen inspecting the work on Zillertalbahn coach B16 in Cammel Laird's workshops at Birkenhead. The new steel interior frame has just been erected.

Waggon und Maschinen Fabriks A.G., of Graz, Austria for most of the Austrian 760mm gauge lines. All coaches are on steel frames, the coupling gear at each end being joined by a rigid steel drawbar, the effect being that each coach '*hangs*' on this continuous drawbar and coupling stresses to the coach mainframe are minimised. Simple vacuum brakes were fitted, as used on the ZB until 1967/8, though in earlier times B24 would have had compound vacuum gear on the SKGLB.

The original ZB Coaches are B14, 16 and 17 (the prefix B is the continental convention signifying second class). Coach B14 has the distinction of being one of the four coaches available at the opening of the very first section of the ZB in December, 1900. It was built at Graz in 1900 as ZB 21, being renumbered 14 in 1933. Two saloons originally had sixteen slatted wooden seats with a central gangway. The gangway is continued at each end via swing doors to outside balconies with drop plates to afford passage from coach to coach. These drop plates are not used on the W&L, however, as they are not considered safe enough for public use. Electric lighting is fitted, operated on the ZB from the locomotive. Steam heating pipes run through the saloons.

Coaches B16 and B17 were built in 1901 and also renumbered in 1933, B17 at least having been designated third class as C17. Coach B16 resembles B14, but has one undivided saloon originally with sliding doors while B17 had two 16-seat sections with a sliding centre door.

In 1989, B16 was sent to the Cammel Laird Shipyard at Birkenhead for rebuilding by a training organisation, receiving a new concealed steel frame whilst retaining much of the original material. Hinged doors replaced the sliding doors and

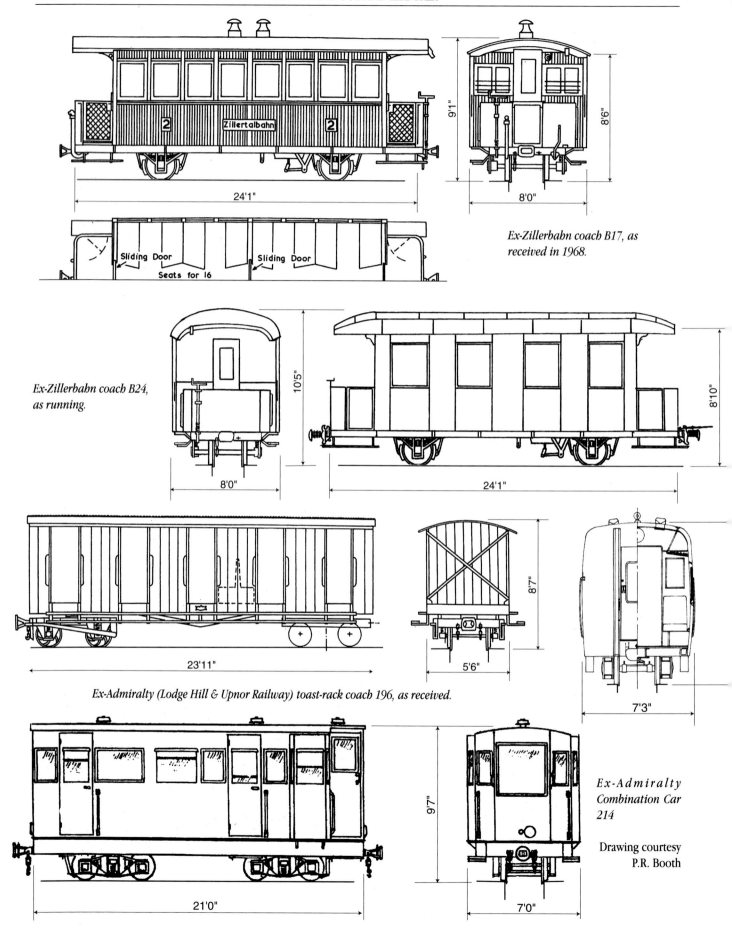

Ex-Zillerbahn coach B17, as received in 1968.

Ex-Zillerbahn coach B24, as running.

Ex-Admiralty (Lodge Hill & Upnor Railway) toast-rack coach 196, as received.

Ex-Admiralty Combination Car 214

Drawing courtesy P.R. Booth

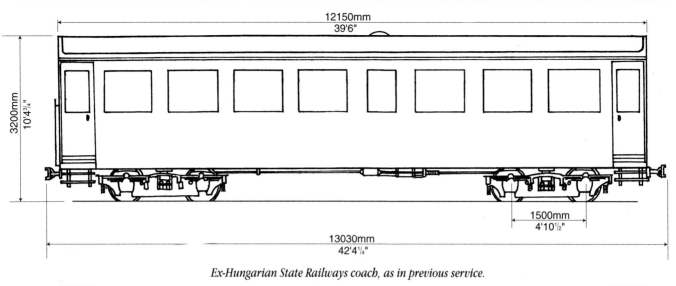

Ex-Hungarian State Railways coach, as in previous service.

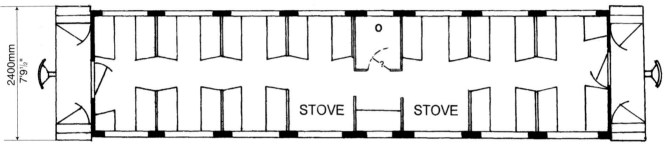

Scale 0   5   10ft

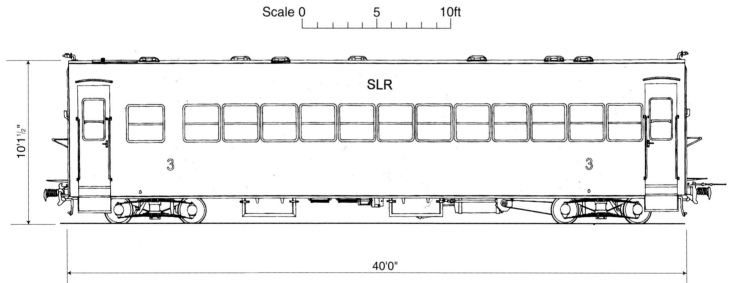

Ex-Sierra Leone Railways third class coach, as built

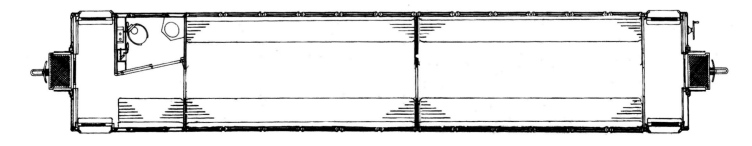

wider balcony gates were provided. Alterations to give access for wheelchairs through new double doors at one end reduced the seating to 30. A year later, the vehicle returned looking immaculate and soon afterwards B14 was similarly rebuilt, returning to the line in May 1992, as sound again as it would have been when outshopped in 1900.

Earlier, in 1977, B17 had needed major attention. Its wooden body frame was renewed at Llanfair, section by section and new matchboard panelling and window frames were made. Five years of painstaking work by volunteers restored B17 to a serviceable condition. The coach worked until 1998 when the condition of the body again made it unfit for public service. The chassis was used as a basis for a replica which was constructed by apprentices at Appleby Heritage and Training Centre. Oak was used for the bodywork on a concealed steel frame with improvements to the suspension. All the internal fittings were refurbished but two seats were sacrificed and a set of double doors fitted to facilitate wheelchair access. It was completed in April 2000.

Coach B24 was built for the SKGLB at Graz in 1925 as No. 166 in a batch of ten third-class coaches, eventually becoming SKGLB No. 572. In 1957, it was bought by the Zillertalbahn and ran on this line for some years as B25 before acquiring its present number. Two saloons seat sixteen and twelve passengers. Four places had been lost about 1947 to make a lavatory cubicle which was converted in Wales to a guard's compartment. Electric light and steam heating are fitted, with individual transverse heaters under each pair of seats.

Coach B27 was also a gift from the ZB and arrived at Llanfair by road in 1975. Movement had suffered delays when the load was deemed to be out of gauge. Although of similar construction to B24, the ventilators over the windows belie a different history as, before Zillertalbahn ownership, it was coach 3660 of the Austrian State Railway. There are signs that it was originally timber clad. The saloon is divided, 16 seats each section, there being no lavatory. Unlike the other ZB stock it was automatic vacuum fitted.

Ex-Sierra Leone Railway Passenger Stock

SLR and W&L No	Type	Date built	Date of arrival
1040	3rd class bogie coach	1961	8th August 1975
1048	do.	1961	8th August 1975
1066	do.	1961	8th August 1975
1207	1st class bogie coach	1961	8th August 1975

Built by Gloucester Carriage & Wagon Company.

These large, steel, modern style coaches, running on bogies with Timken roller bearings, formed the official last train on the SLR from Cline Town to Waterloo on 17th November 1974. They are the last survivors of approximately 45 such coaches supplied by Britain to the Sierra Leone government on attaining independence in 1961 and were ahead of their time in the use of the interior laminate linings. Each coach has a saloon entered from end vestibules and divided halfway by a partition on each side of the aisle. As received, the third class coaches had longitudinal slatted seats while 1207 had 16 (insect infested!) armchairs. Each coach weighs approximately 12 tons.

Three coaches have been re-seated using bus seats, with a capacity of 44 passengers. The other (1040) was used initially

Ex-Zillertalbahn coach B24 in 1999. Built originally for the Salzkammergut Localbahn, the vehicle's steel body panels contrast with the original wooden ZB saloons.

A. Doig

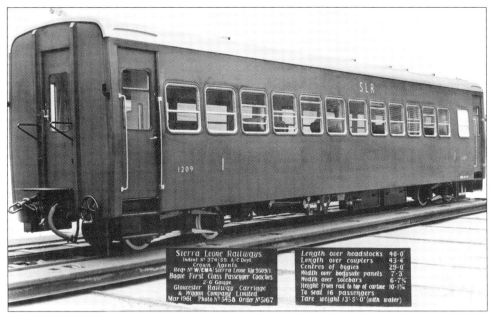

SLR 1st class coach at the makers, 1961.

Gloucester Railway
C&W Co Ltd.

Interior of 1st class coach 1207 on arrival in Wales, 1975. Like the third class coaches, the saloon is divided halfway by a partition on each side of the aisle with entry from end vestibules. The new seating arrangement is two across on one side plus a longitudinal seat opposite.

SLR coach 1066 at Llanfair after restoration. The cream panel around the windows greatly enhanced the appearance of these vehicles and the red (and later marsh umber) of the lower and upper panels made an attractive contrast.

as an exhibition coach in aid of the Welshpool Extension Fund. In 1998, preliminary work began on refurbishing this coach but when the high cost of this became clear, it was decided that the vehicle should remain stored.

The lavatories have been removed from all the coaches but Nos. 1207, 1066 and 1048 have had the space converted to a guard's compartment with vacuum brake valve. Coaches 1048, 1066 and 1207 have been fitted with lighting from 24 volt batteries. A flange lubrication device similar to that on the Docklands Light Railway was fitted to reduce wear (and wheel squeal) on the numerous sharp curves. Coaches 1048, 1066 and 1207 now carry the names 'Bronwen', 'Kathleen' and 'Ursula' respectively.

Ex-Mav (Hungarian State Railways) Coaches

W&L No.	Type	Builder	Date built	Date of arrival
418	Bogie coach	MAV	1958	27th July 1999
430	- do -	- do -	1958	- do -

These two second class coaches (MAV Nos. 418-6 and 430-2) were built in 1958 at Debrecen in eastern Hungary and are from the Nyiregyhaza-Dombrád line, one of the Hungarian State Railways (MAV) 760mm gauge systems. Before the collapse of communism and modernisation of the country began, this railway was the most important of Hungary's several narrow gauge systems in terms of passenger and freight traffic.

They have 40ft (12.2m) long steel bodies on steel girder frames carried on substantial bogies. The tare weight was 15 tons. Two saloons entered from end vestibules were separated by a central compartment with a simple lavatory. As originally designed, utilitarian wooden seating was provided for 54 passengers but in coaches 418 and 430 some seats had been sacrificed to have a primitive coke or wood heating stove in each saloon. Coach No. 430 was designated non-smoking.

The coaches are representative of much of eastern European's post-war output and livery (drab green). They were withdrawn from MAV administration in October 1995, and eventually moved to the Ciernohronska Forestry Railway in neighbouring Slovakia before movement by road to Llanfair. Though basically sound, they needed extensive fitting out with new windows, repairs to internal panels and floors and reassembly of the slatted wooden seats. Restoration was to take place as resources permitted and work started on coach 430 in 2001. The air braking was converted to vacuum operation, Grondana couplings were fitted and the vestibules were converted to open balconies which will give wheelchair access. Big windows, 2 + 2 seating and their high capacity should make them valuable additions to the fleet.

Two spare bogies also arrived with the coaches.

Llanfair Built Stock

Coach 41 was built on the renovated chassis of ex-Upnor bogie flat wagon 41 in 1998-99. Various discarded materials were assembled including some from ZB coach B17 (then being rebuilt) and the vehicle which evolved provides accommodation for permanent way workers.

Passenger Stock Liveries

For the opening season of 1963 the Upnor passenger set was painted plain Brunswick green, but by 1966 the set had acquired the Cambrian Railways livery with deep bronze-green lower panels, white upper panels with a gold waistline and black ends. The company coat of arms appeared on a metal plate centrally placed on each side. Realising that something more suited to the tourism business was needed, the ex-Admiralty coaches were repainted by 1968 in a new livery of cardinal red (BS1/025) lower panels, mid cream upper panels with a black waistline and black ends. The Austrian coaches were painted in the red-brown livery of the Zillertalbahn (except that for a time B24 appeared as 572 in SKGLB green). The SLR coaches, received in mid-green, were repainted cardinal red (later Midland crimson lake) with a cream panel to surround all the window area. In 1999, SLR coaches began appearing in LBSCR marsh umber with GWR cream lined chrome yellow. Roofs in silver grey complete the livery.

General Note on Coupling Gear and Braking

In 1963 a choice had to be made between the original Norwegian 'chopper' type couplings and the link-and-pin couplings of the Upnor and Austrian stock. The link-and-pin was selected and by 1970 most of the stock was so fitted but it was realised that a more rigid coupling was desirable when working to Welshpool. Fortuitously, it was possible in 1977 to purchase from Sierra Leone a complete set of Grondana couplings for the Railway. These couplings, used also, for example, on the Ghana Railways, consist of a conventional screw link coupling mounted over sprung centre buffers (drawbar height 2ft 0ins/615mm). By 1979, all ex-Zillertalbahn stock, like the ex-Sierra Leone coaches, was Grondana fitted. The ex-Lodge Hill & Upnor Railway coaches were still fitted with link-and-pin couplings when sold.

As a further essential step for operation to Welshpool, the fitting of automatic vacuum brakes to all passenger stock was proceeded with. Fully fitted trains commenced in 1977 and all existing coaching stock was fitted by 1979. These two developments greatly increased the standard of safety and smoothness of operation.

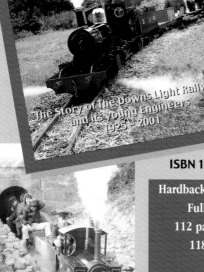

HOW TO ORDER :

To ensure that a copy of this prestigious special edition book is reserved for you, send your cheque/P.O./Bankers Draft for the full amount without delay.

Payments should be in £Sterling payable on a UK bank (Credit cards or Eurocheques not accepted)

Your book will be dispatched as soon as possible after the date of publication.

. . . . . . ORDER NOW TO AVOID DISAPPOINTMENT . . . . . .

POSTAGE :

To avoid any delay, please ensure that you include the correct postage as indicated opposite.

United Kingdom : £3.50
Europe Airmail : £4.47
Worldwide Airmail Zone 1 (incl. USA & S.Africa) : £8.80
Worldwide Airmail Zone 2 (incl. Australia & Japan) : £9.70

ORDER FORM

QTY	TITLE	PRICE
	Don't stand up in the Tunnel ! by James I.C. Boyd	
	ISBN 1-900622-04-1 Postage and Packing	
	Total	

I enclose my cheque/PO/Bankers Draft to the value of £   :

made payable to RAILROMANCES

PLEASE NOTE - IMPORTANT : The publication date is not guaranteed and may be delayed by circumstances outside our control. Books will be dispatched as soon as they are available. Orders are accepted on the condition that no correspondence will be entered into prior to publication and, should you require a receipt prior to delivery, please enclose a stamped addressed envelope. Whilst we generally despatch within two days of receipt of order please allow 28 days for delivery. By placing this order the purchaser accepts these conditions.

MR/MRS/MISS . . . . . . INITIALS . . . . SURNAME . . . .
(BLOCK CAPITALS PLEASE)

ADDRESS . . . .

. . . .

. . . . POSTCODE . . . .

Post your order without delay to

Rail Romances

P.O. Box 85, Chester CH4 9ZH

Chapter 11

The Freight Stock

In October 1901 orders were placed with R. Y. Pickering & Co. Ltd., Wishaw, Lanarkshire for 40 wagons, 4 vans, 2 cattle vans, 2 brake vans and 3 coaches at a total cost of £2,477. The provision of timber wagons, rather surprisingly, was deferred. The 1902 stock was to form the backbone of the Railway for the whole of its commercial existence, being supplemented only by a few timber wagons, cattle vans and sheep wagons, the latter being rebuilds of original open coal wagons. There seems no evidence that proposals to try transporter wagons to carry standard gauge wagons over the branch were ever carried out, but an index to Cambrian wagon drawings does indicate that a transporter wagon was designed for the W&LLR.

The 1902 Pickering Stock

W&L Nos.	Type
1 and 2	Brake Vans
3 to 6	4 ton Closed Goods Vans
7 and 8	Closed Cattle Vans
9 to 48	4 ton Open Wagons

These were all 4-wheeled timber framed vehicles designed by H. E. Jones, the Cambrian's locomotive superintendent. Originally, he had planned unsprung wagons fitted with wooden block buffers. These rudimentary ideas had dismayed the wagon makers who had offered to provide sprung coupling devices at no increase on the £25 basic cost. They reminded Jones of the necessity of all the stock having identical fittings in view of the intention of running mixed trains. Built thus, the set of rolling stock was considered by Jones to be superior to that of other narrow gauge lines.

Chapter 2 has already referred to the difficulties regarding coupling gear. Most of the stock, including the goods and brake vans, was delivered without side chains but following reports from Strachan that wagons on loan to him were breaking couplings, Denniss flatly told the W&L board in December 1902 that he would not work the line without side chains on all stock. There was little option but to agree to this sensible demand, even at 17s 6d (87½p) per set of four chains! Pickering's official print shows that van 8, at least, was delivered new with chains, as of course was all later stock.

The **Brake Vans** appear to have been designed for use on goods (as opposed to mixed) trains. There was an open balcony at one end with only a drop bar to serve as door. From the balcony a plain boarded door led into the van which housed a stove, centrally placed, and a brake pillar (surmounted by a small control wheel) offset towards the balcony end. Two lockers also served as seats. Six-leaf springs were fitted, and brakes acted on all wheels but no sanding gear was provided.

Even before the opening it was clear that these vans would have to serve on the mixed trains. Their scope would thus be greatly enhanced by provision of side doors to improve the miserable accommodation for 'smalls' traffic in the passenger stock. In April 1903, Oswestry Works completed drawings for provision of 3ft 6ins (1.06m) wide sliding doors giving a 3ft (0.91m) opening on each side, the interior space being cleared by moving the stove towards the balcony and opposite the brake pillar. These modifications were carried out soon after the official opening of the line. Through vacuum piping was added but there was no actual vacuum brake on the vans, the purpose of the fitting being solely to enable the van to be sited between the engine and passenger coaches and so enable shunting to be minimised in the absence of goods wagons.

Between 1905 and 1922 both vans were further modified, the van body being extended to cover the area of the former open balcony. The sliding doors just referred to were removed, but in compensation access to the van was by sliding doors in place of the former drop bars. The brake pillar was moved to a position between the doors. Sanding gear was added, probably by the GWR.

The **Goods Vans** were simply constructed in oak, clad with white pine, with a sliding door each side to give a 4ft (1.22m) wide doorway. The braking gear was simple in the extreme, a brake handle on one side only acting on one wheel! Enthusiasts

Brake Van No. 2 as built, with open balcony. These vehicles were supplied at a cost of £120 each, significantly more than the goods vans. But the design was flawed and the vehicles were twice modified to suit the traffic.

Goods Van No. 4, at the makers, 1902. The price tendered for four in November 1900 was £150 but when the order was placed the following October, with an improved specification, the cost was £120 for two.

4-ton Open Wagon, at the makers, 1902. Note plain bearings and lack of safety chains. The rudimentary design contributed to a runaway on the bank in November 1902. Some of the new wagons sustained crash damage at the Standard Quarry turnout.

Private Owner Wagon, at the makers in 1903. Note the owners' name lettered boldly in white.

for detail should however note that the original crude lever shown on the maker's drawings was later modified on all wagons to the improved linkage shown in the cattle wagon drawing. Six-leaf springs were fitted.

The **Cattle Vans**, similar in design to the goods vans, had slatted sides and ends and hinged drop doors to afford an easy access slope for the animals. The official capacity was seven animals. Later, some of the spaces between the lower slats were closed up and others reduced. Pickering original drawings (ref. 2164 and 2194) show both goods and cattle vans as 9ft 0ins (2.74m) rail-rooftop height.

The **Open Wagons** as built were devoid of bearing springs, the frame-axlebox spacing being taken up by a wooden block. The effect of this on both track and freight was no doubt soon revealed, and as early as February 1904, Oswestry Works had designed new axleguards to take axleboxes and six-leaf springs. All wagons were so modified, probably by 1906 if the axlebox cover dates are a good guide. The wagon bodies were of white pine, four planks giving 2ft 1in (641mm) inside height, with full length drop doors. The brakegear was similar to that fitted to the goods vans. Originally the side planking was secured with curved strapping with an inverted 'V' strapping on the ends. All surviving open wagons were rebuilt at Oswestry circa 1928-30 by the GWR with vertical straight strapping. Certain wagons, detailed below, were rebuilt into a form more suitable for the conveyance of sheep, cattle and timber.

J.LL. Peate & Sons Wagons

Private Owner Wagons have always been rare on British narrow gauge lines apart from the early tramroads, so it was an unusual development when in August 1903 Messrs Pickering designed an open wagon for Messrs J. Lloyd Peate and Sons,

Coal and Lime Merchants of Llanfair. Although the main dimensions were identical to the W&L opens, there were several detail differences, principally (a) only a 3ft 0in (0.91m) middle section of the side was arranged as a drop door, (b) the side strapping was straight, (c) the wagon was the first open type on the W&L to be designed with bearing springs and (d) Wood's Patent axleboxes were fitted. Eventually five of these wagons were built, being J. LL. Peate numbers 2, 5, 6, 7 and 8 (the missing Peate numbers were filled by standard gauge wagons). The Cambrian Railways fitted 4-ton registered plates. The wagons were scrapped at Llanfair in 1935. A registered plate from No. 2 (Cambrian 601/1903) was dug up in Llanfair yard in 1970.

Timber Bolster Wagons (W&L Nos. 49 to 54)

There was much discussion in 1903 regarding provision of timber trucks for the line. When H. E. Jones of the Cambrian Railways wanted further remuneration before proceeding with the contract, the W&L sent director W. Forrester-Addie to Pickerings' Works in Scotland. He discussed designs for an ordinary truck without either bearing springs or centre couplers. On the builders' advice, when ten wagons were ordered, the specifications included these fittings and safety chains too. In April 1904, six trial bolster wagons were received. The order for the remaining four was cancelled in May 1906. About this time, some open wagons appear to have been cut down to act as match wagons. The bolster wagons followed in the style of the earlier stock, with wooden frames and the single brake handle acting on one wheel only. All of these wagons were converted to small four-planked open wagons by the GWR at Oswestry Works in 1946. By this time, timber traffic had virtually ceased.

Timber Bolster Wagon, at the makers in 1904. Eventually, only two timber wagons remained. Other survivors were rebuilt as open wagons.

Collection: James I.C. Boyd

Below: *View of cradle on GWR-built Timber Wagon.*

PEK Morgan/G&D NG

Sheep Wagons
(W&L Nos. 10, 16, 17, 19, 24, 27, 36, 37)

In February 1911, the Cambrian Railways accepted terms to convert six open wagons for carrying sheep or other livestock. The conversion cost £18 10s 0d (£18.50) per wagon. Two further wagons were later converted, so that the GWR inherited a total of eight sheep wagons in 1923, recorded by them as having the above W&L numbers. Essentially they were flat wagons fitted with removable slatted sides and ends which fitted into sockets at the edge of the floor. The doors were fully planked, dropping to form a ramp for easy access, and the official capacity was 25 sheep. By 1956, GWR wagons 34163, 34172 and 71619 (W&L wagons 16, 19 and 27) had six-plank sides, the others five planks. This could be due to the open cattle wagon conversions carried out on these wagons and referred to below. In later years at least, sheep wagons were usually stored at Cyfronydd station loop.

GWR - Built Cattle Vans
(GWR Nos. 38088, 38089)

These closed vans were built in December 1923 at Swindon Works (Lot 914) for the Vale of Rheidol Railway. Curiously, it seems that the GWR did not realise that the Rheidol line in fact had no cattle traffic, and they were actually sent to Aberystwyth. After years of disuse, they were returned to Swindon, regauged and sent to the W&L in April 1937. In general the outline of these wagons closely resembled the 1902 cattle vans, but the sturdy steel frames and steel body framing set a new standard for the W&L. The brakegear was unusual. The two brakelevers, one to each side, were unconnected, each lever acting on only one brakeblock, a duplicated form of the 1902 arrangement. After closure, 38089 became the only

ex-W&L vehicle to survive away from the line, on the Festiniog Railway.

GWR - Built Timber Bolster Wagons
(GWR Nos. 17349 to 17354)

Built at Swindon Works in June 1924 (Lot 928), these were a steel framed version of the 1904 bolster wagons. Following a decline in timber traffic four of these wagons were rebuilt at Oswestry Works in 1946 to four-planked open wagons, as were all the earlier batch. This left only Nos. 17349 and 17353 as timber wagons on the W&L.

GWR Open Cattle Wagon Conversions
(GWR Nos. 34143/63/72, 71584, 71619/87/99)

To cope with increasing cattle traffic, seven wagons were strengthened by lining the sides of the interior with sheets of corrugated iron, a cheap and rapid solution to the problem. In March 1930 three former sheep wagons (34163/72, 71619) and three former open wagons (34143, 71584, 71687) were so fitted, sheep wagon 71699 following in September 1937. Most of this cladding was removed during the war years.

Cattle Van No. 8, at the makers in 1902. The oak chassis and uprights were not copied when the GWR built additional cattle vans. The result of carrying many animals over the years must have had a corrosive effect!

GWR-built Cattle Van No. 38088 newly restored, June 2001. Grondana couplings replace the original type.

Six-plank Sheep Wagon No. 34163 at Welshpool in 1951. This version may also have been used for carrying cattle.

James I.C .Boyd

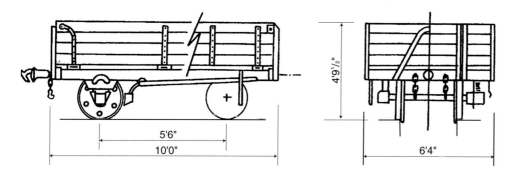

STANDARD OPEN WAGON

Left: *as built in 1902 (Pickering drawing No. 2087)*; Right: *with springs fitted by the Cambrian Railways and showing the body as rebuilt by the GWR.*

J.LL. PEATE & SONS' OPEN WAGON

As built 1903
(Pickering drawing No. 2613)

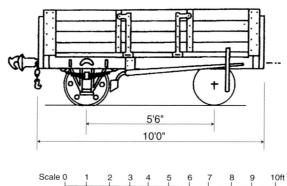

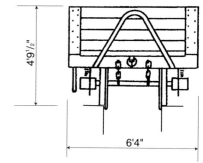

Scale 0 1 2 3 4 5 6 7 8 9 10ft

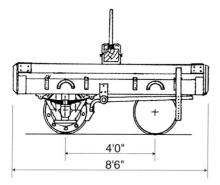

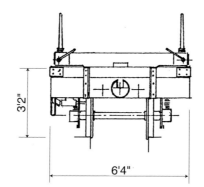

TIMBER BOLSTER WAGON

As built 1904

BRAKE VAN

As first rebuilt, 1903

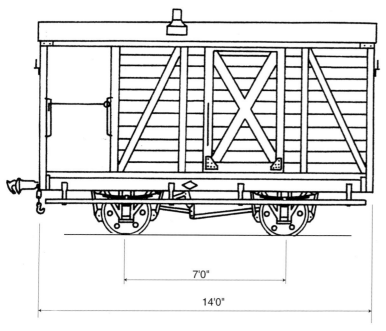

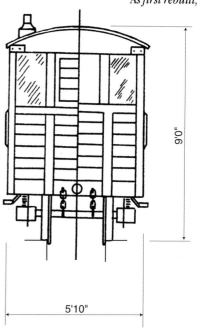

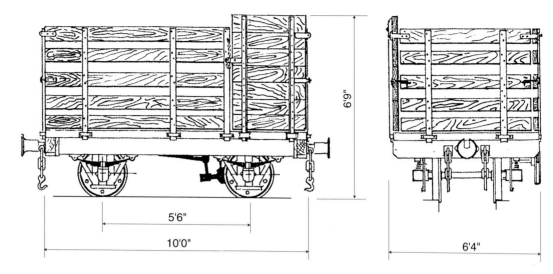

**OPEN SHEEP
WAGON**

*Wagon converted for
sheep carrying, 1911*

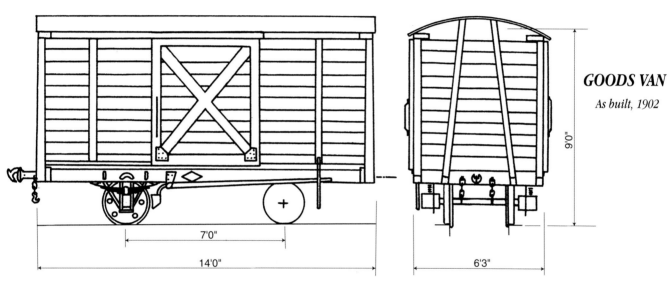

GOODS VAN

As built, 1902

Drawings courtesy Michael Christensen and Ralph Cartwright

CATTLE VAN

As built, 1902

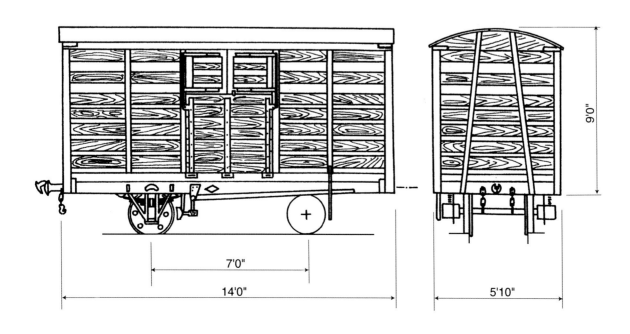

Right: *Open Wagon 71758, in service, 1951. This was supplied in 1902 as W&L wagon 44.*

Hugh Ballantyne

Below: *Llanfair yard in the 1950s was very much in use and illustrates the stock in service at that time. Wagons awaited the collection of coal by local coal merchants and the old coachbodies on the left continued in use as stores for other goods. There was often much shunting to retrieve the empties before the train returned to Welshpool each day.*

GWR Conversions to Open Wagons (GWR Nos. 8514 to 8516, 8518/21/23) (17350 to 17352, 17354)

These were the ten conversions from timber bolster wagons already described, the official conversion date being 5th September 1946.

Wagon Liveries and Axleboxes

The original goods stock was painted in the Cambrian Railways style. Bodywork was grey, roofs white and all ironwork black excepting tyres which were picked out in white when new. Lettering was bold, in white, usually comprising the title 'W&L', the capacity and tare weight of the vehicle. The W&L opens, the Peate wagons and the 1904 timber wagons bore a painted number on the ends when new. A cast oval numberplate carrying the full title of the W&LLR was carried on the mainframe of wagons and vans. Originally the brake vans had vermilion ends, an unusual feature which was soon

discontinued. The GWR adopted graphite grey. Roofs were dark grey or black. The earlier style of large 'G W' lettering on the sides of vans and wagons was changed by the war years to small lettering and numbers all on the left hand of each side. One exception was that goods van numbers were on the doors. The small style lettering was continued by British Railways.

The goods stock used four different types of axlebox at various times, each easily identifiable by its coverplate. The 1902 open wagons had plain bearings with an unmarked coverplate. When springs were fitted to these wagons the new axleboxes were lettered 'W&LR' and usually dated between 1904 and 1906. All the 1902 vans, the 1903 Peate wagon 2 (at least) and the 1904 timber wagons had oil boxes having a small valve over the bearing to feed lubricant. These are dated, clearly lettered 'Wood's Patent' and with the patentee 'Patent Axlebox Co. Ltd.' also shown. Finally, the GWR designed boxes for use on both the W&L and the Vale of Rheidol line. These are marked 'GWR 6 x 3 W & L V R'. Only the 1902 unmarked boxes may no longer be seen in service.

The Preservation Company's Freight Stock

Apart from the original W&L stock, which was renumbered on acquisition, it has been the policy to retain the running number of the former owner of both coaches and wagons, unless duplicate numbers would result.

Ex -British Railways (W&L Section) Stock

W&L No.	Original W&L No.	BR (& GWR) No.	Type
1	2	8759	Brake Van
2 (4*)	1	8755	Brake Van
3 (8*)	-	38088	Cattle Van
4 (2*)	4	10664	Covered Van
5 - allotted to cattle Van 38089 (see below)			
6 (3*)	6	100666	Covered Van
7	46	71794	4 ton Open Wagon‡
8	42	71738	4 ton Open Wagon
9	14	34159	4 ton Open Wagon‡
10 (5*)	34	71692	4 ton Open Wagon
11	11	34154	4 ton Open Wagon

* these numbers carried 1959-60.   ‡ Scrapped circa. 1970.

With the exception of wagon 11, all this stock was obtained from British Railways in 1959 and removal from the graveyard in Welshpool yard was effected by horse power in September of that year. Cattle van 5 had been sold in error and in fact was the property of the Festiniog Railway which had purchased it earlier. It lay in Castle Caereinion station loop until early 1962 with the wheels removed and then the body was taken on a flat wagon to Welshpool for rail transit to Minffordd. The FR ultimately rebuilt it into a stores van of very changed appearance. Wagon 11 was recovered from the standard gauge yard at Welshpool on 17th August 1960, necessitating the laying of temporary track across the yard followed by lifting and carrying the wagon by crane to the existing narrow gauge line at the far end of the Cattle Market yard.

The brake vans and the covered vans were the mainstay of the maintenance trains in the 1960s and 1970s. Sadly, both brake vans were largely destroyed by fires, one in 1977 and one in 1990. However, original chassis members and roof ribs were used for rebuilding and in 1996, brake Van No. 1 reappeared in its later Cambrian form, ready for service. The remains of the other were preserved. Fire also destroyed much of covered van 6, in 1998, in the blaze which damaged the new buildings at Llanfair station. The remains were stored for use in a future replica.

In 1959, the wooden frames of most of the wagons were in poor condition, and in any case with their side drop doors they were not very suitable for ballasting work. Inevitably, they became neglected in the early years of passenger working. Despite the little use they received, two of them had broken frames by 1969. Two wagons (7 and 9) were condemned for spare parts. Wagon 10 was rebuilt in 1971 with new wood throughout, including a frame to the original pattern and wagon 8 was also rebuilt though it needed further restoration in 1988.

In 1997, the offer of grant aid from the Heritage Lottery Fund was the signal for a programme to start involving the restoration of eight of the original freight vehicles. From the beginning the Company had always been short of resources and had never been able to undertake anything other than *essential* maintenance to the wagon fleet. Rather primitive facilities meant that work was slow and often uncomfortable and it was difficult to attract volunteers to this area of work. Furthermore, the surviving Pickering wagons were not now needed for civil engineering purposes. The Lottery project completely changed this scenario and enabled the problem to be tackled in a purposeful and systematic way for the first time.

Under a newly appointed volunteer supervisor, the vehicles were carefully examined to assess their condition and a plan of work was drawn up. A search unearthed copies of the original general arrangement drawings so that parts drawings could be compiled together with a cutting list of materials. Though the vehicles originally had oak frames with whitewood planking, similar oak in the quantity, size and quality needed was hard to find and very expensive. However, an acceptable alternative was discovered called Iroko - a West African hardwood from managed forests.

New (and second hand) machinery was installed in new workshops at Tanllan. A l4ins tilt arbor circular saw, a 16ins x 9ins planer/thickener, a hollow chisel mortiser, a l0ins bandsaw and a large drilling machine, together with a dust extraction system, expedited the work. Timber was bought for the first time in large sections and cut down to size on site, accurately and quickly which saved money and time. Furthermore, components could be machined, joints cut accurately and whole frames assembled under cover in warm and dry conditions. Whilst the construction and assembly of the timber components was fairly straightforward, refurbishing, assembling and refixing the original metal components was time-consuming and comparison of existing vehicles and their drawings showed that a lot of fitting had been done on the job. Matching the original sides and ends to the new frames of the wagons also showed up some interesting differences between the drawings and reality!

Open wagon 8 was rebuilt first including the provision of new frames. Of open wagon 11, only the wheels and metal fittings remained but this was completely rebuilt by early 2000 while open wagon 10, rebuilt in 1971, needed little more than repainting which was done later that year while covered van 4

Lodge Hill & Upnor Railway Brake Van 212, as received.

Ex-Bowaters Bogie Wagon 610, adapted for ballast carrying, 1997.

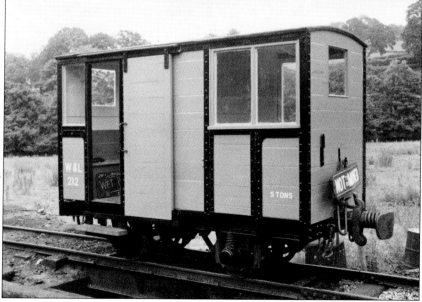

Lodge Hill & Upnor Railway Brake Van 212 in 1984, with doors, windows and new coupling gear.

was being reconstructed. This work incorporated the original roof bearers and chassis. Now brake van 2 began to emerge from the ashes of its fire with reconstruction to the 1903 verandah design with side doors, previously seen of course only in photographs. It was outshopped in September 2001, whereupon work commenced on the rebuild of covered van 6, again starting with little more than the wheels and metal fittings.

Another task completed in 2001 was the provision of a new floor and roof (with ash bearers) in the GWR cattle van following the removal of the weed-killing unit it had carried for some years. The only vehicle which needed little attention was brake van No. 1 laboriously rebuilt a few years previously. The rebuilding of all these vehicles in such a short period of time, and all with volunteer labour, was a remarkable achievement.

As rebuilding was completed, the stock was turned out carrying the GWR numbers. Once again, original W&L wagons and vans can be seen in service if only on demonstration freight trains. Notwithstanding that most of the wagons are now largely replicas, it is arguable that these trains encapsulate the spirit of the old W&L .

Ex-Admiralty Goods Stock
(Lodge Hill & Upnor Railway)

Upnor & W&L No.	Type	Date built	Date of arrival
32	10 ton Low Sided Bogie Wagon	1942	28th July 1961
33	- do -	- do -	- do -
35	- do -	- do -	- do -
38	- do -	- do -	- do -
41	- do -	- do -	- do -
60	10 ton High Sided Bogie Wagon	- do -	25th Nov. 1961
65	- do -	- do -	- do -
212	Brake Van (4-wheel)	?	- do -
213	Breakdown Van (4-wheel)	?	- do -

Built by Cravens Ltd., Sheffield.

The **Bogie Low-Sided Wagons** have steel frames, chassis and bogies (as did the ex-Upnor toastrack coaches), with a useful body width of 6ft 7ins (2.02m). All had single plank sideboards with arched endboards 2ft 3ins (692mm) high. In order to improve the utility of these wagons for ballasting work the endboards were lowered to the height of the sideboards, excepting wagon 41. This was retained in original condition until 1998 when it was converted into accommodation for track workers (see chapter 9). Wagons 32 and 38 were stripped down to carry containers. Wagon 33 was rebuilt in 1999/2000 to restore it to its original condition..

The **Bogie High-Sided Wagons** were formerly ammunition wagons with sides 3ft 7ins (1.09m) over the platform with two

sets of double doors each side and arched endboards 4ft 8ins (1.42m) high. Although the frames and bogies are similar to those of the low-sided wagons, the bodies are only 5ft 5ins (1.67m) wide so that the underframe is visible flush with the body sides. The W&L found these wagons of limited use and in 1969 the sides of wagon 60 were completely removed. This gave a flat wagon with high ends very suitable for sleeper transport.

Brake Van 212 is a small four wheel van with a wooden body on a steel frame. It has bench seats for up to ten persons and is fitted with a central pillar brake screw. In 1979, two of its four cast iron weights were removed and it was rebuilt as an enclosed van with sliding doors though these were later removed.

Breakdown Van 213 has a similar steel chassis to 212, including the central brake pillar. Like 212 it has a cast iron block at each end forming massive sandboxes, but there are no supplementary iron blocks to boost the weight further. The body is a closed van, with double doors on one side only. On the Upnor line 213 sported a broad yellow band painted horizontally around the waist of the body, no doubt to restrict its use to emergency duties only. The Preservation Company, in 1963, made a double window in the other side, and for three years, 213 served as the regular guard's van (with 214) on the passenger trains turned out in plain brunswick green. It is now normally used as a Tool Van on lineside maintenance trains, recently running in grey livery.

Other Ex-Admiralty Goods Stock

W&L No.	RNAD No.	Type	Origin	Date of arrival
248	212	5-ton 4-wheel Flat Wagon	RNAD Broughton Moor	6th July 1968
249	249	Replica Sheep Wagon	RNAD Broughton Moor	- do -
210	11	4-wheel Brake Van	RNAD Trecwn	October 1973
211	13	- do -	RNAD Trecwn	- do -
40	-	5-ton 4-wheel Flat Wagon	MoD, Broughton Moor	17th June 1992
44	-	- do -	- do -	- do -
45	-	- do -	- do -	- do -
47	-	- do -	- do -	- do -

Wagons 248 and 249 were acquired from store in a Mossbay, Workington, scrapyard. Built as closed vans, they were cut down to flats before disposal by MoD. Brake vans 210 and 211 came to the W&L from the Pembrokeshire depot where they had worked. They had a closed section with side

Former RNAD Wagon No. 249 has been converted into a Livestock Wagon with detachable sides and reminiscent of those used on the line before closure. It carries cycles and items of plant more often than sheep.

doors and an open balcony with brake hand-wheel. Number 210 was rebuilt as a fully closed van in 1975 and carries tools for civil engineering work. Number 211 saw little use and, in July 1988, left to work elsewhere. In 1997, 249 was converted to a replica of a Pickering-built sheep wagon with removable sides and runs in demonstration freight trains.

The small wagons 40, 44, 45 and 47 worked at the NATO ammunition depot in Cumbria and are similar to wagons 248 and 249. They have retained their original link and pin type couplings. Latterly, one has been used to carry weed-killing equipment.

Ex-Bowaters Stock
(Sittingbourne and Kemsley Railway)

SKLR/ W&L No.	Type	Date built	Date of arrival
610	High-ended Bogie Flat Wagon	1951	1st Dec 1978
631	- do -	- do -	2nd Dec 1978

(Both built by the Butterley Co.)

These were standard all-steel Bowaters pulp wagons, capacity 14 tons. During 1979 they were rebuilt, the high ends being cut down and three steel drop doors fitted each side. The resulting very effective ballast wagons were first used on the extensive ballasting on the Welshpool extension works and continue in use for permanent way works. In view of the heavy loads carried, wagon 631 is fitted with vacuum brakes and wagon 610 is through piped.

Llanfair-built Stock

Wagon 70 is a **Bogie Lowloader Wagon** built in the workshops at Llanfair Caereinion in 1993 using the chassis of a redundant Thompson LNER first class sleeping car. Ex-Upnor bogies were fitted and the vehicle is used to carry a tractor fitted with a flail for vegetation clearance and for rail carrying.

Wagon 71 consisted of the frames of 0-4-0 Hunslet diesel No. 2245 of 1941 on which a compressor had been mounted. The locomotive arrived on 16th April 1981 and was cannabalised for spares. The compressor wagon was dismantled in 1999.

General note on Coupling Gear and Liveries.

When acquired, the Pickering stock was fitted with the original Norwegian ('chopper') type couplings (drawbar height 2ft 2ins/667mm) and the Upnor and MoD stock had link-and-pin couplings. However, by 1979 all freight vehicles in regular use were fitted with Grondana screw couplings (drawbar height 2ft 0ins/615mm). The Upnor wagons were adapted to Grondana couplings by moving the couplings from the bogies to an extension of the main frames. Only wagons 40, 44,45 and 47 now have link and pin couplings.

Apart from vans 212 and 213, goods stock was painted grey (BS9/097) with black ironwork and white lettering, so following the tradition of both the W&L and the Upnor lines. In 1999, wagon 11 appeared in medium brown. Vermilion ends have been restored to Brake Van No. 1.

Other wagons

The following vehicles are confined to Llanfair yard and Tanllan sidings and are normally manhandled:

Two 1ton **Tipper Wagons**, W&L Nos. 48 &49, arrived in 1973 ex-Talyllyn Railway (formerly at Cefn Coch Quarry).

Well Wagon (ex-NCB) arrived in November 1999 (from storage at a local haulage contractor).

One of the original Brake Vans was completely rebuilt by volunteers as part of the Heritage Lottery project. It had been almost destroyed by fire, many years previously. In the summer of 2001, it was nearing completion in the workshops at Tanllan. Note that it has been rebuilt to the original Pickering design with an end balcony but as modified in 1903 with side doors.

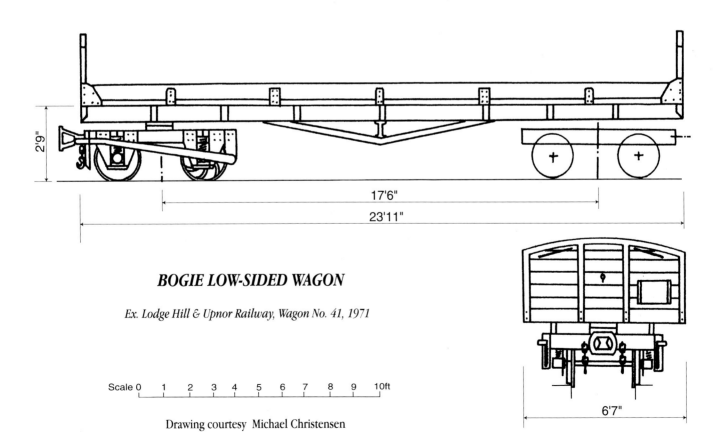

BOGIE LOW-SIDED WAGON

Ex. Lodge Hill & Upnor Railway, Wagon No. 41, 1971

Scale 0 1 2 3 4 5 6 7 8 9 10ft

Drawing courtesy Michael Christensen

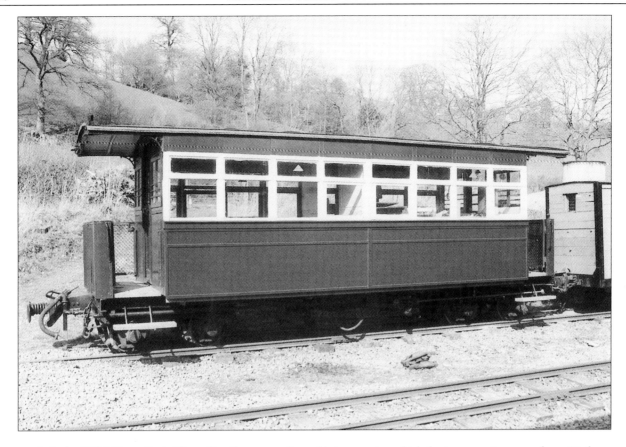

Ex-Lodge Hill & Upnor Bogie Wagon No. 41 was transformed into a service vehicle for permanent way workers. Work started in 1998 making use of materials discarded during the rebuilding of one of the Zillertalbahn coaches. The body was clad with large panels of marine ply.

Brake Vans Nos. 210 and 211 soon after their arrival from Trecwn, Pembrokeshire, still carrying RNAD numbers 11 and 13.

Bogie High-Sided Wagon No. 65, originally used for the conveyance of ammunition on the Lodge Hill & Upnor Railway. Wagon No. 60 was identical on arrival but the sides were later removed.

Axlebox cover on GWR-built Cattle Van No. 38088. Note provision for allocation to the Vale of Rheidol Railway.

Axlebox cover on Pickering-built van.

The Grondana couplings obtained from the Sierra Leone Railway have been fitted to almost all the stock. They are regarded as a very secure device, superior to previous types of coupling used on the Railway.

Passenger-carrying wagons. Open Wagons 343176, 71687 and others, pressed into use with station benches as seats to accommodate enthusiasts. In GWR days, Wagon 71687 was adapted for other 'livestock' - four footed! In October 1956, they have just loaded up besides Smithfield Road, Welshpool.

Courtesy: County Times & Express

Members of the Stephenson Locomotive Society pay their last respects to the Welshpool & Llanfair. Those in the photograph are mainly volunteers from the Talyllyn Railway Preservation Society (North West Area). Standing in the centre on the back row is James I.C. Boyd the well-known author of narrow gauge histories.

Track Layouts

1903 - 2001

Dolrhyd Mill

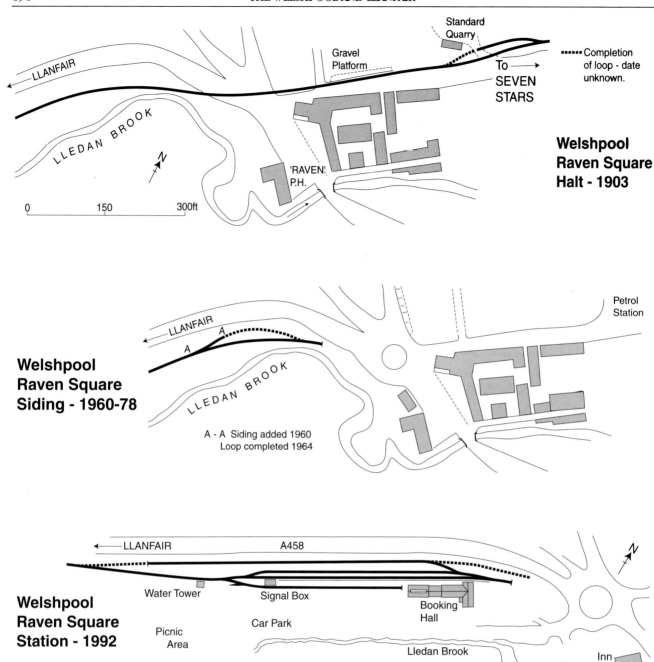

Gravel Platform

Standard Quarry

'RAVEN' P.H.

LLANFAIR

LLEDAN BROOK

N

To →
SEVEN
STARS

······ Completion
of loop - date
unknown.

**Welshpool
Raven Square
Halt - 1903**

0   150   300ft

**Welshpool
Raven Square
Siding - 1960-78**

LLANFAIR

A   A

A

LLEDAN BROOK

Petrol
Station

A - A Siding added 1960
Loop completed 1964

**Welshpool
Raven Square
Station - 1992**

← LLANFAIR   A458

Water Tower

Signal Box

Picnic
Area

Car Park

Booking
Hall

Lledan Brook

N

Inn

········· Former Track

0   150   300ft

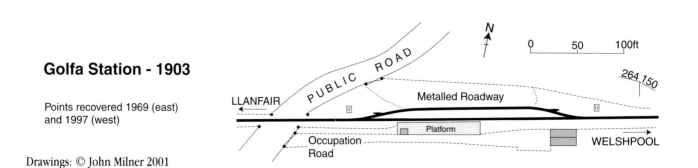

Golfa Station - 1903

Points recovered 1969 (east)
and 1997 (west)

Drawings: © John Milner 2001

PUBLIC ROAD

N

0   50   100ft

264 150

LLANFAIR

Metalled Roadway

Platform

Occupation
Road

WELSHPOOL

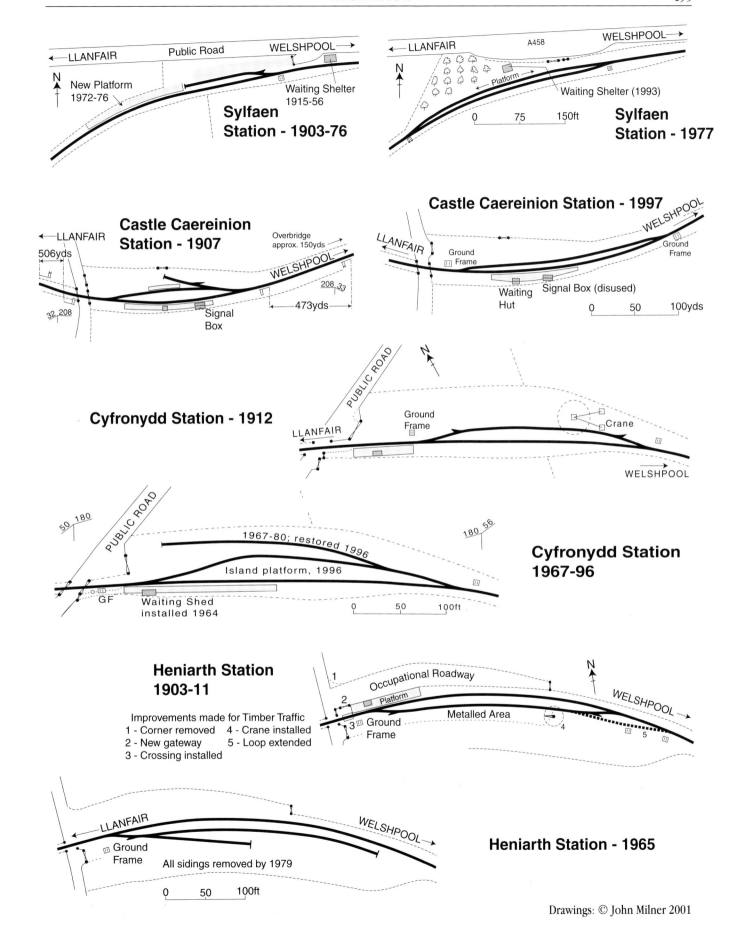

← LLANFAIR   Public Road   WELSHPOOL →

New Platform 1972-76

Sylfaen Station - 1903-76

Waiting Shelter 1915-56

← LLANFAIR   A458   WELSHPOOL →

Platform

Waiting Shelter (1993)

0   75   150ft

Sylfaen Station - 1977

Castle Caereinion Station - 1907

← LLANFAIR

506yds

Overbridge approx. 150yds

WELSHPOOL

473yds

208 33

32 208

Signal Box

Castle Caereinion Station - 1997

LLANFAIR

WELSHPOOL

Ground Frame

Ground Frame

Waiting Hut

Signal Box (disused)

0   50   100yds

Cyfronydd Station - 1912

PUBLIC ROAD

N

LLANFAIR

Ground Frame

Crane

WELSHPOOL

50 180

PUBLIC ROAD

GF

Waiting Shed installed 1964

1967-80; restored 1996

Island platform, 1996

180 56

Cyfronydd Station 1967-96

0   50   100ft

Heniarth Station 1903-11

Improvements made for Timber Traffic
1 - Corner removed   4 - Crane installed
2 - New gateway   5 - Loop extended
3 - Crossing installed

1

Occupational Roadway

2

Platform

3 Ground Frame

Metalled Area

N

WELSHPOOL →

4

5

LLANFAIR

Ground Frame

All sidings removed by 1979

WELSHPOOL →

Heniarth Station - 1965

0   50   100ft

Drawings: © John Milner 2001

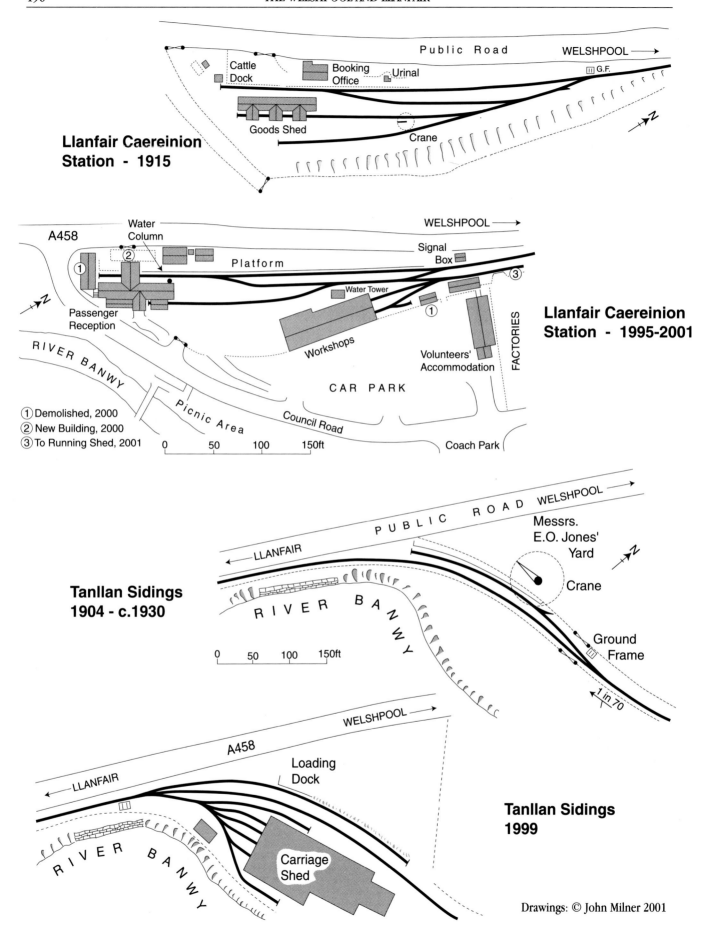

Public Road

WELSHPOOL →

Cattle Dock

Booking Office

Urinal

G.F.

**Llanfair Caereinion
Station - 1915**

Goods Shed

Crane

A458

Water Column

WELSHPOOL →

Signal Box

Platform

① ②

③

Passenger Reception

Water Tower

①

**Llanfair Caereinion
Station - 1995-2001**

Workshops

Volunteers' Accommodation

FACTORIES

RIVER BANWY

Picnic Area

CAR PARK

Council Road

① Demolished, 2000
② New Building, 2000
③ To Running Shed, 2001

0   50   100   150ft

Coach Park

PUBLIC ROAD WELSHPOOL →

Messrs. E.O. Jones' Yard

← LLANFAIR

**Tanllan Sidings
1904 - c.1930**

RIVER BANWY

Crane

Ground Frame

0   50   100   150ft

1 in 70

WELSHPOOL →

A458

Loading Dock

← LLANFAIR

**Tanllan Sidings
1999**

RIVER BANWY

Carriage Shed

Drawings: © John Milner 2001

Appendices

In Welshpool.

Appendix 1

STOPPING PLACES, CROSSINGS AND DISTANCES

Except for the new Raven Square station, passenger facilities were provided at stopping places shown in bold type from 4th April 1903 and ceased as from 9th February 1931. Details of re-opening are noted. LC denotes level crossings.

		Miles	Altitude* (ft)	Notes
Welshpool Station		0.00	243	
Church Street	LC	0.27	—	
Brook Street	LC	0.42	—	
Seven Stars		0.44	264	
Standard Quarry		0.84	—	Mineral siding only
Raven Square (halt)		0.90	305	
	LC	0.96	—	
		0.97	—	Termination of Railway from 18.8.1963
Welshpool (Raven Square) station		0.99	—	Opened 18.7.1981
New Drive	LC	1.57	—	
Golfa		2.82	557	Not re-opened
Cwm Lane	LC	2.85	—	
		3.25	603	Summit of line
Sylfaen Farm		3.66	554	Sylfaen Halt from 1.2.1913. Reopened 6.6.1964 to 6.9.1964. and from 15.7.1972
Coppice Lane	LC	4.42	578	
Castle Caereinion		4.77	538	Re-opened 6.4.1963
	LC	4.81	—	
Dolarddyn Crossing		5.44	470	Appeared as Halt in working timetable from July 1904 and in public timetable from 8.8.1929. Not reopened.
Hydan Fawr	LC	6.01	—	
Cyfronydd		6.71	381	Re-opened 6.4.1963
	LC	6.72	—	
		6.85	—	Brynelin Viaduct
		7.55	—	Banwy Bridge
Heniarth Gate		7.67	360	Heniarth from 1.2.1913. Re-opened 6.4.63
	LC	7.69	—	
Dolrhyd Mill		8.42	365	No Halt shown on working timetables; used for a period prior to World War I - exact dates not known. Not reopened.
Water Tower (GWR)		8.57	—	
Tanllan		8.84	—	Siding(s) 1904-c.1930; from 1975
Llanfair Caereinion		9.06	381	Re-opened 6.4.1963

*From surveys 1970-71.

Appendix 2

DIMENSIONS OF LOCOMOTIVES

PASSENGER LOCOMOTIVES

	The Earl The Countess	Sir Drefaldwyn	Joan	No.14 (SLR No. 85)	Orion (JR No. 5)
Cylinders, dia./stroke (in)	$11^{1}/_{2}$ x 16	13 x $12^{1}/_{4}$	10 x 15	$10^{3}/_{4}$ x 15	$12^{1}/_{2}$ x $17^{3}/_{4}$
Length o/buffer beams	17ft 11in	20ft 7in	19ft 1in	19ft 1in	29ft 2in
Width, overall	7ft 0in	8ft 4in	7ft 5in	7ft 5in	8ft $1^{1}/_{2}$ in
Height, overall	10ft 0in	10ft 6in	10ft 6in	10ft $5^{1}/_{2}$ in	10ft $8^{1}/_{2}$ in
Wheelbase (rigid)	10ft 0in	8ft $10^{1}/_{2}$ in	5ft 6in	5ft 6in	7ft 6in
Coupled wheel dia	2ft 9in	2ft $2^{1}/_{4}$ in	2ft 3in	2ft 4in	3ft $1^{1}/_{2}$ in
Water (gallons)	350	700	530	470	900
Boiler pressure (lb/in²)	160†	200	170	160	200‡
Weight in w/o	c21 ton	27 ton	c21 ton	c21.5 ton	c35 ton
Tractive effort @ 85% b.p.	8,720 lb	13,535 lb	8,027 lb	8,417 lb	12,573 lb

† since 2000 (previously 150)   ‡ since 2000 (previously 184)

OTHER LOCOMOTIVES

	Chattenden	Dougal	Ferret	Scooby (Scwbi)
Cylinders (diameter stroke)	n/a	7in x 10in	n/a	n/a
Length o/buffer beams	16ft $1^{1}/_{2}$ in	14ft 2in	12ft 4in	12ft 9in
Width, overall	5ft 9in	4ft $5^{1}/_{2}$ in	4ft 0in	7ft 1in
Height, overall	10ft 0in	5ft 10in	6ft 4in	10ft 7in
Wheelbase (rigid)	6ft 0in	3ft 0in	4ft 0in	4ft 0in
Coupled wheel dia	2ft 0in	2ft 0in	2ft 0in	2ft 0in
Water (gallons)	n/a	80	n/a	n/a
Boiler pressure (lb/in²)	n/a	140	n/a	n/a
Weight in w/o	12.4 ton	6.5 ton	8.5 ton	(?)
Tractive effort @ 85% b.p.	(150hp)	2430 lb	(50hp)	(50hp)

LOCOMOTIVES DISPOSED OF

	Raven	Upnor Castle	Nutty	Monarch	Wynnstay
Cylinders, dia/stroke (in)	n/a	n/a	$6^{3}/_{4}$ x 9	(4 cyl) 9 x 12	n/a
Length o/buffer beams	9ft $9^{1}/_{4}$ in	14ft 2in	11ft 10in	24ft 1in‡	17ft 1in
Width, overall	3ft 10in	5ft 9in	4ft 10in	7ft 7in	7ft 0in
Height, overall	4ft 9in	ca. 10ft	6ft $0^{1}/_{4}$ in	9ft 6in	10ft 6in
Wheelbase (rigid)	2ft $7^{1}/_{2}$in	4ft 6in	3ft 3in	3ft 3in	7ft 0in
Coupled wheel dia	1ft 4in	2ft 0in	1ft 8in	2ft 0in	2ft 4in
Water (gals)	n/a	n/a	80	500	n/a
Boiler pressure (lb/in²)	n/a	n/a	230	185	n/a
Weight in w/o	3.25 ton	c13 ton	6 ton	28.5 ton	c17 ton
Tractive effort @ 85% b.p.	(16/20hp)	(105hp)	'80hp'	12,737 lb	(100hp)

‡ Over bunker

Appendix 3

DETAILS OF RENUMBERING OF FREIGHT STOCK IN 1923 AND REBUILDING
(from GWR official records).

W&LLR No.	GWR No.	Type	Notes
1, 2	8755, 8759	Brake Vans	
3-6	10663-10666	Closed Vans	
7, 8	13623, 13626	Cattle Vans	
9	34143	Open	With ripple sides for cattle from 4/3/1930
10	34144	Sheep*	
11-15	34154, 34156, 34157, 34159, 34161	Open	
16, 17	34163, 34168	Sheep*	16 - with ripple sides for cattle from 4/3/1930
18	34170	Open	
19	34172	Sheep*	With ripple sides for cattle from 4/3/1930
20-23	34176, 71550, 71551, 71584	Open	23 - with ripple sides for cattle from 4/3/1930
24	71588	Sheep*	
25, 26	71594, 71610	Open	
27	71619	Sheep*	With ripple sides for cattle from 4/3/1930
28-35	71635, 71648, 71668, 71680,71687, 71690, 71692, 71697	Open	32 - with ripple sides for cattle from 4/3/1930
36, 37	71699, 71701	Sheep*	36 - with ripple sides for cattle from 24/9/1937
38-48	71702, 71704, 71728, 71736, 71738, 71743, 71758, 71776, 71794, 71718, 71721	Open	
49-54	8514, 8515, 8516, 8518, 8521, 8523	Timber	Rebuilt at Oswestry to open wagons 5/9/1946
-	38088, 38089	Cattle	
-	17349-17354	Timber	17350-52 & 17354 rebuilt at Oswestry to open wagons 5/9/1946

*Originally open goods wagons

Appendix 4

TRAFFIC FIGURES 1963-2000

Passenger Journeys

1963	9,934	1978	44,500	1993	41,223
1966	17,400	1981	36,050	1996	45,911
1969	32,410	1984	34,806	1999	42,347
1972	39,410	1987	31,302	2000	42,483
1975	46,716	1990	42,109	2001	44,200 (Prov.)

Appendix 5

TIMETABLES

CAMBRIAN RAILWAYS SERVICE TIMETABLE
October 1903 until further notice

Welshpool and Llanfair Light Railway (Narrow Gauge)

DOWN		1§ GOODS Mondays Tuesdays Wednesdays	5 MIXED	3 MIXED	7 MIXED	9 MIXED
		a.m	a.m.	a.m.	p.m	p.m.
Welshpool Station	dep.	5.15	11.45	7.55	3.45	7.10
Welshpool Seven Stars	"		*	*	*	*
Raven Square	"		*	*	*	*
Golfa	"		*	*	*	*
Sylfaen Farm	"		*	*	*	*
Castle Caereinion	"		*	*	*	*
Cyfronydd	"		*	*	*	*
Heniarth Gate	"		*	*	*	*
Llanfair	arr.	6.25	12.55	9.5	4.55	8.20

UP		2‡ MIXED Mondays Tuesdays Wednesdays	4 MIXED	6 MIXED	8 MIXED	10 MIXED
		a.m	a.m	p.m	p.m	p.m.
Llanfair	dep.	6.30	9.40	2.0	5.25	8.30
Heniarth Gate	"	*	*	*	*	*
Cyfronydd	"	*	*	*	*	*
Castle Caereinion	"	*	*	*	*	*
Sylfaen Farm	"	*	*	*	*	*
Golfa	"	*	*	*	*	*
Raven Square	"	*	*	*	*	*
Welshpool Seven Stars	"	*	*	*	*	*
Welshpool Station	arr.	7.40	10.50	3.10	6.35	9.40

* Trains must stop at all stations to pick up or set down passengers
§ On Llanfair Fairs i.e.the first Friday in each month, No.1 will be run as a Mixed train, stopping at all stations.
‡ On Llanfair Fair Days No. 2 will run as a Goods

EXTRACT FROM GWR SERVICE TIMETABLE

October 1942 until further notice (Goods only)

DOWN		Goods MO am	Goods M WS X am	Live-stock MO RR pm
Welshpool Station	dep	7.30	11.30	4.0
Welshpool Seven Stars		-	-	
Standard Quarry Siding		-	CR	
Raven Square		-	-	
Golfa		-	CR	
Sylfaen Halt		-	CR	
Castle Caereinion		-	CR	
Dolarddyn Crossing		-	-	
Cyfronydd		-	CR	
Heniarth		-	CR	
Llanfair Caereinion	arr	8.20	12.30	4.50

UP		Live-stock MO am	Goods M WS X pm	Goods MO RR pm
Llanfair Caereinion	dep	9.0	1.0	5.15
Heniarth		-	CR	
Cyfronydd		-	CR	
Dolarddyn Crossing		-	-	
Castle Caereinion			CR	
Sylfaen Halt			CR	
Golfa			CR	
Raven Square				
Standard Quarry Siding			CR	
Welshpool Seven Stars		-	-	-
Welshpool Station	arr	9.50	2.0	6.5

CR Calls when required
RR Runs when required

MO Mondays only
WS X Wednesdays & Saturdays excepted

ONE OF THE MOST AMBITIOUS W&LLR TIMETABLES EVER, FOR THE ANNUAL STEAM GALA, SEPTEMBER 2000.

TIMETABLE FOR SATURDAY 2nd SEPTEMBER 2000

Note	1, 3										3			3	
Train Set	G	P	P	M	DG	M	P	P	DG	P	M	P	P	M	P
Llanfair C	08.00	09.05	10.00	11.00	11.35	… …	12.00	13.00	13.35	… …	14.00	15.00	16.00	17.00	18.55
Cyfronydd	08.15	09.20	10.20	11.20	11.55	… …	12.20	13.20	13.55	… …	14.20	15.20	16.20	17.20	19.15
Castle C	08.25	09.30	10.35	11.35	—	… …	12.35	13.35	—	… …	14.30	15.35	16.35	17.35	19.25
Sylfaen	08.35	09.45	10.45	11.45		… …	12.45	13.45		… …	14.45	15.45	16.45	17.45	19.30
Welshpool	08.55	10.05	11.05	12.05		… …	13.05	14.05		……	15.05	16.05	17.05	18.05	19.50
Welshpool	09.25	10.30	11.30	… …		12.30	13.30	… …		14.30	15.30	16.30	17.30	18.30	20.15
Sylfaen	09.45	10.50	11.50	… …		12.50	13.50	… …		14.50	15.50	16.50	17.45	18.45	20.30
Castle C	09.55	11.00	12.00	… …	—	13.00	14.00	… …	—	15.00	16.00	17.00	17.55	18.55	20.35
Cyfronydd	10.15	11.15	12.15	… …	12.35	13.15	14.15	… …	14.35	15.15	16.15	17.15	18.05	19.10	20.45
Llanfair C	10.32	11.32	12.32	… …	12.55	13.32	14.32	… …	14.55	15.32	16.32	17.32	18.22	19.27	21.05

TIMETABLE FOR SUNDAY 3rd SEPTEMBER 2000

Note	1			3		3					4	2		
Train Set	G	P	P	M	DG	M	P	P	M	DP	M	P	P	
Llanfair C	08.00	09.05	10.00	11.00	11.35	… …	12.00	13.00	14.00	14.55	… …	16.00	17.25	
Cyfronydd	08.15	09.20	10.20	11.20	11.55	… …	12.20	13.20	14.20	15.15	… …	16.20	17.40	
Castle C	08.25	09.30	10.35	11.35	—	… …	12.35	13.35	14.35		… …	16.35	17.55	
Sylfaen	08.35	09.45	10.45	11.45		… …	12.45	13.45	14.45		… …	16.45	18.05	
Welshpool	08.55	10.05	11.05	12.05		… …	13.05	14.05	15.05		… …	17.05	18.22	
Welshpool	09.25	10.30	11.30	… …		12.30	13.30	14.30	… …		15.45	17.45	18.50	
Sylfaen	09.45	10.50	11.50	… …		12.50	13.50	14.50	… …		16.00	18.00	19.05	
Castle C	09.55	11.00	12.00	… …	—	13.00	14.00	15.00	… …	—	16.05	18.05	19.10	
Cyfronydd	10.15	11.15	12.15	… …	12.35	13.15	14.15	15.15	… …	15.34	16.15	18.15	19.20	
Llanfair C	10.32	11.32	12.32	… …	12.55	13.32	14.32	15.32	… …	15.50	16.40	18.35	19.40	

Whilst every effort will be made to maintain the advertised service, the Company do not guarantee that the trains will arrive at the times stated and reserve the right to cancel, alter or suspend any train without notice and accept no liability for any loss, inconvenience or delay.

TRAIN DETAILS

Train Sets:
- **P:** Passenger train
- **M:** Mixed train with limited passenger accommodation
- **G:** Goods Train
- **DG:** Goods train hauled by *Dougal*
- **DP:** Passenger train hauled by *Dougal* with limited seating

Notes:
1. *The Earl* + W & L goods train on Saturday No 5 + goods train on Sunday
2. Double Headed train on Sunday only *The Earl* + ex-SLR No. 85
3. Bus will follow train
4. Connecting bus departs Llanfair 15.15, arrives Welshpool 15.35

Appendix 6

EXTRACT FROM THE GWR APPENDIX TO NO.16 SECTION OF THE SERVICE TIMETABLES
March 1943 (and until further notice) - page 109:

Instructions as to the loading and conveyance of Round Timber on the Welshpool & Llanfair Narrow Gauge 2ft. 6in. Branch. Vale of Rheidol Narrow Gauge lft. 11½in. Branch.

In connection with the loading and conveyance of Round Timber on the above mentioned Branches, the following instructions must be carefully observed:

1. Before loading timber on bolster wagons, the man in charge must satisfy himself that every bolster has free movement and that the securing chains are in order. Every care must be exercised to ensure equal distribution of all loads over the two carrying bolsters.

2. When the length of timber is greater than two wagons, a match truck should be used, but if the length of timber exceeds three wagons, the first and second wagon must be separated to suit the length of the load.

3. A drag chain will be attached to connect the two wagons. This connecting drag chain must be suspended from the load at intervals by either ropes or chains to prevent mishap in case of the drag chain slackening, but its freedom must not be restricted.

4. The chain or rope put over the centre of the load should only be just taut in order to put no unequal strain on the binding points.

5. In no circumstances must such loads be conveyed by either passenger or mixed trains.

6. The speed of trains conveying the special loads must not exceed 10 miles per hour, and on the V. of R. between Devil's Bridge and Capel Bangor the speed must not exceed 5 miles per hour.

7. The general instructions relating to the loading of round timber *vide* pages 191 to 194 of the General Appendix to the Rule Book must be applied as far as practicable to the loading, securing, and conveyance of this traffic.

Appendix 7

EXTRACT FROM THE GWR APPENDIX TO NO.16 SECTION OF THE SERVICE TIMETABLES
March 1943 (and until further notice) - page 41:

WELSHPOOL AND LLANFAIR BRANCH.

Absolute Occupation of the Line by the Engineering Department for Definite Periods on TUESDAYS, WEDNESDAYS, THURSDAYS and FRIDAYS.

1. In order to facilitate the maintenance of the Welshpool and Llanfair Branch Line the Engineering Department will have absolute occupation of the Branch line from 0m. llch. near Welshpool to the termination of the Branch at Llanfair Caereinion on Tuesdays. Wednesdays, Thursdays and Fridays for the movement of a motor gang trolley during the following fixed periods:

(a) Up to 10.30 a.m.

(b) From 4.0 p.m. (or such later time as may be necessary following the passage of the return Freight train ex Llanfair Caereinion).

2. The Guard of the last return Freight train from Llanfair Caereinion on Monday. Tuesday, Wednesday, Thursday and Friday on arriving at Welshpool will be responsible for placing three detonators 10 yards apart on the Branch line at 0m. llch. i.e. at a point on the Branch line clear of the yard connections. The Guard will also be responsible for fixing a red hand signal near the detonators.

3. The Guard will also be responsible for removing the detonators and red hand signal on Tuesday, Wednesday, Thursday, Friday and Saturday prior to the departure of the Branch Freight train from Welshpool. Under no circumstances must the red flag or detonators be removed before 10.30 a.m. except on the special authotity of the Station Master or person in charge at Welshpool, vide paragraph 5 of these instructions.

4. These instructions do not in any way relieve the Ganger from taking the necessary steps to protect the line in case of emergency, or in connection with the running of ordinary platelayer's trolleys or other Engineering Department work which has to be performed outside the fixed periods of absolute occupation. In such cases the Ganger is responsible for sending out a man in each direction with hand signals and detonators in accordance with Rules 213 and 217. Under no circumstances may the motor trolley be placed on the line except during the times when the Engineering Department have absolute occupation as shcwn in the first paragraph of these instructions.

5. Should the traffic requirements necessitate the running of special Freight trains on the Branch on Tuesdays, Wednesdays, Thursdays or Fridays, the Station Master or person in charge at Welshpool will be responsible for personally making the necessary arrangenients for cancelling the absolute occupation with Permanent Way Inspector or Ganger in charge before any additional train is run. All traffic over the Branch to be restricted to 15 m.p.h.

Appendix 8

Welshpool and Llanfair Light Railway Company.

I am desired to give you notice that a Special General Meeting of the Proprietors and Debenture Stock Holders of this Company will, in accordance with the Railways Act, 1921, be held at the Town Hall, Welshpool, County of Montgomery, on Thursday, the 14th day of December, 1922, at 3 o'clock p.m., for the purpose of considering and, if thought fit, of approving a Preliminary Scheme in pursuance of the said Act, for the absorption of this Company and other Railway Companies by the Great Western Railway Company.

The Scheme provides as follows :—

That cash shall be paid by the Great Western Company in exchange for the Mortgages of this Company and in discharge of the Loans in respect of which such Mortgages were issued, including arrears of Principal, if any, thereon in the following proportion :—

$3\frac{1}{4}$ per cent. Mortgages	...	£81 for each £100.
$3\frac{1}{2}$ per cent. do.	...	£80 „ £100.
$3\frac{5}{8}$ per cent. do.	...	£80 „ £100.
$3\frac{3}{4}$ per cent. do.	...	£80 „ £100.

That the Great Western Company shall pay Cash to the holders of the $4\frac{1}{2}$ per cent. Debenture Stock of this Company in the proportion of £90 for each £100 of such Stock.

That a Cash Payment of 4s. 11d. per Share shall be paid by the Great Western Company for each Ordinary Share of £1 of this Company.

That the absorption shall take effect as from the 1st January, 1923.

ISAAC WATKIN,
Secretary.

Welshpool and Llanfair Railway Company's Office,
38, Park Avenue,
Oswestry.

29th November, 1922.

The notice calling a Special General Meeting on the 29th November, 1922, to approve the takeover by the Great Western Railway with effect from 1st January, 1923.

Collection: John Milner

Index

THE
WEYMOUTH HARBOUR
TRAMWAY
IN THE STEAM ERA

BY GERRY BEALE

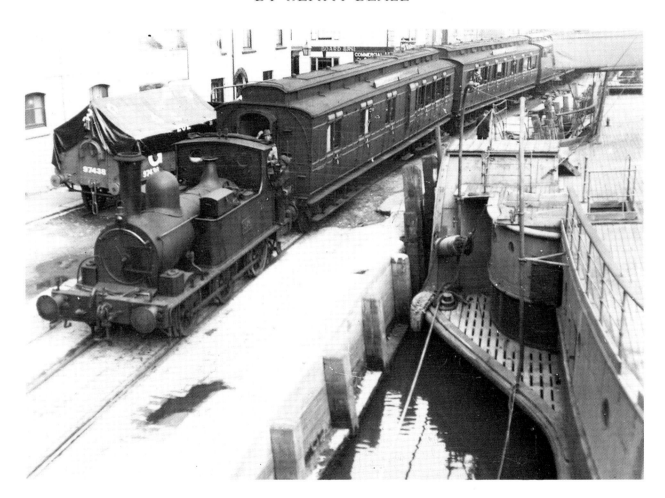

WILD SWAN PUBLICATIONS LTD.

JERSEY BOAT AT WEYMOUTH.

C.M. 1011

The Weymouth Harbour Tramway was inextricably linked with the Channel Islands steamer service. Indeed, its very existence was dependent on the service and when, in the 1980s, the centre of marine operations moved away from Weymouth, the tramway became redundant. This postcard was issued in the early 1930s when the future for both the tramway and the steamer service seemed assured. Within only a few years, however, the German occupation of the Channel Islands caused the cessation of both operations for the duration of the war. The picture shows St. Helier at the landing stage recently arrived from the Channel Islands with the boat train at the platform.

AUTHOR'S COLLECTION

INTRODUCTION

The Channel Islands boat train leaving Weymouth about 1936. The train was a regular Old Oak Common duty and is seen here in the charge of the streamlined 4-6-0 No. 5005 Manorbier Castle. LENS OF SUTTON

One of the most distinctive features of the Wessex railway scene was the Weymouth Harbour Tramway. Connecting Weymouth station with the quay to serve the Channel Island steamers, the line ran through the streets of the town and along the waterside, thus giving it a quite unique character. Although there were harbourside lines elsewhere, Weymouth was the only place in Britain where full-length trains of mainline corridor stock worked along public thoroughfares, competing with the regular road traffic for space in the congested streets.

Opened in 1865, upgraded for use by steam locomotives in 1880 and improved again to allow passenger trains to work over the line in 1889, the Weymouth Harbour Tramway had a useful existence until 1988, albeit little used in its last years. By the 1980s the Channel Islands service had been privatized and the centre of operations moved away to other south coast ports. At the time of writing, the Tramway remains available for use and, indeed, the metals are occasionally disturbed by a special train, usually run for the benefit of railway enthusiasts.

I first made the acquaintance of the Tramway in the early 1960s when the ex-GWR pannier tanks were still to be found at work on the line. I was immediately captivated by it and on visits to Weymouth I would far rather observe operations on the Tramway than spend my time on the beach! Much time was spent watching the cargo vessels being unloaded at the landing stage — the vessels must have been the *Roebuck* and the *Sambur* although I have no clear recollection of them in particular. Whenever a train set off from the quay to Weymouth station, I would walk alongside it along the full length of the line and I was fascinated to watch the train negotiate the Town Bridge. There was often water lying on the track beneath the bridge and the line climbed at a gradient to Ferry's Corner. Although the corner had been eased in the 1930s, it was still very sharp and it must have been quite a feat of enginemanship to keep a lengthy train of corridor coaches on the move over such a line. The junction between Commercial Road and Westham Road was another interesting point as Westham Road was a main route into the town from the west, and traffic congestion caused by the train could be extensive even then. There was also the quite perceptible increase in speed by the train as it made its way along the final straight

section of Commercial Road into Weymouth station yard — in excess of the permitted 4mph I suspect!

Sadly, the pannier tanks moved away from Weymouth soon after I first came to know the line and it is diesel locomotives that I recall most of all. The Tramway continued to be well used throughout the 1960s — indeed, the era was something of a heyday for the line — use which carried on into the 1970s. Freight traffic remained extensive throughout this period and another recollection is of lengthy trains of 'Conflat' wagons — special flat wagons for carrying containers which could be craned off the railway wagons directly onto the cargo vessels — winding their way through the streets to the cargo landing stage.

My continued interest in the line meant that eventually I would make the acquaintance of John Lucking. John was a senior customs officer at the quay and he had followed developments of both the tramway and the Channel Island boats for many years. He also extensively researched the history of the tramway and the service to the Channel Islands and had written a series of articles and a book covering both subjects. In 1986 he published a history of the Weymouth Harbour Tramway which will certainly be the final word on the subject. Following the publication of his book, John had promised to prepare an article on the tramway for Wild Swan Publications but his untimely death prevented this happening. Eventually, I decided to undertake the task myself, in the full knowledge that it would be very much in the shadow of John's own work, and I can only hope that he would have approved of my efforts.

The present work started out with the intention of appearing in article form but, as is so often the case, the amount of material gathered together meant that a rethink was necessary. Thus it was decided that the work would be better served by publication in the form of a book which would allow the mass of attractive material to be better presented. The fact that John's book is now out of print was another factor in making this decision.

The Weymouth Harbour Tramway has a lengthy history of useful service to the town, the GWR and its successors, had its own unique working instructions, was set in an interesting, attractive and photogenic location, and over the years employed a fascinating range of locomotives. Who could resist it?

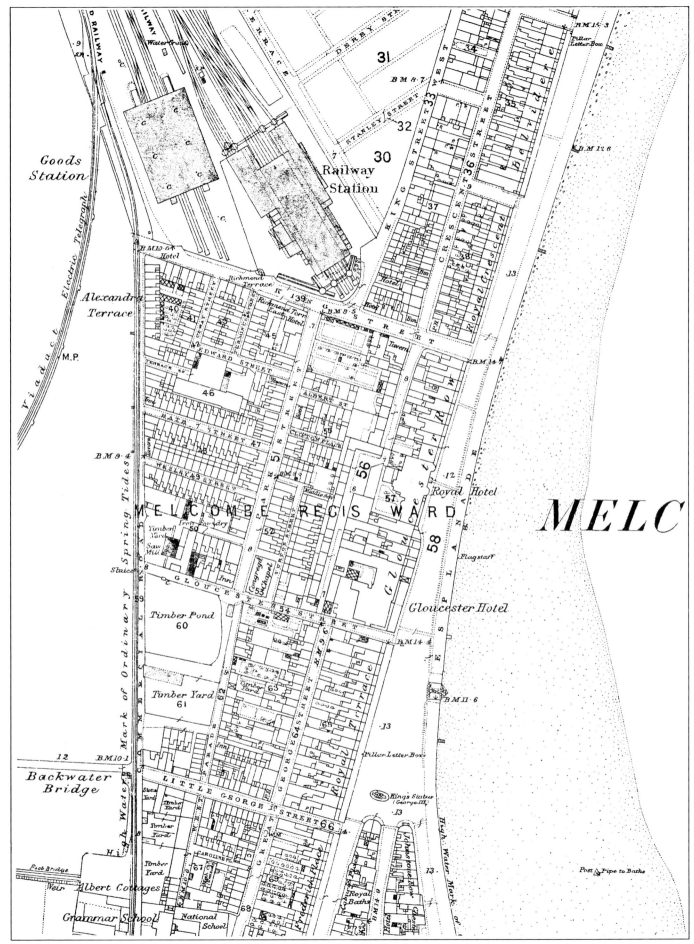

Taken from *First Edition 25-inch Ordnance Survey for 1890. Crown copyright reserved.*

CHAPTER ONE

THE TRAMWAY IN THE NINETEENTH CENTURY

IN its earliest form, the Great Western Railway connected the cities of London and Bristol, both then of great importance as major ports. As the system expanded, it came to serve many more ports and harbours, ranging from small coastal trade or fishing anchorages to those involved in heavy mineral export or those with transatlantic traffic. The company also developed holiday traffic, and became renowned for its services to the West Country and other resorts. However, it was unusual to find both forms of business fully established in a single location, but the Dorset town of Weymouth was one exception.

Weymouth had developed as a genteel, select resort, becoming almost a 'Bath-by-the-Sea' in Georgian and early Victorian society; the necessary 'royal seal of approval' was firmly given between the years 1789 and 1805, when King George III brought the royal family to the town for fourteen lengthy summer visits. During this time, much property development occurred in Weymouth, especially the renowned 'Georgian' terraces along the Esplanade. But the old fishing town also possessed an important harbour which handled a significant coastal trade, and served as a packet port for the Channel Islands mails; the combination of these assets naturally attracted the attention of railway companies.

The intention to reach Weymouth had been established in 1844 with the formation of the Wilts, Somerset & Weymouth Railway, with 'assistance' from the Great Western company. The railway opened in sections from Chippenham, Thingley Jct. to Westbury during 1848, and on to Frome in 1850, being taken over by the GWR in the latter year. It was not until 1856 that the Great Western opened the next section, to Yeovil.

In January 1857, the final, 27-mile section of the broad gauge was opened southwards from Yeovil, the last seven miles of the route, from Dorchester, also accommodating the 'narrow' gauge rails of the London & South Western Railway. With the arrival of the much-delayed railway, the fortunes of the town were transformed, and Weymouth very soon became established as the destination for shorter visits and day trips. In the twentieth century, the accents of Bristol, South Wales and Birmingham often dominated the town during the summer months, though in recent years the growth of cheap foreign travel has affected the town's income from this source. Generations of GWR employees from Swindon works also became familiar with the resort, Weymouth being the most popular destination during 'trip week', with a relatively short rail journey and cheap accommodation forming an attractive proposition to the workers.

Weymouth harbour c.1860 was described by Measom in his *Illustrated Guide to the Great Western Railway*, in which he informed the traveller that 'the channel to the tidal harbour is about fourteen feet deep at high water; at the quays at each side the vessels lie aground at low water. The bay is well sheltered by surrounding hills'.

With the opening of the railway, a regular steamer service to the Channel Islands commenced. Operated by the Weymouth & Channel Islands Steam Packet Co., this was an independent company, in which the GWR had a holding, and by agreement their sailing times were scheduled to correspond with the Great Western's trains to and from Weymouth station. But the distance from the station to the quay posed a problem, and involved a carriage ride or a walk of about a mile for passengers, and the cartage of goods through the town to or from the harbour.

MacDermot, in his monumental work, *History of the Great Western Railway*, indicates that the WS&W obtained a supplementary Act in 1846 authorising a short extension to the quay, but in the subsequent battles with the L&SW, the intention would seem to have lapsed. It was not until the Weymouth & Portland company was promoted in 1861, that the prospect of a tramway between the station and quay serving the cross-Channel steamers was raised once more. During the following year, the W&P Act received the Royal Assent, authorising not only the construction of the Portland line but also the Weymouth Harbour Tramway.

As first built, the tramway was a single line laid to the mixed gauge, terminating in a pair of sidings at the harbour, and was worked by horses. A Board of Trade inspection was not required as the tramway was to convey goods traffic only, and the line opened for traffic on 16th October 1865, along with the Weymouth & Portland Railway. The benefits to the harbour trade were immediate, dispensing with the need for double-handling of goods between railway, road and shipping.

The tramway commenced in the yard at Weymouth station at a junction with the W&P line, which itself diverged from the main line some four chains to the north of Weymouth station at Portland Junction (renamed Weymouth Junction in 1899, prior to the opening of the new Goods Junction signal box at Portland). On leaving the station yard, the tramway passed directly onto the public highway at Commercial Road, along which the line ran for about 600 yards, beside the 'Backwater'. At that point the road finished, and the railway continued southwards on an embankment constructed with fill taken from the Backwater, running in front of a number of yards and other premises that faced the water for about 250 yards as far as Ferry's Corner (named after the adjacent property of James Ferry & Sons). At the corner, the line made an abrupt change of direction to the east by means of a 220ft radius curve, passing in front of a number of warehouses to reach the Town Bridge, which spanned the harbour, connecting the two portions of the town. As the road approach to the bridge on the eastern side (from St. Thomas Street) was by a gradient, the tramway was required to pass underneath by means of an archway, which gave very limited clearance for broad gauge vehicles. Having negotiated the arch, the line passed onto Custom House Quay, which forms the northern side of Weymouth Harbour. A little further, at the George Corner, the old George Inn (c.1550) obstructed the quayside, and necessitated another sharp curve in the line. The tramway terminated at the rear of Devonshire Buildings, the southernmost end of the terraces on Weymouth Esplanade, near the point where the Channel Islands steamers berthed in the harbour. Except for the first few yards within the station boundary, the tramway was constructed on land which remained the property of Weymouth Corporation. This situation was to be the cause of a number of disputes between the Corporation and the GWR over many years, especially with regard to the liability for maintenance of the harbour walls and the road surfaces.

Some nine years after the opening of the tramway, the GWR lines in the district were converted from broad to the narrow gauge, the last broad gauge service running on Thursday, 18th June 1874. According to MacDermot, the broad gauge element of the mixed gauge 'between Dorchester Junction and Weymouth and the joint Portland Railway and Weymouth Tramway were soon afterwards removed'. This brought further benefits to the operation of the tramway in that the Jersey potato traffic, which was largely to the Midlands and the North, was offloaded into Great Western 'narrow' gauge wagons at the quay, and these were able to run through to their destination without the inconvenience of the break of gauge. This 'enhanced' service flourished, and extra boats soon had to be run to cope with the additional demand; this in turn required temporary sidings to be laid down on the tramway to accommodate the additional rolling stock. By 1877, traffic had increased to such an extent that a wooden landing stage, measuring 200ft in length, was provided to ease the handling of the seasonal cargoes. The GWR also supplied a steam-powered crane to assist in the unloading of ships.

Traffic on the tramway at this time was still entirely horse-drawn, an arrangement which severely limited the capacity of the line. There had been a proposal to commence a new GWR steamer service to Cherbourg, but the tramway was clearly unable to accommodate any extra traffic at peak times without considerable improvements. Amongst the ideas suggested was one to introduce a small locomotive to work traffic over the line, which it was hoped would increase the number of wagons able to be moved, and a trial was accordingly carried out in March 1878; this confirmed the shortcomings of the tramway, and the need to convert the two sidings at the end of the tramway into a loop to allow the engine to run round its train. In the same year, the Cherbourg service was introduced and the timber cargo stage was extended to almost double its original length to accommodate the vessels on that service.

Steam locomotives were introduced onto the tramway in 1880 and were, not surprisingly, subject to strict regulations

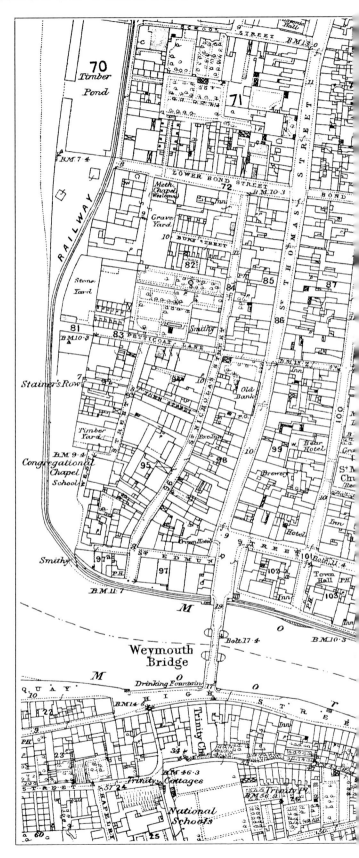

governing their use. A document, *Regulations for Working the Weymouth Tramway with Locomotive Engines*, specified that:

'The speed of the Engine must not exceed four miles an hour, and it must travel slower where it is necessary to ensure safety.

'The Engine must always be accompanied by a Policeman in uniform, who will be responsible for seeing that the road is clear in front of the Engine, and who must warn every one on or about the Tramway of the Engine's approach, and must also see that the Engine does not travel faster than the specified speed. He must either walk in front of the Engine, or ride on the front buffer plank. In going round sharp curves, and at those places where there are many people or Children on or about the Tramway, the Policeman must always walk a short distance ahead of the Engine, so as to be able to warn people of its approach and to keep the road clear. Where the road is straight, and there are no people about, he may ride upon the engine.'

These regulations, considerably extended over the years, continued to form the basis of traffic working over the tramway until services ceased. Indeed, any special workings even today are subject to the same regulations.

Two additional loop sidings were added between the cargo landing stage and the Town Bridge, both being available for use by traders and merchants who conducted their business around the harbour, and this further increased the traffic working over the line. One of the loops, known as Templemans Siding (named after a nearby flour mill), was built at a narrow part of the quay, and the additional line was laid upon timber staging along the quay wall. A severe weight restriction was thus imposed, which meant that only horses could be used for shunting at that point; indeed, horses continued to be used for shunting on the tramway

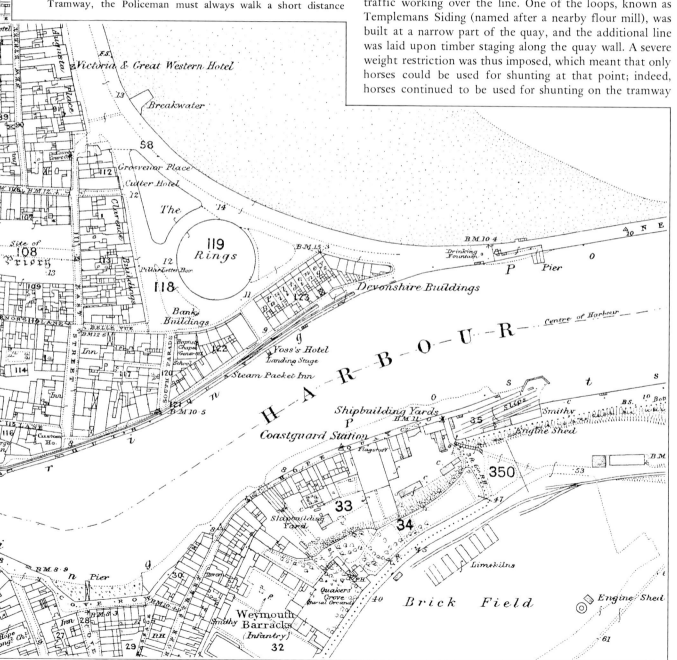

Taken from First Edition 25-inch Ordnance Survey for 1883. Crown copyright reserved.

until early in the twentieth century. When locomotives were used for shunting such restricted sidings, a tow-rope would be employed to enable the engine to move wagons to or from those sidings from the adjacent track, a method which was often used by tramway engines until the early 1950s when improvements eventually did away with the need to employ such means.

Unfortunately, the Cherbourg service did not prosper, and had ceased by 1885. There was also a great deal of uncertainty over the Channel Islands boats, as the Packet company was in financial trouble. Its steamers were in need of replacement, but there were no funds available. Closure seemed likely but, in 1888, the Great Western agreed to take over the steamer service, supplying new boats for the purpose, and to provide a connecting passenger service through to the quay. Weymouth Corporation would provide new harbour facilities, involving a new passenger

landing stage on the pier, and would arrange for the harbour to be dredged to a sufficient depth to accept the new, larger vessels. The tramway would be extended to the new pier.

The new landing stage was constructed of cast-iron pillars and a wooden deck, with a timber-built baggage examination shed which also incorporated offices and a refreshment room. Passengers would be able to transfer directly from the railway carriages standing at the single-track terminus of the extended tramway, as the landing stage decking was constructed at normal platform height above the rails.

Four bogie carriages could be accommodated at the new landing platform, and modifications to the tramway were made to allow passenger stock to operate over the line. This involved raising the arch of the Town Bridge to afford sufficient clearance, and this was partially achieved by

Ibex alongside the passenger landing stage at Weymouth Harbour in 1901. The fruit vans stabled alongside the platform were ready to be loaded with Channel Islands produce landed from the ship. The grand sweep of the Esplanade forms an imposing backdrop to the harbour.   NATIONAL RAILWAY MUSEUM

lowering the track, although that action increased the possibility of flooding of the line at that point. The wall at Templemans Siding (Custom House Quay) was widened, thus allowing the removal of the wooden staging on which the extra rails had been built. Various other curves were realigned, but the severe restriction at Ferry's Corner remained, and bogie stock could only be worked over the tramway after the normal screw couplings had been replaced by special three-link couplings.

At Portland Junction, the layout was remodelled to include a 'scissors' crossing, which permitted greater flexibility in the operation of traffic on both the Portland and tramway lines. A new signal box was provided at the junction to control access to both routes, this containing a frame of 43 levers.

Prior to the commencement of passenger services to the quay, the tramway was inspected by Major General Hutchinson for the Board of Trade. He largely approved of what he found, but there were a number of items which required attention before passenger services could begin over the line. In particular, he required 'that the engine should carry a bell which should ring as the train advanced', thus establishing a tramway tradition which remained a feature beyond the days of steam traction.

The new passenger service commenced on 3rd August 1889, with the first passenger train being the 9.15 p.m. Paddington (a New Milford service, conveying through coaches for Weymouth), which connected with the 2.10 a.m. departure for the Channel Islands on 4th August, worked by the new steamer *Lynx* on her maiden voyage. In 1892, the Weymouth coaches designated to this train were a 6-wheel van, a bogie Third and a bogie Composite, which returned from the Quay with the 'about 3.30 p.m.' Weymouth Boat Special.

Passenger trains destined for the quay would halt on arrival at Portland Junction home signal, and when necessary would be split, one portion proceeding to the Town station with the train engine, the other remaining for the tramway engine to be attached to work forward to the quay. However, there were alternative arrangements in hand periodically. In the summer of 1898, the 8.50 a.m. Paddington to Weymouth train had two coaches for the Town station attached in the rear, and these were detached at Yeovil, being forwarded on the following service to Weymouth. The Quay portion, comprising a Brake Third (3 compartment), Composite, Third and Tri-Compo (Mondays and Saturdays only), and Brake Third (6 compartment) worked through to Portland Junction, where the usual engine change took place. In the opposite direction, trains were usually combined at Portland Junction (later Weymouth Junction) when necessary.

In 1894/5, records show the extensive use of '56' and '481' class 2−4−0s on the Paddington trains between Swindon and Portland Junction, with Barnum '3232' class 2−4−0s and 'Duke' 4−4−0s taking over in the latter years

of that decade. The tramway services were worked by two similar 0−6−0Ts, Nos. 1376 and 1377, built in 1874/5 by the Bristol & Exeter Railway to work the standard gauge Culm Valley line. Following the absorption of the B&E by the Great Western, both engines were extensively rebuilt at Swindon before being sent to Weymouth in 1881, specifically to work the tramway from the commencement of steam traction on the line. The two engines worked all traffic over the tramway, both passenger and goods, and were intensively employed on shunting duties in the various sidings associated with the traffic over the line. Even in quieter periods, eight or nine round trips over the tramway could be made in a turn of duty, in addition to the required shunting. They remained on these duties at Weymouth for well over forty years.

Although the passenger landing stage could accommodate only four coaches, a greater number were regularly seen on the line, and the trains would sometimes tail back along the quay as far as the cargo stage; in this instance, some passengers had to detrain using portable footsteps down to rail level. However, this was both a time-consuming and potentially dangerous practice, and at busy periods it became the normal custom for these passenger trains to be dealt with at the longer cargo stage, the steamers being berthed alongside to permit a cross-platform transfer. Incoming steamers continued to use the passenger landing stage due to the necessary customs formalities, which could only be carried out in the baggage examination hall. When the coaches had emptied, they were generally stabled throughout the day at the passenger landing stage, awaiting the arrival of the next incoming steamer.

To ease the task of loading and unloading, the traders along the quayside would often move wagons standing in the various sidings along the tramway to a more convenient position, and this practice would frequently foul the running line. Before operating a passenger train down the tramway, it was therefore necessary to run a light engine in the charge of a pilotman, to ensure that the line was clear of such obstructions.

In spite of the efforts of the competing L&SW steamers from Southampton, traffic to and from the Channel Islands at Weymouth had grown to such an extent that the existing facilities were proving to be severely limiting. In 1892, the Great Western had applied to Weymouth Corporation for permission to use the passenger landing stage for the transfer of ordinary goods traffic when the cargo stage was being utilised for new potato traffic. This request was granted, and it soon became regular practice to handle goods at the passenger landing stage. In due course, both the landing stage and the cargo stage were extended, but neither of these improvements really made an impact, and the facilities at Weymouth Quay remained woefully inadequate. Although these shortcomings were readily apparent at the turn of the century, it was to be another thirty years before substantial improvements were made.

Weymouth landing stage and pier at the turn of the 20th century.   AUTHOR'S COLLECTION

An up boat train passing Alexandra Terrace in Commercial Road during the mid-1900s in the charge of one of the ex-Bristol & Exeter Railway 0—6—0Ts.
E. H. SEWARD

CHAPTER TWO

TWENTIETH CENTURY DEVELOPMENTS

SIR Frederick Treves, in his fine topographical description of Dorset, published in 1906, described the harbour at Weymouth thus: 'The picturesque parts of Weymouth are about the quay and in the older settlement across the harbour. This harbour, which leads to the backwater behind the town, is spanned by a bridge, from which can be seen the old cobblestone quay, the crowd of sketchy ships and of blue-jerseyed loafers, together with ancient warehouses of faded brick belonging to the time when Weymouth was a town of commerce. Here, about the harbour side, or huddled together in narrow, absent-minded lanes, are cosy old houses with round bow windows of many panes, comfortable lodging-houses, such as pilots use, where a telescope can often be seen projecting from an open casement, and where reefer jackets and oilskins half fill the narrow hall.' This graphic description is recognizable to us today as the harbour and surrounding area have not changed a great deal, but his suggestion that Weymouth was no longer a town of commerce was perhaps a little premature. As we shall see, traffic to and from the Channel Islands and, to a lesser extent, with France, and the servicing of the means by which that traffic was carried out, occupied Weymouth harbour for much of the twentieth century.

Regular and seasonal traffic continued to increase during the Edwardian era, and from time to time, the *Great Western Railway Magazine* would report on events at Weymouth Quay. In June 1908, it reported that hundreds of tons of 'narcissi, tulips, lilies and other spring flowers' had been dealt with at Weymouth over the previous few weeks, nearly all of which had been grown in Guernsey. The magazine also announced that 'on April 14th the "Lynx" and "Roebuck" landed 7,250 packages representing about 20,000 boxes, weighing about seventy tons; thirty vans were requisitioned for the special train. London and Manchester received the largest quantities, but heavy consignments were also despatched to Edinburgh, Glasgow and the North of England'. The cargoes were by no means confined to perishable traffic, and in the June 1909 issue, the *GWR Magazine* reported that 'baskets containing pigeons from Lancashire, Yorkshire, Cheshire, etc.' had been conveyed for flying contests. On the heaviest days, 'nearly 25,000 birds are carried to the islands by special steamer, and there liberated'. But the normal traffic continued unabated, with early potatoes from Jersey forming the heaviest, and one chartered steamer was reported with a deck cargo of 400 tons of the vegetables. Guernsey sent flowers in March and April, with over 22,000 boxes being received at Weymouth on 15th April 1909.

The daily train from Paddington conveying passengers for the Channel Islands left London at 9.35 a.m. during the summer months, arriving at the landing stage at 1.33 p.m., with around sixteen minutes being allowed for the transit over the tramway from Weymouth Junction. In 1909, this train conveyed a Van and a Brake Tri-Compo from Bristol, and a Van, Corridor Third, Lav. Brake Compo, Lav. Brake Tri-Compo and Corridor Van Third from Paddington. Corridor stock had been introduced to the Channel Islands Boat Train service toward the end of the 1890s and, as before, it was necessary for the couplings to be extended by the addition of special three-link couplings. The corridor vestibules also had to be locked and the gangways disconnected to enable the vehicles to negotiate Ferrys Corner, a chore that had to be repeated at the commencement and termination of every journey by a passenger train over the Tramway. The steamer left the landing stage some ten minutes or so after the arrival of the train. A Saturdays-only excursion train also ran in the summer of 1907, leaving Paddington at 8.52 a.m. and arriving at the landing stage at 12.54 p.m.; this presumably gave sufficient time for the passengers to detrain and the empty stock to be removed from the tramway before the arrival of the regular service at Weymouth Junction. Several other through trains and coaches ran to Weymouth Town station, though these were largely concerned with the holiday and domestic arrangements of the town, and had little direct connection with the boat services; the two were entirely separate from an operational point of view at this time.

In the winter months, coaches destined for the boat left Paddington on the 9.15 p.m. train to Neyland, running onwards from Swindon as the 11.28 p.m. to Weymouth Quay, due in at 2.0 a.m.; the steamer left at 2.15 a.m. A four-coach set (Van Third, two Lav. Brake Compos and a Van Third) was normally used in this instance.

The return trip in both instances was made after the arrival of the steamer, due in at around 3.0 p.m., though with Customs to clear, the train's departure was around 45 minutes to an hour later, due into Paddington at about 7.15 p.m. Motive power to or from Weymouth Junction was now largely 'Bulldog', though with 'Atbara' and 'Badminton' 4—4—0s appearing from time to time. On the tramway, the two ex-B&E engines continued their reign, with No. 1377 being recorded at the quay with the 9.40 a.m. Paddington on Tuesday, 27th June 1905.

With the possibility of a revitalised service to France in mind, and the inadequacy of the facilities at Weymouth Quay apparent, a proposal had been made in 1897 to construct a new dock and connecting railway. The new complex was to be constructed at Newtons Cove, directly to the south of Weymouth and within the naval anchorage of Portland Harbour; this was to be served by a new double-track railway that would leave the main line at Upwey Junction, two miles to the north of Weymouth station. Land was acquired and some constructional work carried

THE HARBOUR AND PAVILION WEYMOUTH

Ibex alongside the passenger landing stage in 1908 with the Cosens paddle steamer Victoria moored ahead of her. Cosens steamers operated day and half-day excursions along the coast for holidaymakers and were also chartered by the Royal Navy for tendering duties when the Fleet was at Portland. The Pavilion Theatre appears quite new in this view, thus dating the postcard precisely, and the Palm Court Ballroom had yet to be built.

E. H. SEWARD

Another postcard view showing the Pavilion Theatre, with Reindeer *alongside the passenger landing stage and a boat train at the platform.*
AUTHOR'S COLLECTION

The Pavilion Theatre was built in 1908 and in February 1909 the Great Western Railway Magazine *reported that it had recently been formally opened by the Earl of Shaftesbury. It was constructed by Weymouth Corporation and included an assembly room to accommodate 1,200 people.*
AUTHOR'S COLLECTION

The cargo stage in the 1900s with one of the ex-Bristol & Exeter 0–6–0Ts and a train of vans. The cargo was probably Jersey potatoes.
LENS OF SUTTON

out, but the GWR was already over-committed with extensive engineering works during this period of expansion and, once preliminary works had been completed, the project was shelved. Then, from 1909, the GWR operated a steamer service from Weymouth to Nantes (Brittany), no doubt with a view to justifying the construction of the new facilities. But it was soon apparent that the Nantes service would not prosper, so it was suspended in 1911, and the Great Western's interest in the new docks waned. In 1913 the works were formally abandoned, but a number of physical reminders of the project remained: an approach road to the site of the docks was constructed, and spanned by a steel footbridge of unmistakeable GWR design — later replaced by a concrete structure — whilst a number of GWR boundary markers were dotted around the area. A public house was even constructed, bearing the name 'Railway Dock' in anticipation of the GWR's efforts, but this has been demolished in recent years.

The outbreak of the Great War in August 1914 thwarted any further attempts at improving matters, and the company soon found itself on a war footing. One steamer was left to maintain the Channel Islands service — the *Ibex* — whilst others were requisitioned by the Admiralty and equipped for minesweeping duties in the Mediterranean. *Ibex* was assisted when necessary by other railway-owned or chartered vessels, but in 1916 was joined by a second boat in the form of a tender from Fishguard. In that year,

the steamers received guns for defence against U-Boats, and *Ibex* was credited with sinking a submarine during one such confrontation in mid-Channel during March 1918.

By October 1914, the service had been reduced to three night sailings each week, leaving Weymouth on Wednesday, Friday and Sunday mornings at around 2.15 a.m., served again by the 9.15 p.m. Paddington to Neyland train of the previous evening. The return trips to London left from the landing stage at 4.10 p.m. on Tuesdays, Thursdays and Saturdays, with the four-coach set still in use. By April 1917, the steamer's departure time from Weymouth Quay on its 80-mile, 6½-hour journey to Guernsey had moved to 12.30 a.m., but trains no longer connected with it on the tramway. Instead, passengers had to use the 5.5 p.m. from Paddington, or an L&SW service, to the Town station and find their own way to the quay. The steamer returned at about 3.0 p.m., allowing passengers time to catch the 4.20 train from Weymouth Town to Paddington. Perishable traffic continued unabated, assuming a heightened importance in the prevailing situation, though the cargo shipping arrangements were officially described as 'irregular until further notice'. The steamer service was further reduced to twice-weekly later in that year.

During the summer of 1919, passenger trains were once more to be seen on the tramway, with a Van and a Composite being detached from the rear of the 5.5 p.m. Paddington service at Weymouth Junction on Tuesdays, Thursdays

Ex-Whitland & Cardigan Railway No. 1386 shunting wagons on Custom House Quay in 1909.   E. H. SEWARD

No. 1337 Hook Norton *setting off from Weymouth landing stage in 1921 with an up boat train.*   R. BROOKMAN

and Saturdays, with a balancing service leaving the quay to connect with the 4.15 p.m. Weymouth Town train on the same days. The last GWR vessel was returned to the company's service in April 1920, and from that time it was possible to run a schedule virtually the same as in the days before the Great War.

Perishables were again being carried in increasing quantities during the early 1920s, with new potatoes, tomatoes, beans, peas and flowers originating from Guernsey. In 1920, steamers carried 18,000 tons of tomatoes and fruit from St. Peter Port, over twice the weight conveyed in 1900. New potatoes and fruit were the main exports from Jersey, and the steamship *Pembroke* was recorded as carrying 45,861 packages from the island on a run in September 1921, the largest amount of fruit ever exported from the Islands up to that time. Additional traffic from France was also handled, and the limitations of the quay were again made painfully apparent, some traffic even being turned away; as it was, much night work was

required to handle that traffic which could be accommodated.

The steamers, too, were life-expired, and worn out by their wartime exploits. In the mid-1920s the GWR directors addressed the problem, and during 1924 four new steamers — two passenger & mail and two cargo — were ordered. These became available from May 1925, the first two being the cargo vessels *Roebuck* and *Sambur*, whilst the first of the mail boats, *St. Julien*, made her maiden voyage from Weymouth on 24th of that month. In the following month, the second passenger boat, *St. Helier*, entered service, giving the Channel Islands route a fleet of modern ships.

To coincide with the new steamers, new articulated passenger stock was introduced onto the boat trains, and during the summer service in the latter 'twenties comprised a Brake First and First pair, and a Third, Third, Van Third triplet, with a 60ft Third sandwiched between. These ran on the 9.30 a.m. Paddington to Weymouth Quay, which also conveyed three other vehicles (including a dining car)

The Pavilion Theatre and the landing stage viewed from Alexandra Gardens in the early 1920s. This picture shows a train and the Ibex *present whilst the Nothe Fort dominates the farther side of the harbour.*
NATIONAL RAILWAY MUSEUM

Ibex *leaving Weymouth for the Channel Islands circa 1922.*

E. H. SEWARD

St. Julien *leaving Weymouth. The flags suggest this may have been her maiden voyage to the Islands on Sunday, 24th May 1925.*

E. H. SEWARD

Articulated passenger rolling stock on the Channel Islands Boat Express' at Ferry's Corner. This view graphically illustrates the sharpness of the curve and what a handicap to operations it was. The timbers intruding into the photograph suggest a date between 1928 and 1930 when Weymouth Town Bridge was rebuilt and that this view was taken from the temporary bridge erected across the harbour for use by pedestrians.

A. R. BELCHER

for the Town station at the head. The articulated set duly arrived at the landing stage at 12.56 p.m., the steamer leaving shortly afterwards. The return trip left the landing stage at 3.50 p.m., picking up a Dining Car at Weymouth Junction. The employment of these vehicles alleviated, to a certain extent, the chore of slackening off the screw couplings of each passenger coach, and their replacement by the special three-link couplings, to enable the train to negotiate the sharp curve at Ferry's Corner. The 'Channel Island Boat Express' was one of the first services on which these vehicles were employed, and they replaced a five- or six-coach set of 57ft vehicles.

During the winter months, the boat train portion reverted to the practice of being attached to the 9.25 p.m. Paddington to Neyland mail train, running as the 11.20 p.m. from Swindon to Weymouth Quay. This arrangement worked daily during September, and on Tuesdays, Thursdays and Saturdays from October onwards, with three coaches (Van Third, Compo and Van Third, 57ft stock) forming the normal service. Again, the coaches returned as the 3.45 p.m. from the landing stage, and were attached at Weymouth Junction to the 4.15 p.m. train from the Town station for Paddington. The steamer connecting with the service left Jersey at 7.30 a.m., and Guernsey at 10.0 a.m. that morning, and was due into Weymouth at about 3.20 p.m. On Monday, Wednesday and Friday evenings during the winter months, the Southern Railway provided the service to the Islands from Waterloo via Southampton, though at other times of the year competed for traffic with the Great Western. Unlike the Great Western, their service remained an overnight crossing during the summer months, with a very much shorter rail journey, but a considerably longer boat trip (at 103 miles to Guernsey, 32 miles and around two hours more than the GWR route).

Improvements and alterations were made along the tramway during the 1920s. To permit the use of the articulated stock, small areas of land were acquired in the vicinity of Ferry's Corner, and alterations in alignment made to provide greater clearances, whilst along Commercial Road, the Backwater was filled and reclaimed to allow the construction of a new embankment in connection with the reconstruction of Westham Bridge. Where the tramway had once run between the houses and the waterfront, the line now passed the newly-constructed pleasure gardens.

Plans to reconstruct the pier were drawn up in 1925, but it was another six years before agreement was reached between the Great Western and the Weymouth Corporation. In the meantime, further modifications were put in hand, with the Town Bridge being reconstructed in 1928-30. The new structure incorporated two arches in addition to the main span across the river, one spanning the railway and the other the water, and was provided at the expense of the GWR with an eye to a future widening of the quay.

The spirit of modernisation extended beyond replacement of the steamers and modifications to the tramway route for in August 1925 the *GWR Magazine* reported improvements to the engine shed at Weymouth, indicating

Ex-Bristol & Exeter Railway 0–6–0T No. 1376 at Weymouth locomotive shed in the mid-1920s. P. Q. TRELOAR COLLECTION

No. 1337 Hook Norton *with an up boat train in Commercial Road during the summer of 1925. Comparison with the photograph on page 13 shows that the engine had been fitted with a replacement smokebox door.* R. S. CARPENTER COLLECTION

that the old 45ft turntable 'is to be replaced by a 65ft table, in order that the Weymouth Boat Train service may be improved by the use of "Castle" class locomotives'. Examples of 'Castles' on the services were recorded in the latter 'twenties; the Old Oak Common engine turn during the summer months involved both the down and up trains, a working that remained mostly unchanged until the mid-1950s. Although a 'Castle' was specified, in practice it was not uncommon to see other 4–6–0s on this duty, including 'Stars' and 'Halls', especially in the quieter periods or when Old Oak's 'Castles' were otherwise engaged.

On the tramway, the long reign of the two ex-B&E locomotives came to an end, with No. 1377 being withdrawn from service in 1927, and No. 1376 moving away in the following year, transferring to Oswestry (almost a retirement home for small, ageing tank engines). Over the years, they had been assisted by various small engines, probably the best-known of which was the Manning Wardle 0–6–0ST No. 1337 *Hook Norton*. Their replacements were a pair of

No. 2194 Kidwelly at the quay around 1930. This view clearly illustrates the extended gap between the coaches resulting from the disconnection of the screw couplings and replacement by three-link couplings; to increase flexibility, the links were 16in long instead of the usual 12in. The gangways were also disconnected, and the vestibule doors locked, to allow the train to negotiate Ferry's Corner. AUTHOR'S COLLECTION

No. 2194 Kidwelly ready to depart with the boat train in the early 1930s. AUTHOR'S COLLECTION

Weymouth Quay in August 1929 with St. Julien *at the landing stage. The boat train had been split to allow detraining passengers access to the vessel whilst a temporary Locomotive Department steam crane can be seen at work. Passengers in much of the train had to use portable steps to reach ground level, a dangerous and time-consuming practice. Expansion of the facilities was clearly long overdue.*

NATIONAL RAILWAY MUSEUM

0–6–0STs absorbed in 1923 from the Burry Port & Gwendraeth Valley Railway, Nos. 2194 *Kidwelly* and 2195 *Cwm Mawr*, which were assisted from time to time by other small, absorbed tank engines.

In order to run the facilities at the quay, a total regular staff of around 40 were employed in 1929, plus casual staff when circumstances dictated. The overall responsibility rested in the hands of the Traffic & Maritime agent, who, as his title suggests, was in charge of both passenger and goods movements, and all aspects of shipping operations. In the Traffic Department, his staff comprised 4 clerks, 2 station inspectors, 18 dock porters, 2 senior dock checkers and 6 dock checkers. The Docks Department staff in the Maritime Office comprised 3 clerks, with a berthing master and a tubesweeper as shore staff. A steam launch, *Armine*, was provided with a coxwain and a driver, the latter being subsequently dispensed with.

The two passenger steamers *St. Helier* and *St. Julien* were operated as one 'running vessel' with a Master and 43 crew members, and a 'standby vessel' with a Master and 15 crew, probably forming the basis of the staff should a second steamer be required. In the summer months, an additional sailing staff of 36 was utilised, doubtless to bring the second boat up to operating strength. The cargo steamers *Roebuck* and *Sambur* were operated in a similar manner, with a Master and 15 crew in the 'running vessel', and a Second Officer and 7 crew on the 'standby vessel'. Again, in the summer months a Master and a further seven crew were added to the cargo complement. A small 'factory' was provided for the general maintenance of the vessels, being staffed by a foreman carpenter, a clerk/time & storekeeper, a blacksmith and a striker, a carpenter/shipwright, a fitter and a painter. With the increase in traffic in the mid-'thirties, a further twenty staff were employed as 'regular', having previously worked as 'casual', and the numbers were further strengthened as and when the traffic situation warranted it.

With its new steamers, trains and engines, the service became even more popular. Imports of seasonal perishables increased dramatically, and the need to improve facilities at the quay grew ever more urgent. As a temporary measure to assist in loading and unloading at peak times, steam cranes were provided when required by the Locomotive Department for use on the landing stage. But there was no real option open to the company other than to rebuild the quay.

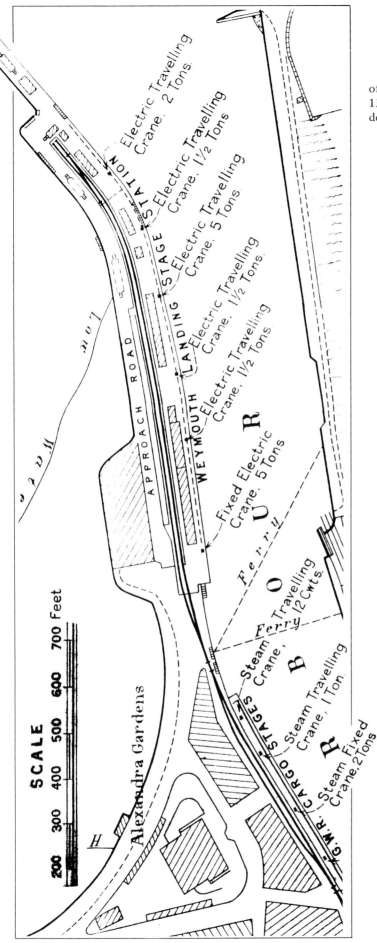

Work eventually started in February 1931, and was officially opened by the Prince of Wales on Thursday, 13th July 1933. The new pier and its facilities were fully described in the July issue of the *GWR Magazine*:

Pier and Harbour Improvements at Weymouth

Weymouth will be *en fête* on the thirteenth of the present month, on which date His Royal Highness the Prince of Wales has consented to open the pier and harbour on completion of a comprehensive scheme of improvements.

The scheme, which has involved a total outlay exceeding £120,000, is one in which the Great Western Railway, as the principal contributor of dues to the Corporation's harbour revenue, is closely interested.

Following upon negotiations between representatives of the Great Western Railway Company and the Weymouth Corporation, an arrangement was arrived at for financing the scheme, under which the cost was divided into three categories, viz.,

> (1) The main harbour works to be financed by a Corporation loan, sinking fund and interest being guaranteed by the Great Western Railway Company;
> (2) The cost of permanent way, cranes, capstans, etc., to be met by the Company, and
> (3) Such works as widening of quay road, pier extension, dredging, and provision of additional public amenities, to be met by the Corporation.

The need for improved accommodation at Weymouth for the Channel Islands and French traffic has been apparent for a number of years. Heavy seasonal imports of flowers, new potatoes, and tomatoes are received from Jersey and Guernsey, and broccoli and other vegetables from France, and the nature of this and other traffic dealt with at the port calls for the utmost speed in discharge from vessels and despatch by rail.

Although excellent service has been given by the Company, the work was often accomplished under extremely disadvantageous conditions, and the continued expansion of traffic tended still further to increase congestion and working difficulties.

Some idea of the extent of the increase in traffic dealt with at Weymouth will be gained from the fact that the harbour dues paid by the Great Western Railway Company to the Weymouth Corporation increased from £4,099 in 1922, to £8,541 in 1928, when French broccoli from Roscoff was first imported to Weymouth, and in each of the past three years the sum exceeded £10,000.

Previous to the completion of the present scheme, cargo vessels arriving at Weymouth were berthed at what is known as the cargo stage, use being made also of the passenger stage when necessary, and when not in use for passenger purposes.

The improvements effected include the construction of a new pier, with a general width of 100ft., following very much the same line as that taken by the old structure, which was only 30ft. wide. As shown on the accompanying diagram, the portion of the new pier, 100ft. wide, ends abruptly in approximately the position of the extreme end, or round head, of the old pier, but continues further seawards, 40ft. in width, for a distance of about 260ft. The total length of the new pier is nearly a quarter-of-a-mile.

The work, which was of considerable magnitude, is carried out entirely in reinforced concrete of two types: a solid portion, in which filling is held by retaining walls built on piles, and an open portion built entirely on piles under which a half-tide bank has been constructed to prevent silt from the bay entering the harbour.

The new pier has been designed to accommodate one passenger, three cargo, and two pleasure steamers simultaneously; berths for the latter, at the extreme end, are on either side of the extension, access to these being provided down the public promenade portion on the north side.

Up-to-date facilities exist in the shape of six electric cranes (one fixed and five travelling), capable of dealing with loads ranging from 30 cwt. to 5 tons, with a maximum radius of 60ft, and capstans electrically operated. The additional berths and cranes, together with an extended double line of track in place of the former single line, will enormously facilitate the handling of cargo traffic at the port.

Weymouth Harbour improvements in progress and photographed on 3rd August 1932, looking east. NATIONAL RAILWAY MUSEUM

Photographed on the same occasion as the view above, this looks towards the Pavilion Theatre and the Esplanade. The beach was busy on this lovely summer day.
NATIONAL RAILWAY MUSEUM

The reconstruction was finished in 1933 and this postcard view shows St. Helier *alongside the largely completed pier. The new buildings on the pier were mirrored by similar new structures at St. Peter Port, Guernsey, built at the same time. By an agreement of 1932, the formerly separate GWR and SR staffs in the Channel Islands were amalgamated, the GWR assuming control in Guernsey and the SR in Jersey.*
P. Q. TRELOAR COLLECTION

No less valuable will be the improved accommodation for dealing with the Channel Islands passenger traffic, which has also substantially increased in recent years. During the peak period of the holiday traffic, reached in the months of July, August, and September, the additional facilities will be of particular benefit.

The platform accommodation, which was formerly adequate for only four coaches, is now sufficient to accommodate 36 coaches.

The baggage shed, directly opposite the passenger boat berth, has been extended and renovated, and gives excellent facilities for Customs examination.

A new refreshment room for passengers has also been provided.

At intervals along the pier, a number of other buildings have been erected. These include mess rooms and offices for the Customs and other staff.

The whole of the pier and buildings will be lighted by electricity.

On the promenade pier every effort has been made to provide for the needs of the public. Reinforced concrete shelters, of pleasing design, have been constructed, with accessible flat roofs protected by ornamental railings; bathing facilities have been provided in the way of dressing accommodation and an elaborate diving stage; and stairways down to the water constructed at intervals along the pier for the use of small craft.

These amenities will be greatly appreciated by the thousands of holiday-makers who patronise Weymouth each year. Whatever of business may be in process, it will be to the landward of the holiday-maker enjoying sea breezes on the pier extension. A wide vista of blue sea is before him, with delightful views of Portland Bill on the one hand and a long range of Dorsetshire coast on the other.

An admirable breadth of comprehension in the scheme has done justice to the claims of business and pleasure, in both of which sides of Weymouth development the Great Western Railway is interested.

The construction of the new pier and buildings was entrusted to Messrs. Bolton and Lakin, Ltd., contractors, Birmingham, the work being supervised by a resident engineer, on behalf of the Great Western Railway Company's Chief Engineer, in whose office the whole of the plans were prepared.

With full-length platforms now available at the landing stage, long boat trains could at last be conveniently handled. During that summer, the 9.30 a.m. Paddington and the 3.45 p.m. Weymouth Quay trains were joined on the tramway on Saturdays by a new service from and to Birmingham. This left Snow Hill at 9.30 a.m., arriving in Weymouth at 2.10 p.m., returning from the Quay station at 4.10 p.m. for Birmingham. The boat portion of the train comprised a five-coach set (Van Third, two Thirds, Compo and Van Third), whilst a Town portion of another six vehicles (including a Dining Car) catered for those travelling no further than the beach. This service was scheduled to continue into the winter season of that year, with six coaches working on the 8.10 a.m. Birmingham to Weston-super-Mare as far as Stapleton Road, with three coaches for Weymouth Town and three for the Quay forming the 10.35 a.m. hence, again returning as the 4.10 p.m. Weymouth Quay (and 4.25 Town).

In the summer of 1934, changes were made to the timings, with the London train now leaving at 8.30 a.m. for a steamer departure of 12.10 p.m., and the Birmingham train at the same time on Saturdays only, with the connecting steamer leaving the quay at 1.30 p.m. The 8.30 a.m.

steamer from Jersey (10.45 Guernsey) connected with both return trains (3.45 for London, 4.5 to Birmingham [Saturdays]). The second steamer left Jersey on Saturday nights at 9.0 p.m., giving a 6.30 a.m. departure from the Quay station, with a Third and Brake Compo for Bristol, and a Third, Compo and Van Third (together with a Dining Car from Weymouth Jct for breakfasts) to Paddington. The three boats advertised for the services were 'Fast Turbine Steamers' *St. Helier*, *St. Julien* and *St. Patrick*, each attributed a speed of 19 knots and accommodation for 1,000 passengers.

From the winter service of 1934, the traditional connection on the 9.25 p.m. Paddington to Neyland train was discontinued, and a direct service instituted on Tuesday, Thursday and Saturday nights. This train left Paddington at 10.15 p.m., reaching the landing stage at 1.57 a.m., the balanced working of the 3.40 p.m. Weymouth Quay train earlier in the day. A four-coach set was utilised (Van Third, Third, Compo and Van Third), with an extra Van being added for the winter 1935 timetable. From the winter of 1936, a Dining Car was added to the formation, this probably being the first such vehicle to work onto the tramway on a regular basis.

The articulated stock on the summer service would appear to have been withdrawn after the 1936 season, being replaced from 1937 by a five- or six-coach rake and a Brake Van, with the dining facilities being removed at Weymouth Jct. Thus, the summer and winter arrangements remained until the outbreak of the Second World War.

In 1934, the Great Western introduced a small number of 0–6–0PT dock tanks, the '1366' class. One of these engines, No. 1367, joined *Kidwelly* and *Cwm Mawr* at work on the tramway line during 1935, thus commencing an association with the line by the class that was to last for twenty-eight years.

Despite all the improvements made, there still remained one major problem on the line – that of Ferry's Corner. As early as 1928, the Great Western's general manager had obtained permission from the Board for this restrictive curve to be eased, but it was 1938 before work was commenced, due largely to the difficulties experienced in negotiating a suitable agreement with Weymouth Corporation. There were also protracted discussions with Cosens & Co., whose premises were adjacent to the line, and who would lose the use of their crane by the construction of the realignment. In addition to easing the curve, it was intended that the quay should be widened between Ferry's Corner and Custom House Quay.

In 1938, work began at the Town Bridge, where a new quay wall was constructed and infilled. At Ferry's Corner, the reclamation was far more extensive, to allow for the larger radius of the tramway line, but this had been completed by July 1939. The new alignment now took the tramway under the Town Bridge by the arch closest to the water (which had been reclaimed from the river, as planned), whilst the new curve at Ferry's Corner was

eased to some six chains. At the latter point, the old alignment was retained as a loop, and was occasionally used for through running, though it was primarily intended as a siding for the use of Cosens.

With the completion of Ferry's Corner, the tramway reached the zenith of its prewar development. Passenger rolling stock could now work over the line virtually

These views, taken on 7th March 1939, show the new harbour wall at Ferry's Corner under construction with infilling already started. Wagons were standing on Cosens and Webb Major's sidings.
NATIONAL RAILWAY MUSEUM

Reconstruction work completed at Ferry's Corner on 19th July 1939. The new line can be seen sweeping round on the left whilst, on the right, the line of the former harbour wall is clearly defined with the original route and Cosen's siding remaining in use.
NATIONAL RAILWAY MUSEUM

A sequence of photographs illustrating the widening of the quay between Ferry's Corner and the Town Bridge. Work commenced in March 1938 and the realigned tramway was brought into use in March 1939.
NATIONAL RAILWAY MUSEUM

No. 1367 with an up perishables train, on 31st August 1938, passing the Town Bridge whilst reconstruction of the quay was in progress.
L&GRP

Widening of Custom House Quay in progress with the tramway still on the original alignment.
NATIONAL RAILWAY MUSEUM

This view shows workmen standing aside as No. 2195 Cwm Mawr was easing her short train through the reconstruction work in August 1938. AUTHOR'S COLLECTION

A view of the reconstruction work now more advanced on 7th March 1939.

NATIONAL RAILWAY MUSEUM

An up boat train, possibly the 4.5 p.m. to Cardiff, ascending the 1 in 51 climb to Bincombe Tunnel in the charge of an unidentified 'Star' class 4–6–0, in the late 1930s. The train had passed Upwey Junction station and was approaching Littlemoor Road bridge.   N. SHEPHERD

Such trains were routinely banked from Weymouth and this view shows the banker of the above train – on this occasion a 'Hall' class 4–6–0 crossing Littlemoor Road.   N. SHEPHERD

unhindered, although some of the longer and wider vehicles remained prohibited. As set out in the 1936 *Appendix to the Working Timetable*, the articulated stock, vehicles not exceeding 60ft 6½in over buffers with 7ft bogies, and coaches not exceeding 9ft 3¼in width and 59ft 4in length (or bogie centres not exceeding 42ft, or with a bogie centre to buffer measurement of not more than 10ft) could work the line. To clarify the rules for the staff, all qualified vehicles were provided with a plate marked 'WXQ' on their ends. In 1937, this was eased to include vehicles not exceeding 63ft 6½in over buffers with 7ft bogies, and otherwise 60ft 6½in length (bogie to bogie centre measurement being increased to a maximum of 43ft 6in, though with the 10ft overhang still limiting). Stock could now also operate over the line without the requirement of replacing the couplings at Weymouth Junction.

The perishable traffic continued apace, with a total of over 40,000 tons being imported annually in the latter 1930s. In 1937, Weymouth handled 11,500 tons of potatoes and 12,000 tons of tomatoes from Jersey alone, which required prompt and careful handling at the quay on arrival. Indeed, a considerable organisation was in place to deal with this traffic. At peak periods in 1938, five 'C' headlamp trains were scheduled to leave Weymouth yard at 2.0 and 10.50 a.m., 1.40, 5.5 and 9.15 p.m. for Westbury. After an engine change (in most cases), the trains were worked onwards variously to Southall, Paddington, Bordesley Jct,

Oxley Sidings or Cardiff (via Bristol) as required, with connections en route to many other destinations. At the quay, each boat would be offloaded where possible so that the wagons left in a specific order, with traffic for the North and Midlands first, then South Wales, London, and finally Bristol. If there was insufficient traffic to warrant any of the specials (normally fifteen wagons minimum), the wagons would be forwarded by regular services from Weymouth yard, including the 12.40 or 4.30 a.m. to Bristol, 11.12 to Swindon (for the North), 12.40 p.m. to Bristol, 1.10 to Severn Tunnel Jct., 3.15 to Westbury (for the West Country), 6.35 to Paddington and 8.8 p.m. to Bristol. A considerable supply of empty wagons was required to handle the traffic, and 'Oil Box Opens, Opens "A", Opens "B", Vacuum Vans and Non-Vacuum Vans' were specified; these were worked into the Weymouth area as 'C' or 'D' headlamp trains. Such was the requirement for additional rolling stock to convey this perishable traffic that in 1937-38 200 new fruit vans were built at Swindon largely for the Guernsey tomato traffic. Most were dedicated to work from Weymouth Quay but they were also employed on the extensive fruit traffic from the Vale of Evesham. Wagons destined for the quay would often convey empty fruit and vegetable baskets and packages for Guernsey or Jersey, and were carefully marked accordingly.

With the tramway improved throughout its length in the summer of 1939, the season looked set to be the best ever.

2–6–0 No. 7305 on an up Weymouth 'C' class freight conveying Jersey potatoes near Witham on 23rd July 1935.   L&GRP

No. 2195 Kidwelly *(left) and No. 2194* Cwm Mawr *(right) at Weymouth Quay in August 1938.*   AUTHOR'S COLLECTION

Indeed, the deteriorating international situation induced a 'now or never' atmosphere, and the August Bank Holiday traffic to both Weymouth and the Channel Islands broke all previous records. The boat train on Saturday, 5th August 1939, ran in two heavy parts, the first part (No. 106) conveying a twin dining set as far as Weymouth Junction, with the normal five coaches (Van Third, two Compos, Third, Van Third) and an extra seven Thirds and a Brake Van working through over the tramway; this part carried registered seat passengers only. The second part, train No. 105, was formed of fifteen vehicles (Brake Compo, twelve Thirds, Compo, Van Third), and conveyed both seat-registered and unregistered passengers for the Channel Islands. The two sets of coaches returned as parts of the 3.40 p.m. Weymouth Quay (trains Nos. 330 and 331). The Saturdays-only 8.30 a.m. Birmingham service also ran (train No. 715, with the returning boat portion leaving the quay that afternoon at around 4.30 to connect with the 4.45 p.m. Weymouth Town at the Junction. Another Saturday train (No. 340) was scheduled to leave from the quay station on summer Saturday afternoons — the 4.5 p.m. to Cardiff, consisting of three Thirds, a Compo and a Van Third; this connected with the 4.20 Weymouth Town to Cardiff train at the Junction. The Cardiff service had been introduced around 1936, but had no equivalent down service, though passengers could connect with the 9.30 a.m.

Bristol to Weymouth Town, which also conveyed three coaches (Van Third, Compo, Van Third) for the quay, arriving at midday. At August Bank Holiday weekends, it had also become the custom to run an evening train from Wolverhampton to the quay, connecting with an additional boat.

The year also saw the departure of *Cwm Mawr* from Weymouth — she was withdrawn from service in March 1939, but was reinstated in December of that year for war service though she did not return to her old haunts; in her place, No. 1371 arrived from Danygraig.

On 3rd September 1939, the nation found itself at war again, causing the immediate curtailment of the Channel Islands passenger service; the last 'up' boat arrived at the quay at 2.20 a.m. on Wednesday, 6th September, although *Roebuck* and *Sambur* continued on the cargo services, and the tramway remained open for goods traffic. The passenger and mail steamers were requisitioned by the Admiralty, and in due course both distinguished themselves at Dunkirk.

A passenger service to the Islands was maintained from Southampton by the Southern Railway, but this, together with the cargo boats from Weymouth, ceased abruptly on Monday, 1st July 1940, when the Germans occupied the Channel Islands. The GWR Marine Department was suspended 'for the duration', but the tramway continued to run as required for the use of the military. The Royal Navy had requisitioned the pier and the passenger stage in May 1940, and, following the withdrawal of the cargo services, also acquired the cargo stage. A fence was constructed across the quay adjacent to the cargo stage, with a gate set in to allow access for trains using the tramway, but the entire area was closed to civilians, and military checkpoints established to control entry.

In 1940, the second of the BP and GVR engines, *Kidwelly*, was transferred away, leaving Nos. 1367 and 1371 to carry out duties throughout the war.

At first, Weymouth Harbour's function was that of a contraband control station for the examination of merchant shipping in the Channel, but, as the war progressed, its importance increased dramatically. As plans were laid down for the invasion of Europe, it was proposed that both Weymouth and Portland harbours would be major embarkation ports for the allied armies. Included in those preparations was the construction of a new pier into the harbour, to be used for loading locomotives and stock onto train ferry boats for use in Europe after the invasion;

the loading pier was constructed by the Army, but the permanent way was provided and maintained by the GWR. It was so arranged that the loading ramp could be used to load a train ferry berthed at the cargo stage but, in the event, the facility was never used.

During early 1944, many thousands of allied servicemen began to congregate in southern England, and it became apparent that Weymouth Harbour was to play a major part in the invasion of Normandy. In the frenetic months prior to the invasion, the various units received a number of distinguished visitors who came to view the preparations. Amongst these was General de Gaulle who, in May 1944, inspected a detachment of French marines (which included his own son) on the cargo stage at Weymouth Quay. In the months that followed D-Day, over 517,000 troops and 144,000 vehicles passed through Weymouth and Portland Harbours, many of the first to leave being American soldiers bound for 'Omaha' beach and all the difficulties encountered there at that bloody shambles.

Weymouth Quay in May 1944 with preparations underway for Operation Overlord, the Allied invasion of Europe. These men were loading supplies but the combat troops of Force 'O' who sailed from Weymouth and Portland harbours, were bound for 'Omaha' beach. The presence of railway wagons in the background reveals that the Weymouth Harbour Tramway played its part in these momentous events.
U.S. ARMY

By the time this view was taken, on 28th July 1950, traffic to the Channel Islands had returned to, and indeed was exceeding, pre-war levels. In this immediate postwar era of affluence, paid holidays and restrictions on foreign travel, the Islands were a popular destination – a means of 'going abroad' without actually doing so! No. 1370 is seen here waiting at the Quay with an up boat train.

W. GILBERT

THE POSTWAR ERA

FOLLOWING 'VE' Day, a very limited GWR cargo service was reinstated to the recently-liberated Channel Islands. Four months later, *Sambur* reopened the full service, on 14th September 1945, being joined shortly afterwards by her sister ship, *Roebuck*. However, it was not until Sunday, 16th June 1946 that the first passenger and mail steamer returned to the Islands, with *St. Helier* inaugurating the service — rather appropriately, as she had been the last GWR passenger steamer to leave Jersey in those uncertain days of 1939. *St. Helier* had received an 'austerity' refit following her war service; she was joined by *St. Julien* in November 1946.

On the tramway, goods traffic recommenced in September 1945 with the de-requisitioning of the pier area and the return of the cargo boats. The reintroduced passenger trains ran into the quay station at around 1.5 a.m. on Wednesday, Friday and Sunday mornings, the first one in connection with the return of *St. Helier* on 16th June 1946; not surprisingly, this was fully reported by the *GWR Magazine*, and the following excerpt appeared in the August 1946 issue under the heading 'A Ship Comes Home':

> Our Channel Islands steamship *St. Helier* has had her own Victory Parade, and well she has deserved it. It is fitting that as the last mailboat to sail from Jersey in September 1939, she

should be the first to return to the island with the restoration of the Weymouth—Channel Islands passenger steamer service. The years between these voyages have been studded with danger and high adventure for *St. Helier* and her crew; readers will recall the story of her exploits which we published in the January Magazine.

Gleaming after her austerity refit, *St. Helier* had a right royal welcome at Weymouth, her home port, when she arrived to inaugurate the resumed service. There were flags and bunting on the pier; *Sambur, Roebuck* and *Empire Seasilver* had 'dressed ship' for the occasion; the Great Western house-flag flew from the Company's marine offices. As *St. Helier* entered the harbour, every siren sounded, and even the ships of the Home Fleet, anchored at Portland, saluted her.

A Memorable Send-off
A large crowd of holidaymakers and officials were waiting on the quay. After the ship berthed a party went on board, led by the Mayor of Weymouth (Councillor C. H. J. Kaile), and Mr. Leslie E. Ford, OBE, Chief Docks Manager. Included in the group were Mr. Davie Blee, Chief Goods Manager, Mr. R. G. Pole, divisional superintendent, Bristol, Mr. E. A. Glayzer, Staff Assistant to the Superintendent of the Line, and other officers.

After the visitors had been greeted by the master of *St. Helier*, Captain R. R. Pitman, DSC, Mr. Ford asked the company to drink a toast to this brave officer who was awarded his decoration for his conduct at Dunkirk.

With the boat train from Paddington pulling into Weymouth prompt to time, the ship was invaded by an eager crowd of holidaymakers, and shortly afterwards, at 2.0 a.m. on Sunday, June 16, *St. Helier* set out on her maiden peacetime voyage to the Channel Islands.

A box-camera holiday snapshot of Weymouth Quay with St. Julien *alongside, about 1950. The boards on the right advertised boat trips around Portland Harbour to view HM warships; such trips were taken by generations of holidaymakers and were a highlight of their stay in the town.*

JOHN HARRISON

The regular train left Paddington at 9.10 p.m. (Tuesday, Thursday and Saturday evenings) and consisted of a Van Third, two Thirds, three Compos, two Thirds and a Van Third. The return journey departed from the quay for Paddington at 3.40 p.m. on Tuesdays, Thursdays and Saturdays. So popular was the service that the figures for the latter part of 1946 were only slightly less than the last full year of prewar sailings — 10,796, as compared with 12,748 for the whole of 1938. Goods and parcels tonnage were also only slightly down on the full 1938 figures. Once again, the Southern Railway provided alternate services from Waterloo on Monday, Wednesday and Friday nights in connection with their steamer from Southampton.

By 1947, the staff complement was fully back to prewar levels, an indication of the activity which was taking place at Weymouth Quay:

Staff
Quay Superintendent (Special Class)
Chief Clerk (Class Two)
Woman Clerk/Typist (Class Two)

General Office
Clerk (Class Three)
6 Clerks (Class Five)
Woman Clerk (Class Two)
Junior Messenger

Customs & Correspondence Office
Clerk (Class Four)
6 Clerks (Class Five)
2 Women Clerks (Class Two)
Junior Messenger

Cargo Office
4 Clerks (Class Five)

Uniformed Staff
Inspector (Class Three)
2 Supervisory Foreman (Class Five)
6 Dock Checkers
23 Dock Porters

The two '1366' class 0–6–0PT engines on the tramway, Nos. 1367 and 1371, were joined in June 1946 by No. 1370 in readiness for the reintroduced passenger services over the line. No. 2195 (formerly *Cwm Mawr*) had also previously returned to Weymouth to work on the tramway for a short period.

For the summer service of 1947, the company reverted to prewar practice with daily sailings from Weymouth each afternoon. The boat train left Paddington at 8.45 a.m., reaching the quay at 12.30 p.m. to connect with the 1.0 p.m. sailing, which was due into Guernsey at 5.15 p.m. and Jersey at 7.45. A balancing service left Jersey at 8.30 a.m. and Guernsey at 10.15, due into Weymouth at around 3.0 p.m., connecting with the 3.40 to Paddington. The London boat train was formed as in the winter service, but with the addition of a buffet car. In addition, the Saturdays-only Birmingham train was reintroduced, departing from Snow Hill at 8.0 a.m. and comprising nine coaches (Brake Compo, Third, Compo, Third, Van Third, Brake Compo, Third, Compo, Van Third); curiously, this stock returned

from the quay that afternoon as the 4.5 p.m. to Bristol and Cardiff, any Birmingham passengers being directed to the London train and advised to change at Reading. Perhaps this was a way of sharing any inconvenience, as Cardiff and Bristol passengers bound for the Islands were catered for by having to change into the down London boat train at Westbury.

Coaching stock restrictions were altered at this time to allow the passage of more modern rolling stock, and now specified the limits as those GWR (or other companies') stock not exceeding 63ft 6in length over buffers by 9ft 3in width over body, 64ft 6in length over buffers by 9ft 0in body width, or GWR stock 66ft 8in length over buffers by 8ft 11in width over body. Screw couplings had to be 'slackened 3 or 4 threads'.

The immediate postwar period was a time of reconstruction for the tramway, with a continuation of work done in the 1930s. Contemporary GWR and BR Western Region documents reveal a large number of derailments on the line, and work commenced on relaying the track; by 1952, the entire tramway had been relayed, with check rails added to those sections which had not been dealt with in the 1938 work. Another project undertaken was the complete reconstruction of the timber cargo stage — deemed life-expired in 1939 — which had been completely ruined by heavy wartime usage. This work was completed in 1951, and was followed by the installation of splendid new electrically-powered cranes from Stothert & Pitt of Bath, replacing the steam-driven relics formerly in use. The harbour wall was reconstructed between the cargo stage and the end of St. Mary Street, the point at which the wall reconstruction carried out by the GWR in 1938 had finished; this involved the temporary removal of Templeman's siding, and when completed had widened the Custom House Quay by 13ft.

Following Nationalisation in 1948, on 2nd April 1950, all ex-GWR lines to the south of Sparkford, including the Bridport, Abbotsbury and Easton lines, were transferred to the Southern Region of British Railways. Accordingly, all commercial, engineering and other functions were transferred along with the operating staff, although trains continued in the hands of the Western Region as penetrating services. Boat trains continued to run from and to Paddington, Birmingham and Cardiff, with three of the '1366' class engines working them over the tramway. In the case of the latter, the daily working was shown as the 12.3 p.m. from the Junction to the Quay (12.20), and the 3.40 p.m. Quay (12.20), and the 3.40 p.m. Quay to the Junction (3.57), with two parts on Saturdays, plus the down Birmingham and up Cardiff portions.

The perishable traffic from the Channel Islands continued to flow, with the 'Perpot' (GWR telegraphic code for special train of potatoes, vegetables and other perishable traffic from Weymouth) trains being as familiar a sight as in prewar days. These would again run at short notice, and often require several trains each day in order to clear

57XX 0–6–0PT No. 5784, on 28th August 1954, crossing the junction with King Street before entering Weymouth station yard with an up boat train. The pub on the corner of King Street and Commercial Road was the Portland Railway Hotel.   AUTHOR'S COLLECTION

the incoming cargoes. The extra vehicles for this traffic would be accommodated in the extensive sidings to the east of the engine shed and in the 'Jersey' sidings to the west of the main line at Radipole, and in the 'Jubilee' sidings by the main station yard at Weymouth; the empty vehicles would be worked onto the quay as required.

At busy times, cargo vessels would discharge their loads at the berths at the seaward end of the pier, beyond the passenger berths. Some shunting was undertaken at the quay by the tramway engines, but very often vans would be drawn up from the far end of the pier at the rear of a departing boat train, and left in a more convenient position for loading, thus saving a shunting movement. Trains of loaded vehicles were then worked along the tramway to Weymouth yard, where they would frequently be remarshalled in the 'Jersey' or 'Jubilee' sidings, the brake van attached to the rear, and the train sent on its way. 'Hall' class 4–6–0s and '28XX' class 2–8–0s were the favoured power for 'Perpot' trains, and often worked through to Bristol (East Depot), though engine crews usually changed at Westbury. Shunting in the yards at Weymouth was usually undertaken by the pilots, larger pannier tanks of the '74XX' and '57XX' class, whilst the '1366' engines were generally restricted to work on the tramway.

The journey from the quay to the yard generally took about sixteen minutes, the maximum speed allowed being 4 mph. On occasions this time could be exceeded; at high tide, the line was often flooded beneath the Town Bridge, and at spring tides to a considerable depth. Trains would then have to wait for the water to recede, often for forty or fifty minutes. A train standing in the streets at such times was vulnerable to idle vandalism – it was not unusual for juveniles to remove the tail lamp from the last vehicle which was simply hung from the drawhook, and to throw it into the harbour. Delays could also be caused when up trains arrived at Weymouth yard gates; a telephone (housed in a cabinet just inside the gates) was used to advise the Weymouth Junction signalman that the train had arrived, but the trains often had to stand, trailing along Commercial Road, until a conflicting movement on the adjacent Portland line had been completed.

In the days before mass motoring, a train standing in the middle of a poorly-lit street at night was not too much of a problem, but as road traffic increased, so, too, did the number of incidents. On one occasion in 1948, a train was held at the gates to the station yard, awaiting clearance to enter, with its tail lamp unofficially removed. A car containing a number of sailors crashed into the back of the train, but no blame was attached to the railwaymen or the car driver, although the investigating police officer did comment on the lateness of the hour and the fact that the sailors were off-duty!

As the numbers of vehicles on the roads around the tramway increased, so did the difficulties for the operating staff, with parked cars and lorries becoming a perennial problem. The working of loose-coupled goods trains could also be a hazard; road vehicles would impatiently follow the slow-moving train far too closely, and a car driver would be unpleasantly surprised if the train engine suddenly stopped and the wagon buffers compressed and the train then rebounded back towards him! In due course, notice boards were carried on the rear of loose-coupled goods trains carrying the warning 'Danger — Keep 50ft Clear'.

Down boat trains from Paddington arriving at Weymouth would be brought to a stand on the main line at the Junction inner home signal, where the train engine (usually a 'Castle' class 4—6—0 from Old Oak, working Turn No. 22) would be removed with the dining car and any vehicles destined for the Town station. The '1366' engine would then move onto the train, couple up, and move off past the

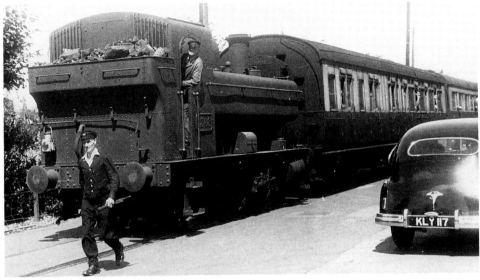

No. 1368 amongst the road traffic in Commercial Road, on 8th August 1952, with a down boat train bound for the quay. A. B. CROSS

This view shows No. 1368 on the final leg of its journey, passing the cargo stage, with the rear elevation of Devonshire Buildings dominating the background.
G. F. BANNISTER

No. 1370 shunting wagons at the quay in the mid-1950s.
I. D. BEALE

Junction signal box and down the line to the quay; a total of seven minutes were allowed for the engine change.

Up boat services would be brought into Weymouth yard and, with the train standing on the up Portland line, engines would be changed using the scissors crossing. The *Appendix to the Service Timetable* contained five pages of specific instructions for the working of the tramway, and included a provision for the changing of engines of special trains from the quay: 'When necessary, through Trains from the Tramway Line must be brought to a stand clear of and on the Quay side of the Approach Road to Melcombe Regis Station, at which point the Train Engine may be attached. The Train Engine, however, must not be taken beyond the corner of the Gardens'. By the mid-1950s, it had become the practice for boat trains to pull into the yard, and the engines changed using the loops on the tramway just inside the yard gates.

With the tramway under the control of the Southern Region, it became increasingly apparent that economies would be made, particularly as the former competing route via Southampton was also in the hands of the same body. In due course, it was decided that the Channel Islands service would be concentrated on Weymouth, but that major changes would be made which would remove the remaining influence of the Western Region on tramway operations. On Saturday, 26th September 1959, 'Castle' class No. 7010 *Avondale Castle* took the 'Channel Islands Boat Express' on its final journey to Paddington; thereafter, the boat train was routed to and from Waterloo. New steamers were ordered to replace the now elderly *St. Helier* and *St. Julien*, which finished their working lives in September 1960 after 35 years of service, though *Sambur* and *Roebuck* continued at work until 1965.

In 1960, agreement was reached with the Weymouth Corporation for the reconstruction of the quay. An addi-

tional platform road was to be added but the original 1888 baggage examination hall was retained. The rebuilding work was completed in 1961.

Another link with the GWR was severed in 1962 with the transfer of the '1366' class tank engines to Wadebridge, where they took over the Wenford Bridge line from the ex-L&SWR Beattie 2—4—0WTs. Of the '1366s', No. 1367 stood out as the engine which had served the tramway for twenty-seven continuous years (apart from periods of repair). Thereafter, only a few '57XX' 0—6—0PTs remained at Weymouth to fly the Great Western flag, and these were occasionally used on the tramway; the last such engine to work over the line was No. 4610, which hauled the boat train on Christmas Eve 1963.

The Channel Islands service prospered during the 1960s, with as many as three trains occasionally being accommodated at the quay. Motor cars were transported to the Islands in increasing numbers, and the author has clear recollections of vehicles being craned aboard the vessels using the electric cranes at the cargo stage. In due course, a roll-on, roll-off car ferry terminal was built, but the tramway continued to carry the connecting boat trains for passengers from and to Waterloo. In the 1980s, the privatised 'Sealink' service was transferred away from Weymouth, and the tramway thereafter had no regular use. At the time of writing, the line remains in situ and available for traffic. With all sidings and loops removed, it now stands as a single line from Weymouth yard, much as it was when first built in the 1860s. At Weymouth, a single red colour light signal glows steadfast along Commercial Road, controlling access to the station yard from the silent tramway and, where they are not disturbed by passing road traffic, the rails are covered by a heavy coat of rust, with no engines, coaches or wagons to polish them.

4–6–0 'Castle' class No. 5093 Upton Castle, of Old Oak Common shed, getting away from Weymouth with an up boat train. T. G. HEPBURN

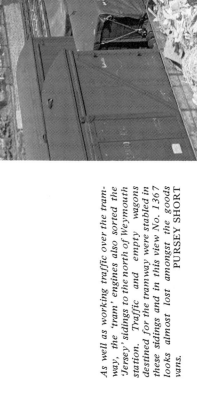

As well as working traffic over the tramway, the 'tram' engines also sorted the 'Jersey' sidings to the north of Weymouth station. Traffic and empty wagons destined for the tramway were stabled in these sidings and in this view No. 1367 looks almost lost amongst the goods vans.   PURSEY SHORT

CHAPTER FOUR

ALONG THE LINE
A PICTORIAL JOURNEY

General view of Weymouth Junction around 1950. The Weymouth Harbour Tramway and the Portland line passed behind the signal box and joined the main line beyond. The main arrival and departure lines to Weymouth station feature on the centre right with the up and down engine roads to Weymouth locomotive shed on the far right.

J. H. MOSS

No. 1368 awaiting her next tramway duty alongside Weymouth Junction Signal Box.

WESSEX COLLECTION

A fascinating view of Weymouth goods yard in 1956, taken from the tower of Christchurch shortly before it was demolished. The tramway entered the yard by crossing King Street (on the left of the photograph) and passed behind the goods shed before joining with the Portland line. Visible beyond the goods yard are the Jubilee sidings used for stabling passenger rolling stock. As well as the regular passenger services, carriages for the large number of excursion trains arriving at Weymouth were stabled in these sidings. This view illustrates a typical town goods yard shortly before the road motor lorry took this traffic away from the railway.
GRAHAM HERBERT COLLECTION/DORSET COUNTY LIBRARY

Weymouth looking towards Portland.

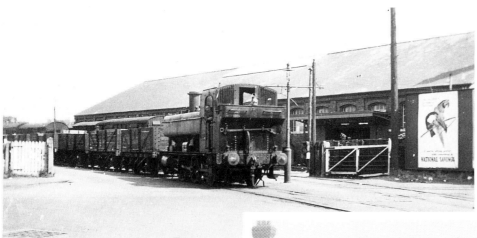

An aerial view of Weymouth, photographed in 1946 and issued as a postcard in the years immediately after the Second World War. The tramway left the goods yard and, passing in front of Alexandra Terrace, ran along Commercial Road before reaching Ferry's Corner. Capital ships of the Royal Navy are visible in Portland Harbour including the distinctive outline of HMS Nelson, recently returned to home waters after wartime service in the Far East.
AUTHOR'S COLLECTION

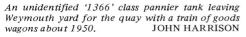

An unidentified '1366' class pannier tank leaving Weymouth yard for the quay with a train of goods wagons about 1950. JOHN HARRISON

No. 2195 Cwm Mawr arriving in Weymouth yard on an up boat train with the shunter riding on the leading footstep. The presence of a passenger luggage van at the head of the boat train was a regular feature in the pre-war years. AUTHOR'S COLLECTION

SWANS, WEYMOUTH

An early postcard view of the tramway passing in front of Alexandra Terrace before entering Weymouth yard. The entire area of water visible was reclaimed following the reconstruction of the Portland branch 'Backwater' viaduct and the establishment of Melcombe Regis station.
AUTHOR'S COLLECTION

No. 1370 arriving at Weymouth yard with an up boat train on 28th August 1954 and passing Alexandra Terrace.
AUTHOR'S COLLECTION

No. 1367 on 6th June 1956 approaching the junction with King Street under the watchful eye of the shunter. The Weymouth & District Co-operative Society coal delivery lorry would have had to wait for the lengthy train to pass before continuing on its round. On the right the well-established gardens were laid out on land reclaimed from the Backwater.
AUTHOR'S COLLECTION

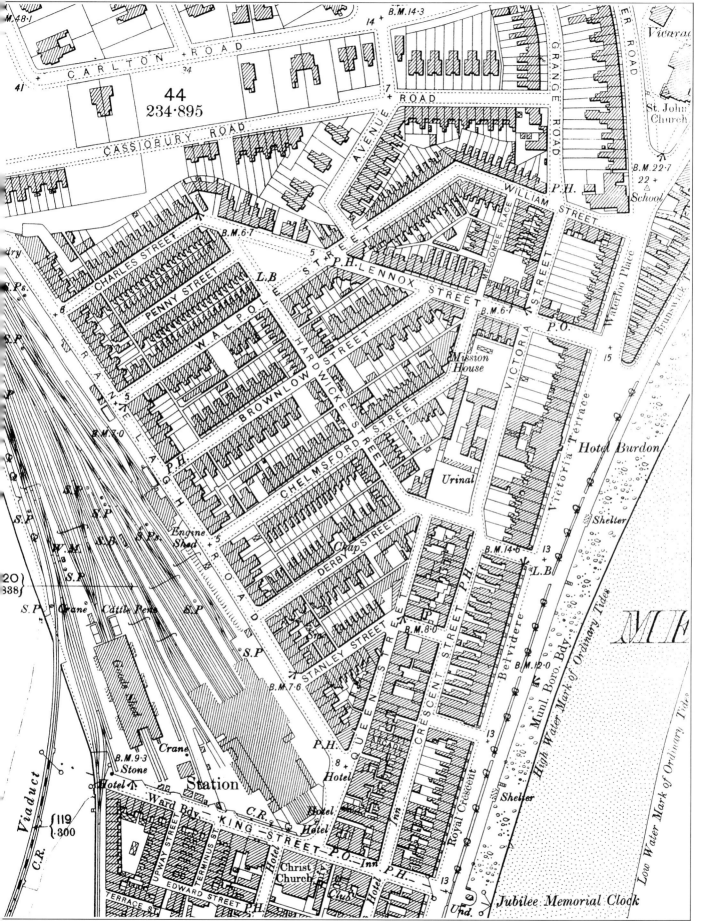

42

Looking along Commercial Road on 31st August 1938 towards Weymouth station.

L & GRP

57XX 0−6−0PT No. 7780 running light along an unusually quiet Commercial Road in the early 1960s.

I. D. BEALE

No. 1370 crossing Westham Road and passing the New Bridge Hotel on 2nd May 1957 with an up boat train.   P. H. WELLS

The shunter holding up the road traffic on Westham Road, on 10th July 1951, while No. 1367 passed with an up train of Fruit Vans. The building on the right of the photograph was the former Melcombe Regis Boys School built in 1912 and now demolished.   R. H. TUNSTALL

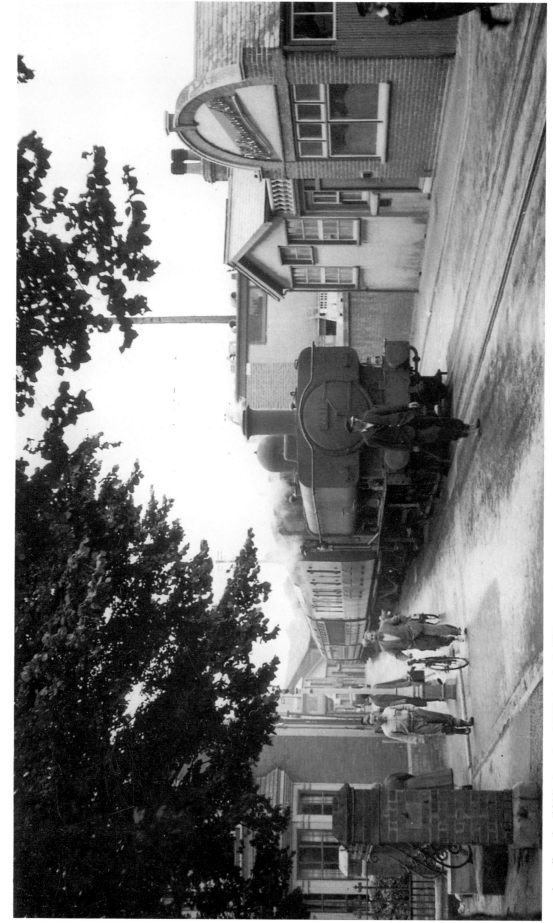

As well as the '1366' class, the '74XX' class 0–6–0PTs were also permitted to work on the tramway. This view shows No. 7418 in Commercial Road, approaching Westham Road Crossing on an up boat train. No. 7418 is recorded as the first of the class to have worked on the tramway in July 1951 but for a period in 1953, when the '1356' class was temporarily banned, the '74XX' class took over all workings.

AUTHOR'S COLLECTION

The tail-end of a down boat train in Commercial Road about 1950, with cyclists weaving along behind the slowly moving train.
JOHN HARRISON

A view along the tramway in Commercial Road on 29th June 1932. NATIONAL RAILWAY MUSEUM

An unidentified Drewry 204 hp diesel shunter making its way along Commercial Road on a damp day in the early 1960s. This photograph was taken during the transition period between steam and diesel traction.
I. D. BEALE

This photograph, taken on 9th April 1946, shows No. 2195 running without her Cwm Mawr nameplates. She returned to Weymouth from November 1945 until June 1946 as a temporary supplement to the two '1366s' that had served throughout the war. The train is seen here standing on the tramway — the siding in the foreground was formerly known as Bagg's siding and served the extensive timber yard of John Bagg. By the time this photograph was taken, it was known as Webb Majors siding and yard.

R. K. BLENCOWE

A view along the tramway towards Weymouth station, with Webb Majors siding and timber yard on the right. Photographed on 31st August 1938.

L&GRP

In the 19th century, coal for bunkering the steamers was worked down to a siding near the cargo landing stage where it was transferred to barges and taken down to the ships. In 1898 it was proposed to construct a new Marine Coal siding near Bagg's siding but, before construction could commence, the harbour wall required strengthening and some dredging to enable the barges to come alongside the wall. This view, taken on 1st March 1938, shows wagons standing in Webb Majors siding and, on the extreme left, Fruit Vans on the Marine Coal siding.

NATIONAL RAILWAY MUSEUM

This view from Webb Majors yard, also taken on 1st March 1938, shows the same Fruit Vans standing on the Marine Coal siding. Introduction of oil-fired steamers in 1925 reduced its use and from 1932 the siding was no longer required for coaling. It remained available for use as a traffic siding until about 1947.

NATIONAL RAILWAY MUSEUM

Looking along Commercial Road on 31st August 1938, with the tramway in the foreground, Fruit Vans stabled on the Marine Coal siding directly ahead, a sheeted wagon standing on Webb Majors siding and Cosen's siding on the right.
L&GRP

The tramway passing in front of Cosens yard on 21st September 1938 before work commenced on easing the curve at Ferry's Corner. The wagon was standing on Cosens siding and prominent in the centre is the crane, the cause of much negotiation, which was made redundant when the tramway was realigned.
NATIONAL RAILWAY MUSEUM

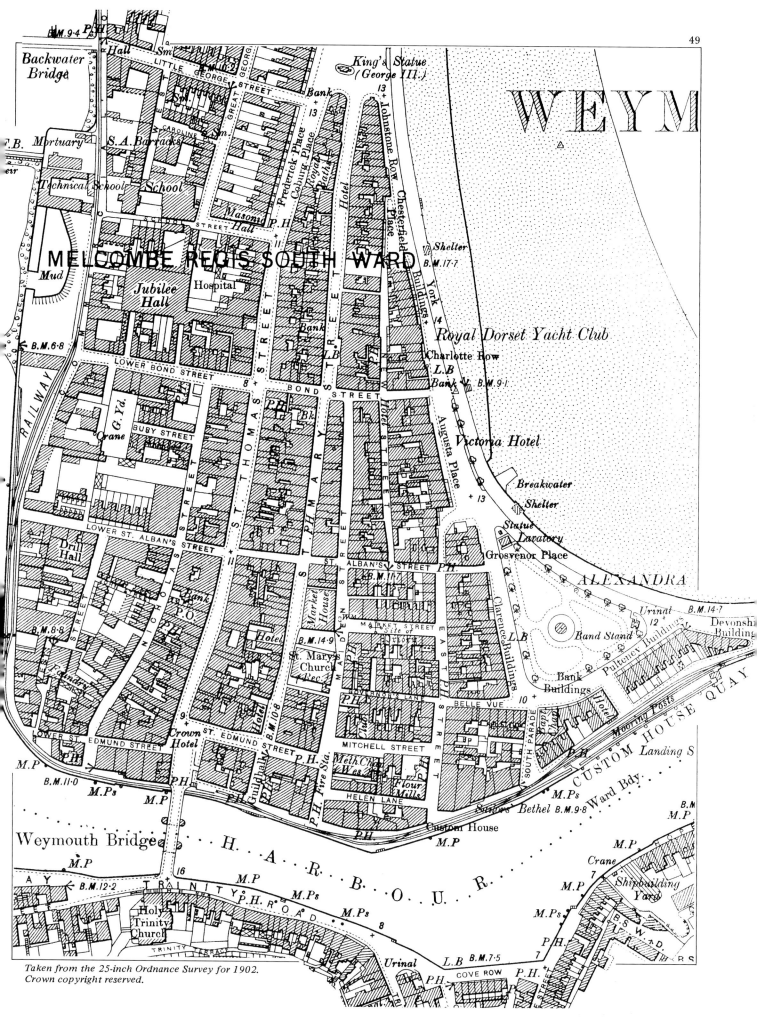

Backwater
Bridge

King's Statue
(George III.)

WEYM

F.B. Mortuary
S.A. Barracks

BM.9·4 P.H.
Hall Sm.
LITTLE GEORGE
GREAT GEORGE STREET
Bank
13

CAROLINE

Technical School School
Masonic Hall
STREET
P.H.
Frederick Place
Coburg Place
Royal Bath
Johnstone Row
Chesterfield Place
York Buildings
Shelter
B.M.17·7

MELCOMBE REGIS SOUTH WARD

Mud
Jubilee Hall
Hospital
Royal Dorset Yacht Club
Charlotte Row
L.B.
Bank L.B. B.M.9·1

BM.6·8
LOWER BOND STREET
8
ST. THOMAS STREET
BOND STREET
L.B.
Augusta Place
Victoria Hotel

RAILWAY
G.Yd.
BUBY STREET
P.H.
Bk.
13

Crane
LOWER ST. ALBAN'S STREET
ST. NICHOLAS STREET
ST. MARY STREET
Breakwater
Shelter
Statue
Lavatory

Drill Hall
Bank
P.O.
P.H.
11
ALBAN'S STREET P.H.
B.M.17
Grosvenor Place
ALEXANDRA

BM.8·8
Hotel
Market House
Clarence Buildings
Urinal B.M.14·7
Devonshire Buildings

Foundry
Bank
Hotel B.M.10·8
St. Mary's Church Rec.
MARKET STREET
Site of
L.B.
Band Stand
Pulteney Buildings

LOWER ST.
EDMUND STREET
Crown Hotel
ST. EDMUND STREET
Hotel
P.H.
GOVERNOR'S LANE
BELLE VUE
SOUTH PARADE
Bank Buildings
10
CUSTOM HOUSE QUAY

M.P.
BM.11·0
M.Ps
P.H.
9
Guildhall
P.H.
Fire Sta.
MITCHELL STREET
Meth.Ch. Wes.
HELEN LANE
P.H.
Flour Mills
Mooring Posts
P.H. Landing S

Weymouth Bridge
M.P.
A Y B.M.12·2
TRINITY ROAD
P.H.
Holy Trinity Church
TRINITY TERRACE
M.P.
M.Ps
M.Ps
Custom House
M.P.
Sailors Bethel B.M.9·8 Ward Bdy.
Crane
Shipbuilding Yard
B.S.W.D.

H A R B O U R

Urinal
L.B. B.M.7·5
COVE ROW P.H.
P.H.

Taken from the 25-inch Ordnance Survey for 1902.
Crown copyright reserved.

The harbour wall at Ferry's Corner before the rebuilding work of 1938-39. The caution board marked the point at which one-engine-in-steam working from Weymouth station ended. Beyond this point to the landing stage, more than one engine, or train, was permitted subject to certain safeguards; the regulations were in the Appendix to the Service Time Tables.
NATIONAL RAILWAY MUSEUM

By 7th March 1939, when this photograph was taken, the new harbour wall was complete and had been infilled. The tramway may be seen, still on the original alignment, amongst the contractor's detritus.
NATIONAL RAILWAY MUSEUM

This was the view from the Town Bridge side of Ferry's Corner, also on 7th March 1939. The contractor for these works was A. Jackaman & Sons Ltd of Slough.
NATIONAL RAILWAY MUSEUM

Work had been completed by 19th July 1939 when this view was taken. The new curve was to the left but the original alignment was retained and used as a siding. The Fruit Vans seen here were probably empties waiting to be worked down to the landing stage for loading.
NATIONAL RAILWAY MUSEUM

In conjunction with the work on easing the curve at Ferry's Corner, the quay was widened as far as Customs House Quay. This view, taken on 24th May 1938, shows the line between the Town Bridge and Ferry's Corner when preparations for the rebuilding work were underway.

NATIONAL RAILWAY MUSEUM

Reconstruction work largely complete on 7th March 1939 with the new alignment in use and the old route still in situ and awaiting lifting.

NATIONAL RAILWAY MUSEUM

No. 1370 at Ferry's Corner in the summer of 1957 heading for Weymouth station yard with empty passenger stock. R. S. CARPENTER

No. 1368 with an up perishables train at Ferry's Corner. Weymouth Gas Works, visible across the 'Backwater', was removed during the 1960s.
P. Q. TRELOAR

Weymouth Town Bridge as rebuilt in 1930. This view was taken on 1st March 1938 before work on reconstructing the quay and realigning the tramway had commenced.
NATIONAL RAILWAY MUSEUM

No. 2194 Kidwelly with an up boat train passing through the Town Bridge in 1933. N. SHEPHERD

By March 1939 the reconstruction work was largely complete. The realigned tramway had been brought into use whilst the old route remained awaiting recovery.
L&GRP

Reconstruction work at the Town Bridge completed. This view was taken on 19th July 1939.   NATIONAL RAILWAY MUSEUM

No. 1367 passing the Town Bridge with a boat train in the years immediately after the Second World War.   PURSEY SHORT

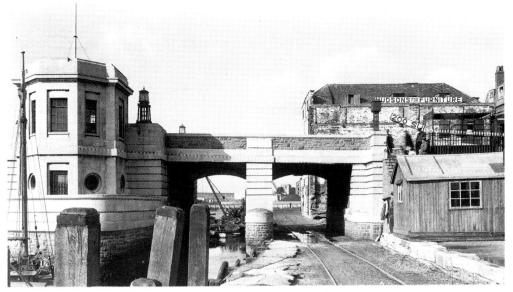

Looking towards the Town Bridge from Custom House Quay on 1st March 1938. Work had yet to start on reconstructing the quay wall and realigning the tramway.
NATIONAL RAILWAY MUSEUM

By 7th March 1939 the work was largely complete. The original route of the tramway and the remnants of Farthings siding are visible on the right awaiting recovery. The Cosens paddle steamer Victoria, *seen on the left, was laid up for the winter.*
NATIONAL RAILWAY MUSEUM

In 1962 the tramway beneath the Town Bridge was raised to alleviate the problems caused by flooding, and this view shows the completed work. The relaying reduced the incidence of flooding but the tramway was always wet at the lowest point beneath the bridge.
AUTHOR'S COLLECTION

The view from the Town Bridge on 1st March 1938 showing the tramway before reconstruction and Farthings siding in front of the Royal Oak public house.
NATIONAL RAILWAY MUSEUM

Another of the series of photographs recording the work on realigning the tramway. This is the view from the Town Bridge, on 19th July 1939, of the completed work.
NATIONAL RAILWAY MUSEUM

58

No. 1368 making her way along Custom House Quay with a lengthy train of Fruit Vans in the mid-1950s. The large brick-built warehouse, between the Royal Oak and Ship Inn public houses, had, amongst other uses, formerly been a bonded store for Eldridge Pope & Co, the Dorchester brewers. It was demolished by the late 1950s.

P. Q. TRELOAR

An unidentified '1366' with the boat train about 1948. Although the railways had been nationalised, the carriages were still in the traditional GWR 'chocolate and cream' livery.
COLLECTION R. K. BLENCOWE

No. 1367 pausing between shunting duties on Custom House Quay on a sunny day in the mid-1950s. Parked cars were already causing problems for the tramway but not on this occasion.
P. Q. TRELOAR

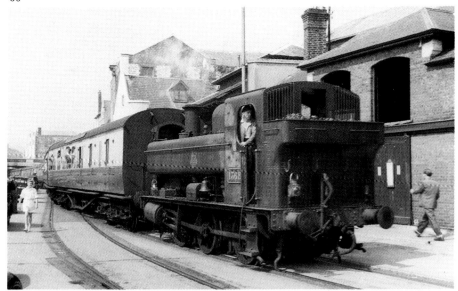

No. 1368 with the down boat train on Custom House Quay in the mid-1950s.
G. F. BANNISTER

On 27th May 1961, 57XX 0–6–0PT No. 8799 shunting vans and catching the attention of passers-by. During 1952 the quay, between the cargo stage and the Town Bridge, was surfaced in concrete to permit the use of mobile cranes such as the one on the right in this view.
COLLECTION
R. K. BLENCOWE

No. 1370 shunting vans on Custom House Quay.

HUGH DAVIES

No. 1368 with empty Fruit Vans in the early 1960s, shortly before the '1366s' were transferred away from Weymouth. COLLECTION R. K. BLENCOWE

No. 1368 again, with Fruit Vans on Custom House Quay in the mid-1950s. The Custom House is the brick building with first-floor bow windows immediately behind the locomotive.

P. Q. TRELOAR

No. 1331 making her way along Custom House Quay with goods wagons on 1st September 1933. The siding occupied by the other goods wagons was known as Templemans siding, named after the nearby Templemans Flour Mills in East Street, which were destroyed by fire in December 1917. The tramway on Custom House Quay remained in the condition shown in the photograph, without check rails and with the quay unsurfaced, until after the Second World War.

H. F. WHEELER

By the early 1950s the tramway on Custom House Quay required urgent attention. This view shows No. 1368 passing the Custom House, seen here receiving a postwar repaint, with Fruit Vans on 11th July 1951. The tramway still retained the original metals but Templemans siding had been removed and the harbour wall rebuilt, thus widening the quay. Both tramway and siding were renewed in 1952 with checkrails throughout.

R. H. TUNSTALL

By June 1955, when this view was taken, the reconstruction work had long been completed. No. 1368 is seen here making her way along Custom House Quay with a perishables train.

J. H. LUCKING

With the cargo stage in the background, this picture shows No. 1370 setting out for Weymouth yard with perishables vans. The headshunt of Templemans siding was often used for stabling wagons and, on occasions, a wagon containing the pump used for bunkering the steamers with fuel oil was kept there.
G. F. BANNISTER

Shunting operations on the tramway could often block the quay to road traffic. This view, taken on 9th July 1956, shows wagons on Templemans siding and the driver of No. 1367 lubricating her slidebars with his oil feeder during a pause in shunting operations.
R. H. TUNSTALL

No. 1367 passing the cargo stage with an up boat train on 6th June 1956. The poster board on the railings advertised day excursions by British Railways steamer to Guernsey; such trips were a regular feature during the summer season.
AUTHOR'S COLLECTION

No. 1367 again, paused during shunting movements at the cargo stage in September 1957. The shunter on the right was replacing one of the loose point levers — several of these were placed at strategic locations along the tramway and were, inevitably, subject to idle vandalism. Therefore, at least one point lever, and often two, were carried on the 'tram' engines and could often be seen lying on the front footplate. T. G. HEPBURN

A busy scene at the cargo stage in August 1929 with Roebuck alongside and Great Western behind her. Further along the quay are visible the four masts of a timber boat from the Baltic — such vessels were regular visitors to Weymouth until the Second World War. On the south side of the harbour a crane and slipway mark the GWR Marine Department workshops and stores whilst Sambur is seen moored in the Cove — the wide area of the harbour by the Cove Inn.

NATIONAL RAILWAY MUSEUM

An Edwardian postcard view of Weymouth Harbour with the cargo stage on the north side, unoccupied on this occasion.
AUTHOR'S COLLECTION

Shunting underway at the cargo stage about 1930.
AUTHOR'S COLLECTION

This was the cargo stage on 31st August 1938 in poor condition and overdue for renewal. It was to be a further ten years, including the heavy usage of wartime, before reconstruction began and the work was not completed until July 1951. The track was also in poor condition with many 'dropped' rail joints and was the cause of frequent derailments.
L&GRP

No. 1367 passing an unusually quiet cargo stage in 1961 with no road traffic and no vessels at their moorings.   COLLECTION C. L. CADDY

In a Weymouth scene typical of the 1950s, No. 1370 with a train of Fruit Vans passing more vans at the cargo stage.   G. F. BANNISTER

Roebuck *at the cargo stage in September 1957. The reconstructed cargo stage with the electric cranes was a great improvement over the old facilities. By the mid-1950s, goods conveyed to and from the Islands was increasingly container-ised, but the 30-year-old* Roebuck *and* Sambur, *were not suited for such traffic. Here* Roebuck's *cargo was being handled using the traditional, labour-intensive methods.*
GRAHAM HERBERT
COLLECTION/DORSET
COUNTY LIBRARY

No. 1368 passing the cargo stage with a down boat train. Passengers leaning from the carriage windows were clearly enjoying the unfolding panorama of Weymouth Harbour.
G. F. BANNISTER

No. 1370 drawing Fruit Vans up from the pier in the mid-1950s. The old Pavilion Theatre (renamed The Ritz in the postwar years) was destroyed by fire in 1954 and in this view only a few girders remained.

G. F. BANNISTER

No. 1368 shunting Fruit Vans at the pier in September 1957. Custom House Quay was very narrow at this point and was later widened as part of the reconstruction work, completed in 1961.

T. G. HEPBURN

No. 2194 Kidwelly arriving at the pier in the late 1930s with a down boat train.

AUTHOR'S COLLECTION

An aerial view of Weymouth Harbour in 1954 and issued as a postcard. The burnt-out ruins of The Ritz Theatre had yet to be removed, whilst on the slipway, on the south side of the harbour, a Trinity House lightship was receiving attention. AUTHOR'S COLLECTION

This view, taken at 3.40 p.m. on Tuesday, 22nd July 1947, shows No. 1368 getting away from Weymouth Quay with an up boat train.

PURSEY SHORT

When this view was taken, in July 1939, war was only two months away. St. Patrick — to become a casualty in the forthcoming conflict — is seen arriving from the Islands whilst the boat train was alongside the platform awaiting the incoming passengers. NATIONAL RAILWAY MUSEUM

No. 1367 shunting Fruit Vans whilst a National Serviceman was contemplating taking the ferry across the harbour to the Nothe Gardens.

P. Q. TRELOAR

No. 1370 shunting during the late 1950s. To the amateur observer of tramway operations, the large iron gates were a bar to further progress and to pass beyond, one had to have a valid travel ticket – or a good excuse! No. 1370 left Weymouth in December 1959 and was scrapped in 1960 – the first of the '1366s' to go.
I. D. BEALE

Shunting with a tow rope was a feature of tramway working for many years but was rarely photographed. This view shows No. 1368, on Saturday 7th July 1951, drawing wagons onto the pier using a tow rope. The oil tank car contained fuel oil for the steamers.
PURSEY SHORT

A fine aerial view of Weymouth pier and harbour in the summer of 1939 with GWR and Cosens steamers in attendance.

This view, taken during the summer of 1957, shows No. 1370 recently arrived with a down boat train, with St. Patrick *and either* St. Julien *or* St. Helier *moored alongside.*

R. S. CARPENTER

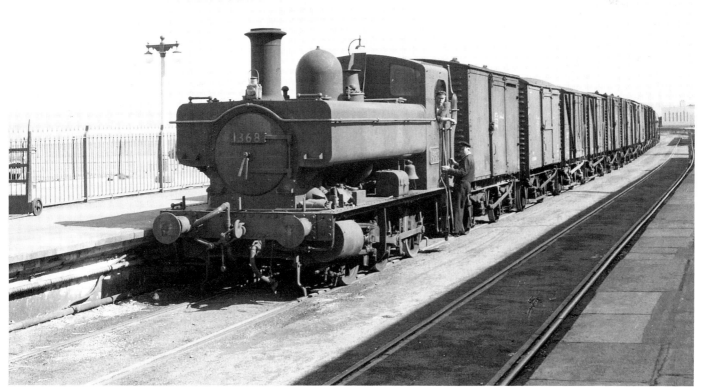

No. 1368 shunting goods vans at the farthest end of Weymouth Pier in 1957.

T. G. HEPBURN

During 1961 further improvements were made to the facilities at Weymouth Quay. An additional platform was provided and is shown here on 6th July 1961 occupied by No. 1368 waiting with an up boat train for Waterloo. The building on the left is the replacement Pavilion Theatre opened in 1960.
H. C. CASSERLEY

The original baggage shed of 1889 was retained and incorporated in the 1961 improvements. This was the scene on 20th January 1962 with the new steamer Caesarea of 1960 alongside.　C. L. CADDY

General view along the quay on 15th May 1961 with St. Patrick *loading prior to departure for the Islands.*　AUTHOR'S COLLECTION

This was the view of the pier on 1st June 1961 with a lengthy train of vans at the platform. Caesarea *is visible in the centre of the photograph with* Isle of Guernsey *behind her. The SR ship was on temporary secondment to Weymouth to stand in for the new vessel* Sarnia *which was delivered later that month.*
AUTHOR'S COLLECTION

The new platform on 15th May 1961 with the recently completed Pavilion Theatre in the background. Green-liveried Southern Region stock formed the boat train, then running to Waterloo instead of Paddington.
AUTHOR'S COLLECTION

No. 2 is thought to have been the locomotive involved in the trial run over the tramway in 1878. The engine was rarely photographed but is seen here in 1892 in the Torquay area when working on the conversion of the broad gauge to standard gauge.
NEWTON ABBOT TOWN
AND GWR MUSEUM

GWR weight diagram of ex-Bristol & Exeter Railway 0—6—0T Nos. 1376 and 1377 as rebuilt at Swindon in 1881.
COLLECTION
P. Q. TRELOAR

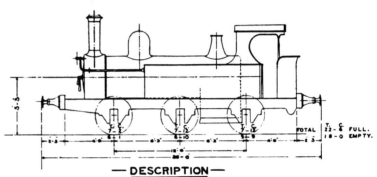

— DESCRIPTION —

CYLINDERS _ _ _ _ _ _ _ _ DIAR 12" STROKE 18" STEAM PORTS 1" X 10 EXHAUST 2½" X 10".

BOILER _ _ _ _ _ _ _ _ BARREL 9'-0½" DIAR OUTS 3'-5½" & 3'-5".

FIREBOX _ _ _ _ _ _ _ OUTS 3'-9" X 3'-6½" INS 3'-2" X 3'-0¼" HEIGHT 4'-2".

TUBES _ _ _ _ _ _ _ Nº 94 DIAR. 2" LENGTH 9'-3¼".

HEATING SURFACE _ _ _ _ _ TUBES 457·3 SQ FT. FIREBOX 54·61 SQ FT. TOTAL 511·91 SQ. FT.

AREA OF FIRECRATE _ _ _ _ 9.7 SQ. FT.

WHEELS _ _ _ _ _ _ _ LEADING 3'-6" .DRIVING 3'-6" .TRAILING 3'-6".

WATER CAPACITY OF TANKS _ _ _ 380 GALLONS.

WORKING PRESSURE _ _ _ _ _ 140 LBS.

TRACTIVE FORCE _ _ _ _ _ 7776 LBS.

—ENGINES 1376—1377—

—CLASS 0 — 6 —0—
T

Both Nos. 1376 and 1377 received new cylinders in 1896 and in due course their appearance was altered by the provision of open cabs and a tall, slender chimney of obvious 'Swindon' origin. No. 1376 is seen here on Custom House Quay on 20th May 1902.
COLLECTION P. Q. TRELOAR

CHAPTER FIVE

TRAM ENGINES AND STEAMERS

No. 1376 posed, along with tramway staff and the engine crew, just inside the yard gates at Weymouth in the 1900s. E. H. SEWARD

WHEREAS the previous notes contained details of some of the locomotives and steamers associated with the Weymouth Harbour Tramway and the Channel Islands service, it is the object of this section to examine them more closely.

TRAM ENGINES

The 'tram' engines are a particularly interesting sequence of locomotives and it was not until 1935 that a purpose-built GWR engine was employed on the tramway. The overriding requirements were that the engine had to be small, have a light axle loading and be capable of negotiating the sharp curves. Fortunately, the GWR was not required to provide fully-enclosed tram engines, such as those found on the former GER Wisbech and Upwell line, and therefore any 'absorbed' oddment with a short wheelbase sufficed.

Although there is no conclusive evidence to prove it, it is generally thought that the locomotive used in the trial run in 1878 was a small 2–4–0 side tank No. 2. Built originally in 1871 to the broad gauge by the Avonside Engine Co for the Torbay and Brixham Railway, and named *King*, it was taken over by the South Devon Railway. Later, when the SDR amalgamated with the GWR in 1876, it became No. 2171 and was rebuilt at Swindon in March 1878 to the standard gauge, whereupon it received the number 2. It was a tiny machine weighing only 13 tons 17 cwt, with driving wheels of only 3ft diameter and leading wheels of 2ft 6in diameter. John Lucking suggests that its rebuilding to standard gauge was with the tramway in mind but the engine does not seem to have been regularly used on the line after the trial. It is thought to

have worked mostly in the Swindon area although recently discovered photographs also show it in the Torquay area working on the gauge conversion in 1892 and in 1898 at work on the newly constructed Lambourn Valley Railway. It is also known to have been employed on the construction of the Bodmin Road–Bodmin line in the 1880s. No. 2 was withdrawn from GWR service in March 1907 and was sold for further use. The RCTS history records it as being last seen working for the Anglo-American Oil Co at Purfleet, Essex, in 1921, after which there is no trace of it.

General working of the tramway with locomotives is thought to have begun in 1880, and in 1881 two locomotives emerged from Swindon Works that were eminently suited for work on the line. GWR Nos. 1376 and 1377 started life as 0–6–0 tanks and had been built by the Bristol and Exeter Railway at their Bristol works in 1874 and 1875. They carried B&ER numbers 114 and 115 and had been built especially to work on the Culm Valley Light Railway. They weighed 20 tons 8 cwt, had an overall wheelbase of 10ft 6in and driving wheels of 3ft 6in diameter. Unusually, they had water tube boilers with the firebox enclosed within the boiler. The absence of a grate allowed the addition of a small well tank between the frames to supplement the small side tanks. A drawing of these unusual machines in their original condition is to be found on page 23 of *The Culm Valley Light Railway* by Michael Messenger, published by Twelveheads Press in 1993.

They apparently served quite satisfactorily on the CVLR until that line became a part of the GWR, but in 1881 both engines were sent to Swindon to be rebuilt. When they emerged, they had been substantially altered

The 'tram' engines were stabled and serviced at Weymouth locomotive shed, seen here in 1921. On this occasion the shed yard was unusually deserted except for No. 1337 Hook Norton resting between her tramway duties.

NATIONAL RAILWAY MUSEUM

and the RCTS states 'it is probable that comparatively little of the originals remained after the 1881 rebuilding'. With new, conventional, locomotive boilers and new frames, they weighed 22 tons 6 cwt in working order and the wheelbase was lengthened to 12ft 6in evenly divided. No photographs have been located showing the engines as first rebuilt but the accompanying GWR Weight Diagram may give an indication of their appearance with their roll-capped chimneys and pillared cabs. They were soon sent to Weymouth specifically to work the tramway and started an association which was to last for over forty years.

There are few records of their years of service at Weymouth; the RCTS informs us that in 1896 both engines received new cylinders whilst, according to John Lucking, No. 1377 was very nearly in serious trouble in 1903 when she ran through open trap points on Custom House Quay and was stopped only inches before toppling into the harbour.

From time to time, other small engines would be sent to Weymouth to assist the ex-B&ER tanks and perhaps to cover for them while one or other was away at Swindon for

periodic overhaul. One of the earliest recorded examples was the 0—4—0 saddle tank No. 1391 *Fox*. Built in 1872 by the Avonside Engine Co at Bristol, it was initially owned by the West Cornwall Railway and had driving wheels of 2ft 7in diameter and a wheelbase of 5ft 10½in. Absorbed by the GWR in 1876, it received a 13XX series number — reserved by the GWR for locomotives absorbed from smaller companies — and was rebuilt at Swindon in 1897. In its rebuilt form it had 2ft 10in diameter wheels and weighed 18 tons in working order. According to the RCTS, *Fox* worked extensively over the Southern Division of the GWR, mostly on engineering and ballasting duties, but she served at Weymouth on the tramway from April 1903 to May 1906 and from March to October 1908. In July 1912 the locomotive was sold to the Gloucester Carriage & Wagon Co Ltd and was finally disposed of to Cashmores of Newport for scrap in 1948. *Fox* outlived the other locomotives absorbed from the West Cornwall Railway by 67 years!

Also sent to work on the tramway was an 0—6—0 saddle tank which carried the name *Hook Norton*. She had been owned by the Hook Norton Ironstone Partnership in Oxfordshire and was employed there until the workings went into liquidation in 1904. *Hook Norton* was a standard Manning Wardle locomotive with the distinctive double-cranked driving wheels, saddle tank over the boiler only, wrap-over cab, and dated from 1889. After the GWR purchased the engine from the liquidators at Hook Norton, it was given the number 1337 whilst the name was retained. She arrived at Weymouth in November 1904 — perhaps she had been purchased specifically to serve as a third 'tram' engine — and worked on the tramway until 1907. In September of that year she was sold to the Fishguard and Rosslare Railways and Harbours Co in which the GWR shared an interest with the Great Southern and Western

Ex-West Cornwall Railway No. 1391 Fox *at the entrance to Weymouth locomotive shed.*
AUTHOR'S COLLECTION

A closer view of No. 1337 Hook Norton *at Weymouth locomotive shed, possibly taken in 1904 when she arrived for her first spell on the tramway. She had yet to have the bell fitted in front of the cab.*
AUTHOR'S COLLECTION

Railway of Ireland. *Hook Norton* was moved away from Weymouth but in October 1913 the engine returned to GWR stock and, in January 1914, came back to Weymouth. Her stay was rather more prolonged on this occasion and she remained for twelve years. In January 1926 she was withdrawn from service and sent to Swindon where she was broken up.

Other small locomotives were sent to Weymouth from time to time to assist or relieve the 'regulars' but not all are recorded. More notable examples included 0—6—0ST No. 1386 — absorbed from the Whitland and Cardigan Railway in 1886 — which was on the tramway from May 1909 to March 1911. She was sold by the GWR in 1911

and passed into the hands of Col. Holman F. Stephens when she became East Kent Railway No. 1. She was eventually scrapped in 1934. Locomotives of the '1392' class — absorbed from the Cornwall Minerals Railway and rebuilt by the GWR — worked on occasions whilst during the Great War ex LNWR 0—4—0 saddle tank No. 3033 was on the line in July 1917.

In January 1927 No. 1377 was withdrawn from service and broken up at Swindon. She had been rebuilt in 1915, receiving a new boiler with a tall dome on the back ring, thus making her different in appearance from her sister. No. 1376 acquired an enclosed cab and in 1928 was transferred away to Oswestry to work on the Tanat Valley Light

No. 1376 with an up boat train in Commercial Road about 1921.
AUTHOR'S COLLECTION

No. 1377 at rest at Weymouth locomotive shed on Sunday, 19th September 1926. By this time the engine had acquired a tapered chimney and her condition appears to have become quite run-down.
P. J. T. READ

No. 2194 Kidwelly at Weymouth locomotive shed about 1937. The tow rope draped along the side of the engine was a characteristic feature of all 'tram' engines until the practice ceased in the early 1950s. COLLECTION P. Q. TRELOAR

Railway. She remained here in semi-retirement until she was withdrawn in 1934 when she, too, made the final, one-way journey to Swindon.

To replace these withdrawals and transfers, two 0–6–0Ts were brought to Weymouth, Nos. 2194 *Kidwelly* and 2195 *Cwm Mawr*. These had been taken into Great Western stock in 1922 from the Burry Port and Gwendraeth Valley Railway. *Kidwelly* formerly carried the BP&GVR No. 4 and was built by the Avonside Engine Co. in 1903. *Cwm Mawr* carried BP&GVR No. 5 and had been built in 1905, also by Avonsides. The two engines were practically identical, although No. 5 had an extended smokebox and was vacuum brake fitted. Following the GWR takeover and renumbering, the two engines were sent to Swindon — No. 2194 in July 1923 and No. 2195 in November 1923. When they returned to traffic in February 1926, both had boilers rebuilt to GWR standards, GW boiler fittings and extended bunkers. The two engines arrived at Weymouth in the same year, *Kidwelly* arriving about April and *Cwm Mawr* in September. They carried out their tramway duties to great satisfaction and remained at work until 1939/1940. No. 2194 *Kidwelly* left Weymouth in 1940 and after a short time allocated to Cardiff Cathays, spent her final years at Taunton. She survived long enough to be taken into British Railways stock, even receiving a smokebox door numberplate, and was withdrawn in February 1953.

No. 2195 *Cwm Mawr* was taken out of service in March 1939 but, in common with many other locomotives withdrawn during this period, instead of being broken up was reinstated for emergency war service in December 1939. She worked during wartime, without her nameplates, in the Bristol division, often at Swindon, but she made a brief return visit to Weymouth from November 1945 until June 1946 and duly reappeared on the tramway.

No. 2195 also survived into BR ownership but does not appear to have received a smokebox door numberplate. She was withdrawn in January 1953.

No. 2195 Cwm Mawr, also at Weymouth locomotive shed in the 1930s with the tramway bell on the footplate ahead of the injectors. AUTHOR'S COLLECTION

A head-on view of No. 2194 Kidwelly in Commercial Road on 1st August 1938. The array of equipment on the front footplate was typical — as well as the tow rope there were usually several shunters poles and at least one of the loose point levers.
AUTHOR'S COLLECTION

A further 0−6−0ST, which worked on the tramway from 1928 until October 1935, was No. 1331. She had been built in 1877 by Fox Walker & Co. for the Whitland and Cardigan Railway, carrying the company's No. 3 and had inside cylinders and driving wheels of 4ft 0in diameter. When absorbed into the GWR in 1886, she initially received the number 1387 and in 1896 the mainframes were lengthened and new cylinders fitted. In June 1902 No. 1387 was removed from GWR stock and transferred as works shunter to the Signal Department at Reading where she remained until 1925.

In February 1926, the engine was returned to GWR stock, receiving the No. 1331, and was taken into Swindon shops for rebuilding. She emerged in 1927 with frames lengthened at the rear to accommodate a larger bunker and an enclosed cab. Prior to her spell of duty at the Reading signal works, the engine had been employed at Gloucester and Pontypool and, following her departure from

Ex-Whitland & Cardigan Railway 0−6−0ST No. 1331 in Commercial Road, on 29th August 1932, with goods vans from Weymouth Quay. The shunter was permitted to ride on the engine, rather than walking in front, where there was a clear view ahead.

AUTHOR'S COLLECTION

No. 1331 again, seen here in Weymouth locomotive shed yard on 14th June 1932.

COLLECTION P. Q. TRELOAR

Weymouth in 1935, was at Swindon until 1941 when she moved to Oswestry. Here she was employed on the Tanat Valley line — following the example set by her Weymouth predecessor No. 1376 — working principally in the quarries around Porthwaen. She was reconditioned again in 1946 at Wolverhampton and was taken into British Railways stock, receiving a smokebox door numberplate. Withdrawal eventually came in January 1950.

Two other locomotives which deserve mention are No. 679 and 1397. No. 679 was built by Peckett of Bristol in 1890 for the Alexandra (Newport and South Wales) Docks and Railway and carried that company's No. 18. She came into GWR stock at the grouping in 1923 and worked on the tramway from January to June 1929. Her usual haunt was Oswestry but she was sold out of service in September 1929 and continued to work in private ownership at various collieries in South Wales, eventually being reported out of use by 1953. Ex-Cornwall Minerals Railway 0—6—0ST No. 1397 was working on the tramway from June to July 1931.

The first GWR-built locomotive arrived on the tramway early in 1935 when Collett '1366' class No. 1367 began an association with the line that was to last for almost 27 years. The '1366' class pannier tanks had been built primarily to replace the former Cornwall Minerals Railway '1392' class which had latterly been largely employed at Swindon Wagon Works. The '1366s' took over the Swindon duties but No. 1367 was sent new to Weymouth to replace the departing No. 1331. When No. 2195 *Cwm Mawr* left in 1939, a second member of the class, No. 1371, was sent to replace it.

Unlike the other members of the class, the Weymouth 'tram' engines were equipped with steam heating equipment for working the boat trains, along with the other traditional 'tram' engine features of warning bell and additional handrail and footstep for the shunter at the front right-hand side of the running plate. By 1947, No. 1371 had moved away, back to Swindon, but Nos. 1368/1370 were at Weymouth. During this period the three '1366s' monopolised tramway duties and although the '74XX' larger panniers were permitted on the line, the smaller engines were preferred. Indeed, during the late 1940s, there was only one '74XX' at Weymouth — No. 7408 — and she was primarily employed as station pilot, shunting carriage stock and vans around the station.

In 1951 the '57XX' class 0—6—0PTs were permitted to work over the line for the first time following the rebuilding of the harbour wall at Custom House Quay. However, the new axle loading regulations also meant that, strictly speaking, the '1366' class were not allowed on the line and for a time, in 1953, the 74XX took over tramway duties. In practice, the harbour wall could accommodate loads well in excess of the specified loadings and the Civil Engineer soon permitted the '1366' class to run again and they were back on their old duties by September 1953, being increasingly joined by the '57XX' class.

No. 679 only worked on the tramway for six months in 1929 but was photographed at Weymouth locomotive shed on 28th May of that year.   H. C. CASSERLEY

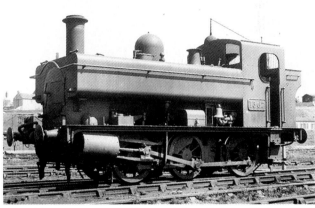

No. 1367 was sent new to Weymouth from Swindon Works in 1935 and was the first '1366' to arrive. She remained until 1962 with only a six-month spell away when the '1366s' were temporarily prohibited from the tramway in 1953. This view was taken in the late 1930s.   AUTHOR'S COLLECTION

No. 1370 was another long-term Weymouth resident — from 1946 until 1959 with a similar six-month spell away in 1953. This view was taken at Weymouth locomotive shed on 18th April 1952.
AUTHOR'S COLLECTION

Weymouth Harbour around 1900. Two GWR steamers, Lynx and the larger Reindeer, are seen berthed in the Cove, the wider area of the harbour also used for turning vessels after they had discharged at the landing stage. One of Cosens steamers features in the centre, and beyond, on the opposite side of the harbour, may be seen the GWR Marine Workshops and Stores at Nothe Parade. A number of houses were demolished in 1888 to allow construction of this yard as part of the general improvement of the harbour to accept the new GWR steamers. The tramway is just visible on the left, at Custom House Quay, behind the white-painted sailing vessel which had probably arrived with timber from the Baltic.

Antelope in Weymouth Bay sometime before 1896 when her appearance was changed by alterations to her accommodation. The Royal Mail pennant can be seen at her forward mast head and the GWR house flag at the aft masthead. SECR SOCIETY, CTY. P. COUTANCHE

Although the '1366' class were built primarily for work at Swindon, by 1948 all except No. 1369 had spent time at Weymouth. When No. 1369 finally arrived for a spell of tramway duty, in March 1960, she still carried 'Great Western' on her tanks, a feature made all the more poignant by the fact that the tramway was now firmly in the grip of the Southern Region. Although the boat trains had stopped running to Paddington in 1959 and henceforth ran to Waterloo, the ex-GWR panniers continued to work the tramway until the summer of 1962 when the '1366s' left. They were transferred to Wadebridge in Cornwall to work china clay trains from Wenford Bridge on the former Bodmin and Wadebridge line. Here they replaced the famous ex-LSWR Beattie 'Well Tanks' but their stay in Cornwall was shortlived and they were withdrawn in late 1964. No. 1369 was sold for preservation and is presently at the South Devon Railway, the only ex-GWR 'tram' engine to survive. Following the departure of the '1366s', the '57XX' continued to work on the 'tram', increasingly assisted by varieties of diesel shunters, until 24th December 1963 when 0—6—0PT No. 4610 became the last GWR-designed engine to work on the line.

It only remains to record that the last steam locomotives to work on the tramway were BR class 2P 2—6—2Ts which arrived at Weymouth in 1964 to take over the duties of the departed '57XX' pannier tanks.

STEAMERS

When the GWR began to operate the service in 1889, they used 'one of the well known fast iron paddle steamers of the old Weymouth and Channel Islands Steam Packet Co.

Three new twin-screw steamers were ordered by the GWR to work the Channel Islands route, but the vessels were not ready when the company took over the service. All were ordered from Laird Bros of Birkenhead, at a cost of £25,000 each, and were to carry the names *Lynx, Antelope* and *Gazelle. Lynx* was launched first, on 29th January 1889, but was delivered too late to inaugurate the Channel Islands service. She eventually made her maiden voyage to the islands on 4th August 1889. Her sisters followed shortly afterwards, the *Antelope* making her maiden voyage on 5th August from Jersey to Weymouth and the *Gazelle* making her first run on 8th September.

These three vessels operated the service until the turn of the century when new larger ships were brought onto the route.

In the first years of the 20th century the *Lynx* and the *Antelope* served at Plymouth, acting as tenders between ocean liners and the GWR Millbay docks, but both made occasional return visits to Weymouth to cover the service when other steamers were temporarily unavailable. The *Gazelle* remained at Weymouth as a spare to the larger steamers until 1907 when she was converted to a cargo vessel, returning afterwards to the Channel Islands service. The *Lynx*, too, was converted to a cargo vessel but the *Antelope* remained as a tender at Plymouth until she was sold in 1913. Both the *Lynx* and the *Gazelle* were requisitioned by the Admiralty in 1914 and left the familiar waters of the English Channel for the Mediterranean where

A postcard view of Weymouth Harbour, with Ibex *and either* Roebuck *or* Reindeer, *taken after 1908 when the Pavilion Theatre was built.*
AUTHOR'S COLLECTION

they served as mine-sweepers for the duration of the Great War. Both vessels returned to Weymouth in 1920 and remained on the service until 1925 when they were sold.

In 1890 a steamer was ordered to supplement the fleet, which was to be bigger, faster and embodying all the points found deficient in the existing vessels. She was named the *Ibex* and was to become one of the most noted steamers to have worked on the route. She made her maiden voyage from Weymouth to the Islands on 9th September 1891.

In April 1897 the *Ibex* was approaching Jersey in 'close company' with the LSWR steamer *Frederica* — there was more than a suggestion that the two were racing — when the *Ibex* struck a rock off La Corbière Lighthouse which caused much damage to the hull and propeller blades. With her decks almost awash, the ship was beached and the passengers taken off in her boats. She was refloated and later repaired at Barrow-in-Furness, returning to service in July 1897.

On 5th January 1900, while en route to the Islands, she again struck rocks and sank just outside St. Peter Port, Guernsey. The winter weather delayed her salvage until July but she was eventually refloated and, after much repair work, she was sent to Birkenhead for a thorough refit. She returned to the Channel Islands in 1901 virtually as a new ship. During the Great War the *Ibex* remained at Weymouth as the GWR's only vessel, maintaining the service single-handed for a considerable time until assistance arrived in the shape of the *Pembroke* in 1916. During the war she narrowly avoided being torpedoed and in October 1916 the *Ibex* was sent to Plymouth where she had a 12-pounder

gun mounted at her stern. On 18th April 1918 she was attacked by a surfaced German U boat and the gun crew of the *Ibex* returned fire, scoring a hit. The enemy vessel submerged and the *Ibex* was subsequently credited with having sunk the submarine. A brass plaque was later fitted at the head of her saloon staircase to record the event.

Two new twin-screw vessels were provided in 1897 to work an additional daylight service from Weymouth to the Channel Islands. First to be completed was the *Roebuck* and her first duty, on 25th June, was to convey the directors and officers of the GWR to the naval review at Spithead, held in celebration of Queen Victoria's Golden Jubilee. She took up the Channel Islands service in July but only operated during the summer months, being laid up at Milford during the winter. In January 1905, while berthed for the winter, she caught fire and the weight of water used to put out the fire caused her to sink at her mooring. She was refloated and refitted, re-entering service in time for the summer season.

In 1911, when the *Roebuck* had just left St. Helier, she became grounded on Kaine's Reef. When the tide receded she was left with her bow high in the air and became the subject of the spectacular photographs, taken by the GWR official photographer, which have appeared in various publications over the years. She was subsequently refloated and, after repair by Harland and Wolff at Southampton, returned to service in January 1912.

In September 1914 she was requisitioned for Government service and converted to an armed cruiser, renamed HMS *Roedene*, initially stationed at Portland. By 1915, however, she was at Scapa Flow — far from her native waters - and on 13th January she dragged her anchor. She was rammed by the battleship HMS *Imperieuse* and sank. It is thought that her wreck remains there.

Sister ship to the *Roebuck* was the *Reindeer* which was likewise built in 1897 by the Naval Construction & Armaments Co. Ltd. at Barrow-in-Furness. Her inaugural voyage was on August Bank Holiday Monday 1897 and she worked the daylight service between Weymouth and the Islands uneventfully for many years. Following the outbreak of war in 1914, the *Reindeer* was temporarily transferred to Fishguard before being requisitioned by the Admiralty. She served as a mine-sweeper in the Mediterranean and as a tender during the ill-fated landings at Gallipoli.

On her return from service in the Mediterranean she served for a while as a troopship between Weymouth and Cherbourg, helping to bring home the demobilising armies from France. Subsequently refitted, she returned to the GWR Channel Islands service in 1920 and again served uneventfully until new vessels arrived in 1925 when she became the relief ship. By 1928 she was redundant and in November was sold to T. W. Ward Ltd. and was broken up at Briton Ferry.

Other vessels appeared on the Channel Islands service from time to time to assist the regular fleet and often reappeared over a number of years during the busy periods. The *Pembroke* has already been mentioned, arriving in

1916 to assist the stalwart *Ibex* and she remained on the service until 1920 although she reappeared annually during the produce season, until 1925 when she was withdrawn.

The *Melmore* was acquired by the GWR in 1905 and was intended for use on both the Irish and Channel Islands services. She worked to Weymouth during the potato season but in 1909 commenced operating the ill-fated Weymouth—Nantes service. When this ceased in 1911, she became surplus to requirements and was sold in 1912.

In 1902 a twin-screw steamer named *Great Western* was brought into service, the second GWR-owned vessel to carry the name. She provided assistance to the regular Channel Island steamers throughout the 1920s and her last appearance at Weymouth was in 1932. Her sister vessel the *Great Southern* also provided occasional relief service on the Channel Islands route — first in 1916 and again in 1920 and 1924 during the produce seasons.

Four new ships were ordered in 1924 to modernise the service, two mail steamers and two cargo steamers. First of the mail steamers to enter service was the *St. Julien* which made her maiden voyage to the Islands on 24th May 1925. At first, the *St. Julien* and her sister ship had two funnels but in 1928 the aft funnel was removed. In this condition she worked regularly and uneventfully on the Channel Islands service until the outbreak of World War Two.

In October 1939 the *St. Julien* was requisitioned by the military authorities and was converted to a hospital carrier. She took part in the evacuation of the BEF from Dunkirk,

Weymouth Harbour in August 1929 with Great Western *(nearest) and* St. Julien *at the cargo stage.* Great Western *carried out relief passenger duties on the Channel Island service between 1921 and 1925. Thereafter she carried only produce and continued to visit Weymouth until 1932, the last GWR coal-fired vessel to work to the Islands.*
NATIONAL RAILWAY MUSEUM

coming under fire from shore batteries and enemy aircraft. In 1943 the *St. Julien* went to the Mediterranean where she steamed nearly 30,000 miles and conveyed upwards of 9,000 wounded and sick soldiers including many from the Anzio beachhead. At D-Day the *St. Julien* was serving as a hospital carrier to the invasion fleet but struck a mine and required repairs. It was not until January 1946 that she was released from government service, whereupon she went to Penarth in South Wales to receive a long overdue refit. Her first postwar voyage was in December 1946 and at nationalisation she became part of the BR(WR) fleet.

She was transferred to the Southern Region of BR on 1st November 1948 whereupon she carried the SR marine colours of yellow funnel with black top band. Her postwar career continued uneventfully until she was withdrawn from service in September 1960. She was laid up for a while before being sold for scrap in 1961, when she was broken up at Ghent, Belgium.

Sister ship of the *St. Julien* was the *St. Helier* which made her maiden voyage on 17th June 1925. In 1928 she received the same alteration as her sister when the aft funnel was removed. An uneventful pre-war career was brought to an abrupt halt in 1939 when she was withdrawn

from the Irish service, on which she had been assisting, and went to Southampton on Government service. She carried troops, mails and cargo, mostly between Southampton and Cherbourg until May 1940 when she, too, went to assist with the evacuation from Dunkirk. Here she had a most eventful time and her exploits were fully recorded, after the war, in the *Great Western Railway Magazine*. An extract from the article reads:

'One evening at Dunkirk, when *St. Helier* was attacked by nine enemy planes, her master avoided hits by repeatedly steering his ship to the spot where the last bomb fell. Three days later *St. Helier* shot down an enemy plane in mid-Channel. Two days later still, outside Dunkirk Harbour, a minelayer crossed her bow, and there was a collision. At the request of the master of the minelayer, *St. Helier* did not withdraw, but steamed into the other vessel at half speed, on one engine, for 40 minutes, to ease pressure on the minelayer's bulkhead, until a tug arrived to assist the latter vessel. Later on the same trip, while enemy planes were continually overhead, another ship struck *St. Helier* on the starboard bow. Though considerably holed by these two collisions, *St. Helier* proceeded — and immediately ran over a wreck. Fortunately she sustained no serious underwater damage, and plodded on to land her troops safely at Dover.

'Next day — and the next after that – *St. Helier* was back at Dunkirk again, braving bombs and shelling from coastal batteries

St. Helier *in St. Helier Harbour, Jersey, as built and as she appeared until 1928 when the aft funnel was removed.*

COLLECTION P. Q. TRELOAR

St. Julien, *dressed overall, in Weymouth Harbour in 1946 making her postwar maiden voyage to the Channel Islands. She is shown passing* Roebuck, *similarly dressed to celebrate the return to service of the mail-boat.*
WELSH INDUSTRIAL AND MARITIME MUSEUM

St. Julien *in Weymouth Harbour in the late 1950s, by now wearing BR colours of buff funnel with black top-band.* I. D. BEALE

for hours on end. When the Naval authorities thought that Captain R. R. Pitman had done enough, and offered to put a Naval Commander in charge, he refused relief, made another trip and brought away the last 2,300 British troops to be evacuated from that "coast of death". Altogether, from May 22 to June 3, *St. Helier* made one trip to Calais and seven into Dunkirk, bringing away 10,200 troops and 1,500 evacuees. Then, with holed bows, damaged docking bridge, manoeuvring awkwardly, and with the crew working at the pumps in relays to keep down the water in her fore peak, the gallant ship limped back at very slow speed to Southampton for repairs.'

St. Helier was taken over by the Admiralty in November 1940 and was converted to a landing ship in 1942. With landing craft suspended from davits on either side, she took Canadian troops to the Normandy landings in 1944. In May 1945 she returned to St. Peter Port, Guernsey, with military personnel for the liberation of the Channel Islands and was passed back to the GWR in 1946 when she received

a long overdue refit. *St. Helier* had the honour of reinstating the regular GWR Channel Islands service following the wartime hiatus and received a wonderful welcome when she returned to Weymouth in June 1946.

As with her sister, her postwar service on the route was uneventful until, in September 1960, she made her final voyage, an excursion from Torquay to Guernsey. She, too, was sold to Belgium shipbreakers and left Weymouth under tow from a Dutch tug on 17th December 1960.

Of the two cargo vessels ordered in 1924, the first into service was the *Roebuck* – the second vessel on the Channel Islands service to carry the name, the first having been lost at Scapa Flow while on Government service. In 1928 she was altered to allow the carriage of twelve passengers whereupon she served uneventfully until the Second World War. She was still conveying produce from the Channel Islands in May 1940 when, at short notice, she

Roebuck *in Weymouth Harbour in the immediate postwar years.*

steamed to Dover to assist in the evacuation at Dunkirk. Again the exploits of the GWR vessel were recorded in a postwar edition of the *GWR Magazine* which read:

> 'Roebuck was a Channel Islands cargo vessel. On May 29, 1940, she unloaded her last tray of produce at Weymouth and was rushed off to Dover, without even waiting to ship any scaling ladders or other equipment. Two days later she was rammed astern by a destroyer, but went right on. Not being degaussed, *Roebuck* was unprotected against magnetic mines, but braved these and survived: threading her way among unmarked wrecks, some wholly submerged, while many others lay beached high and dry and burnt out, she came at last to Dunkirk. She had no proper gangway or ladders, but improvised some and, under fire from a battery, brought off 570 men, including 119 wounded.'

Soon after her activity at Dunkirk she was again involved with more evacuation duties further west along the French coast in company with her sister ship *Sambur*. Both vessels came under fire from shore batteries and casualties were sustained amongst the GWR crews, some being fatal.

Prior to D-Day, *Roebuck* was rammed by a monitor but was repaired in time to take part in the invasion. She, again in company with her sister ship, was used to manoeuvre the huge concrete caissons which formed the temporary harbour at Arromanches. With the completion of the Mulberry Harbour, *Roebuck* was used to convey bridge-work, cranes and other vital cargoes across the Channel to assist in the supply of the invading armies.

She was returned to the GWR in 1945 and in 1948 passed into BR ownership. Her postwar duties continued uneventfully until in 1960, in line with the reorganization of services to the Islands, she commenced calling at South-

Roebuck *at the cargo stage in September 1957 with the electric cranes at work.*

A postcard view of the ill-fated St. Patrick *at St. Peter Port Harbour, Guernsey, in the 1930s.*   PRIAULX LIBRARY, GUERNSEY

ampton. She remained in service until 1965 when she made her last entry into Weymouth Harbour from Guernsey on 27th February. She was the last of the 1925 vessels to remain at work and was broken up in Belgium in December 1965.

The fourth of the vessels introduced in 1925 was the cargo vessel *Sambur* which made her maiden voyage to Jersey on 25th May. She received the same alterations as her sister in 1928 and likewise had an uneventful pre-war career. In 1940 she shared in the evacuation of the BEF and later served as a barrage balloon ship. In 1944 she assisted with the construction of the Mulberry Harbour and later served with the Army in their work on reconditioning the French ports. She was actually the first GWR vessel to re-enter Jersey on 19th September 1945 but at that time she was still on military service. In company with the other vessels in the GWR fleet, she passed to BR ownership in 1948 and continued her service to the Channel Islands. Her last voyage was in March 1964, then, after being laid up at Southampton, she was subsequently sold and broken up in Holland later that same year.

It remains only to describe two vessels which regularly appeared at Weymouth, although not solely used there, both of which carried the same name. *St. Patrick* (1) was completed in March 1930, her owners being the Fishguard and Rosslare Railways and Harbour Co., an undertaking in which the GWR shared an interest with the Great Southern Railway of Ireland. She was built primarily as a relief vessel for the Irish service but appeared regularly at Weymouth during July and August of each year to assist on the Channel Islands service. She was launched by Mrs. Milne, wife of the GWR General Manager, and made her maiden voyage to the Islands on 18th April 1930.

Her peacetime service on both routes passed, for the most part, uneventfully, but with the outbreak of war in

1939 *St. Patrick* left Jersey for the last time on 2nd September. She was employed for a time for troop transport but then took up duty on the Fishguard-Rosslare route. Twice in 1940 she was attacked by German aircraft and in 1941 was able to fight off another using her own gun. However, on 13th June 1941, her luck ran out for she was bombed and caught fire. She sank in six minutes, with the loss of 30 lives, including Captain J. Faraday, her master.

When peace returned, a replacement vessel was ordered by the GWR and was built by Cammell Laird & Co. at Birkenhead. *St. Patrick* (II) was launched on 20th May 1947 but by the time she was completed, the GWR had ceased to exist. Her maiden voyage to the Islands was on 4th February 1948. Like her predecessor, she was owned by the Fishguard and Rosslare Railways and Harbour Co., an undertaking which did not come into Government ownership, so was not part of the nationalized fleet, and she continued to carry GWR colours — red funnel with deep black top — she also carried the GWR coat-of-arms embossed on her bows and picked out in full colour.

In 1949 she worked principally on the Fishguard route and in 1950 passed into the ownership of BR (London Midland Region) when she spent some time on the Holyhead—Dun Laoghaire route. She continued the tradition of spending the summer based at Weymouth for the Channel Islands service throughout the 1950s. In 1959 she passed into Southern Region ownership and was permanently stationed at Weymouth as part of the reorganization of services. With the arrival of new, BR-ordered vessels in 1960/61, to replace the old GWR vessels of 1925, *St. Patrick* was refitted to bring her in line with the new ships.

The revised Channel Islands service took effect in 1961 but *St. Patrick* was required only at weekends. At other

St. Patrick (II) in Weymouth Harbour in the early 1960s with the new Pavilion Theatre in the background.   I. D. BEALE

The GWR crest was proudly carried on the bow of St. Patrick *well into the 1960s.*   I. D. BEALE

times she worked excursions from Weymouth and Torquay to Guernsey. From 1964 her appearances at Weymouth were increasingly intermittent and she was based variously at Newhaven and Dover. She appeared more frequently in the Channel Islands on charter work and visited Jersey for the last time in May 1971. Disposal came in September 1971 — the last GWR vessel to remain in 'railway' service and she was sold to a Greek owner for use around the Greek Islands. She was laid up in 1976 and broken up in 1980.

As I write these final notes before the book goes to press, I am, within a few days, to undertake a journey from Weymouth to the Channel Islands. In 2001 the Condor ferry reaches Guernsey in two hours and, with just twenty minutes in St. Peter Port harbour, it is only another hour to reach Jersey. This, most emphatically, is progress and is a far cry from the GWR service. By recognising this fact, one also realises that the Weymouth Harbour Tramway, and the Channel Islands steamers, have been firmly consigned to history. It is my hope that this book will, in a small way, record the tramway, with all its rituals and traditions, when it remained firmly in the control of the GWR and, its successor at Paddington, British Railways.

Gerry Beale